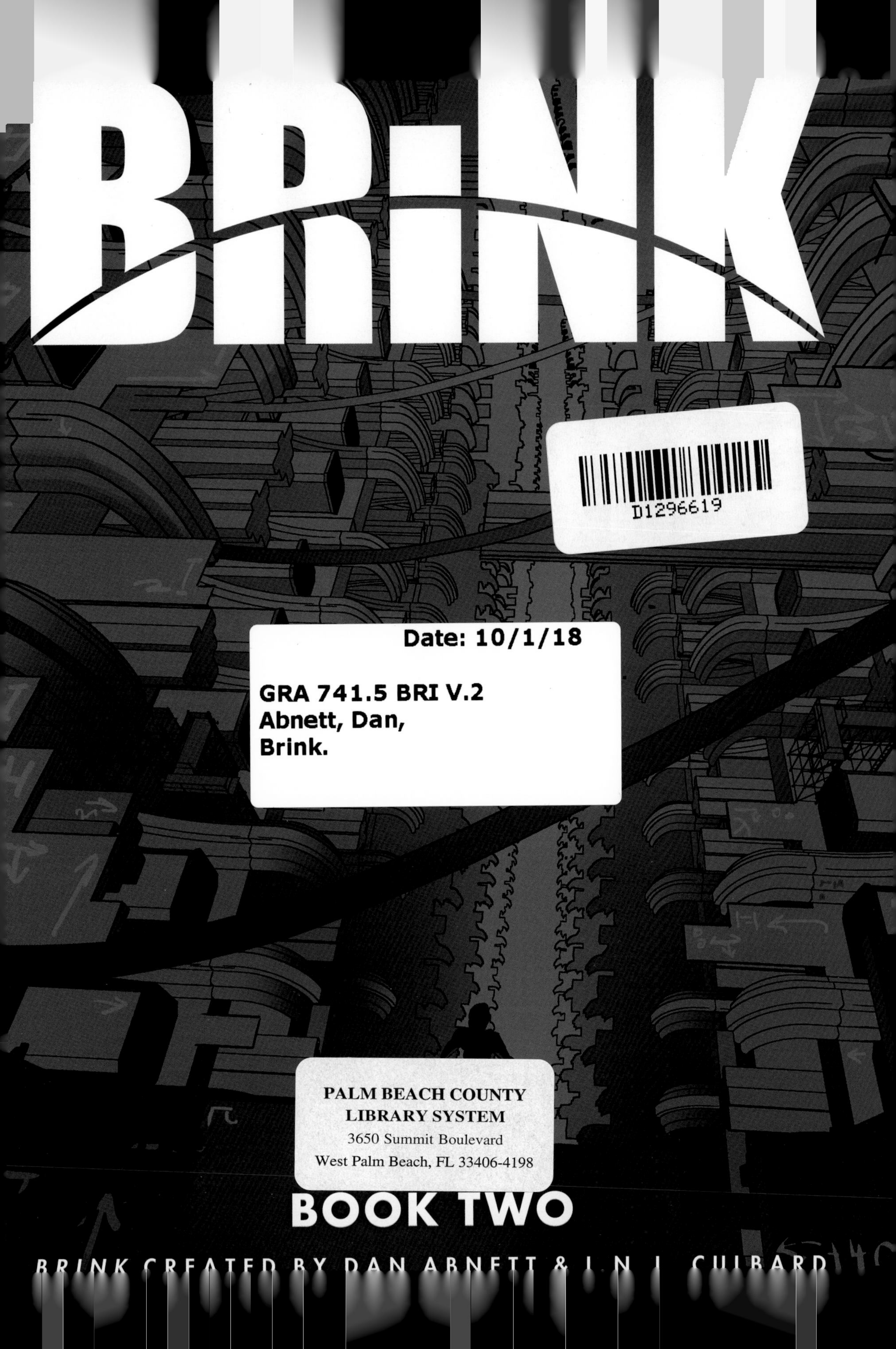

BRINK

BOOK TWO

BRINK CREATED BY DAN ABNETT & I.N.J. CULBARD

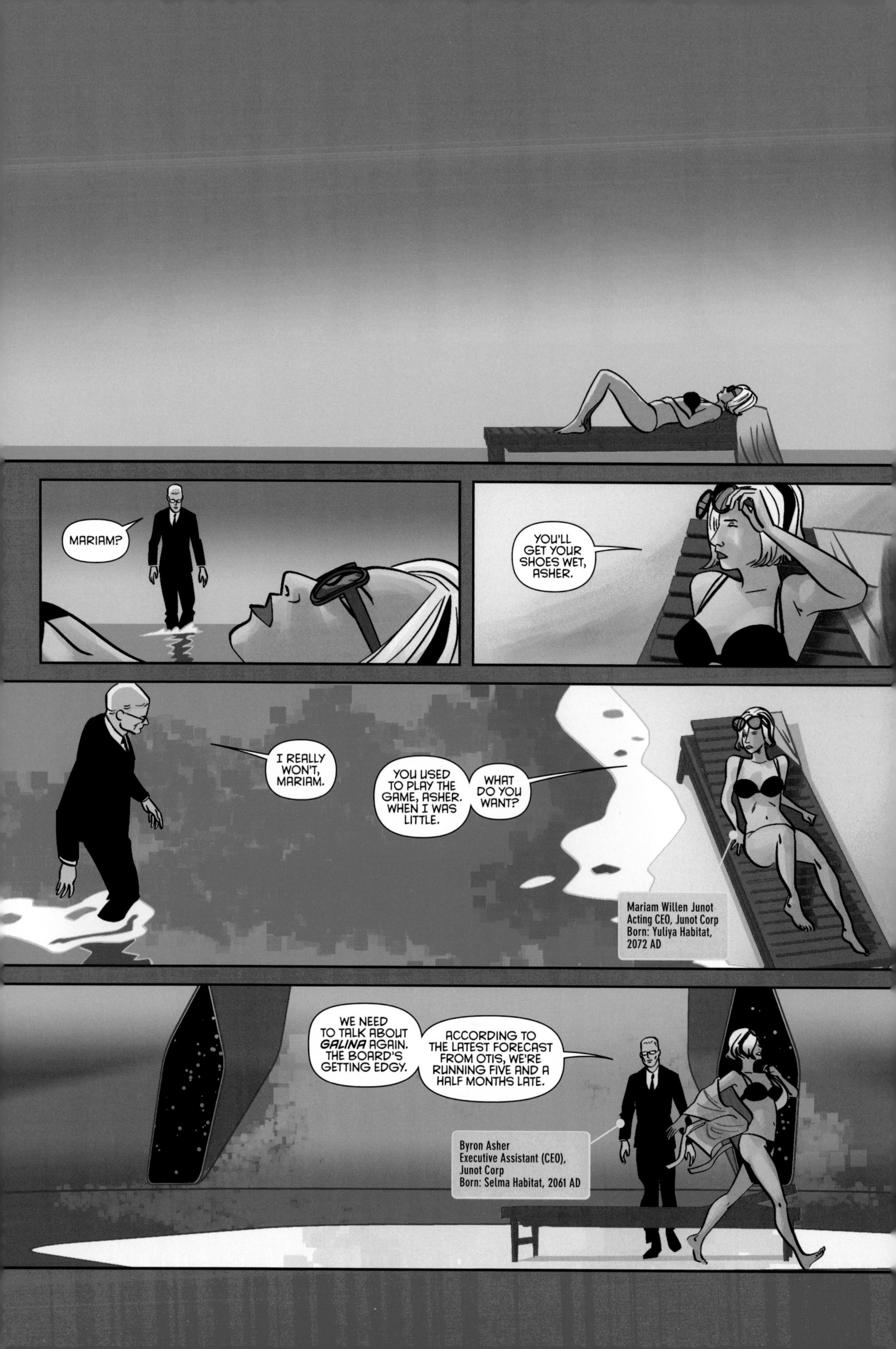
MARIAM?
YOU'LL GET YOUR SHOES WET, ASHER.
I REALLY WON'T, MARIAM.
YOU USED TO PLAY THE GAME, ASHER. WHEN I WAS LITTLE.
WHAT DO YOU WANT?
Mariam Willen Junot
Acting CEO, Junot Corp
Born: Yuliya Habitat, 2072 AD
WE NEED TO TALK ABOUT *GALINA* AGAIN. THE BOARD'S GETTING EDGY.
ACCORDING TO THE LATEST FORECAST FROM OTIS, WE'RE RUNNING FIVE AND A HALF MONTHS LATE.
Byron Asher
Executive Assistant (CEO), Junot Corp
Born: Selma Habitat, 2061 AD

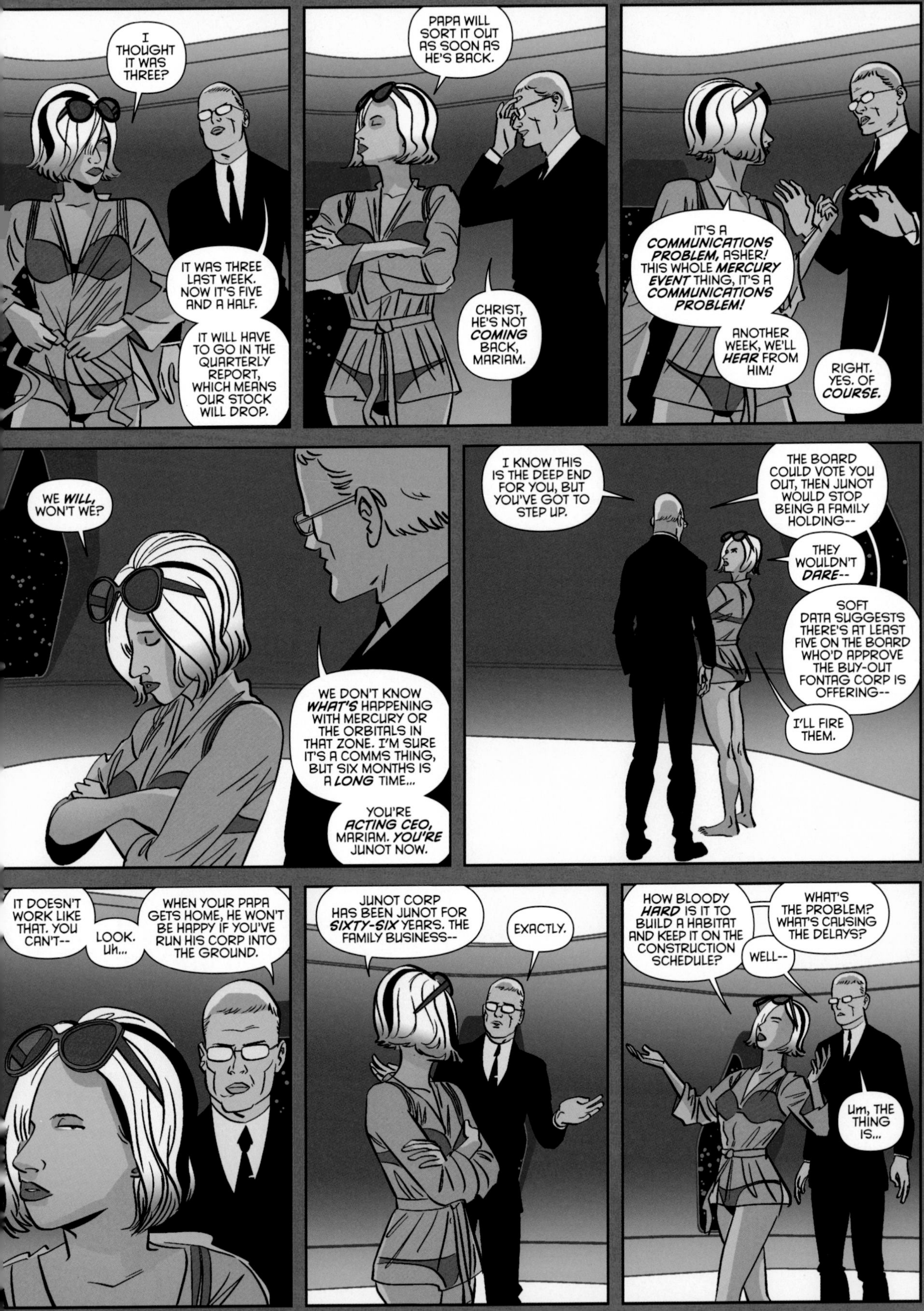
I THOUGHT IT WAS THREE?
IT WAS THREE LAST WEEK. NOW IT'S FIVE AND A HALF.
IT WILL HAVE TO GO IN THE QUARTERLY REPORT, WHICH MEANS OUR STOCK WILL DROP.
PAPA WILL SORT IT OUT AS SOON AS HE'S BACK.
CHRIST, HE'S NOT COMING BACK, MARIAM.
IT'S A COMMUNICATIONS PROBLEM, ASHER! THIS WHOLE MERCURY EVENT THING, IT'S A COMMUNICATIONS PROBLEM!
ANOTHER WEEK, WE'LL HEAR FROM HIM!
RIGHT. YES. OF COURSE.
WE WILL, WON'T WE?
WE DON'T KNOW WHAT'S HAPPENING WITH MERCURY OR THE ORBITALS IN THAT ZONE. I'M SURE IT'S A COMMS THING, BUT SIX MONTHS IS A LONG TIME...
YOU'RE ACTING CEO, MARIAM. YOU'RE JUNOT NOW.
I KNOW THIS IS THE DEEP END FOR YOU, BUT YOU'VE GOT TO STEP UP.
THE BOARD COULD VOTE YOU OUT, THEN JUNOT WOULD STOP BEING A FAMILY HOLDING--
THEY WOULDN'T DARE--
SOFT DATA SUGGESTS THERE'S AT LEAST FIVE ON THE BOARD WHO'D APPROVE THE BUY-OUT FONTAG CORP IS OFFERING--
I'LL FIRE THEM.
IT DOESN'T WORK LIKE THAT. YOU CAN'T--
LOOK. UH...
WHEN YOUR PAPA GETS HOME, HE WON'T BE HAPPY IF YOU'VE RUN HIS CORP INTO THE GROUND.
JUNOT CORP HAS BEEN JUNOT FOR SIXTY-SIX YEARS. THE FAMILY BUSINESS--
EXACTLY.
HOW BLOODY HARD IS IT TO BUILD A HABITAT AND KEEP IT ON THE CONSTRUCTION SCHEDULE?
WHAT'S THE PROBLEM? WHAT'S CAUSING THE DELAYS?
WELL--
UM, THE THING IS...

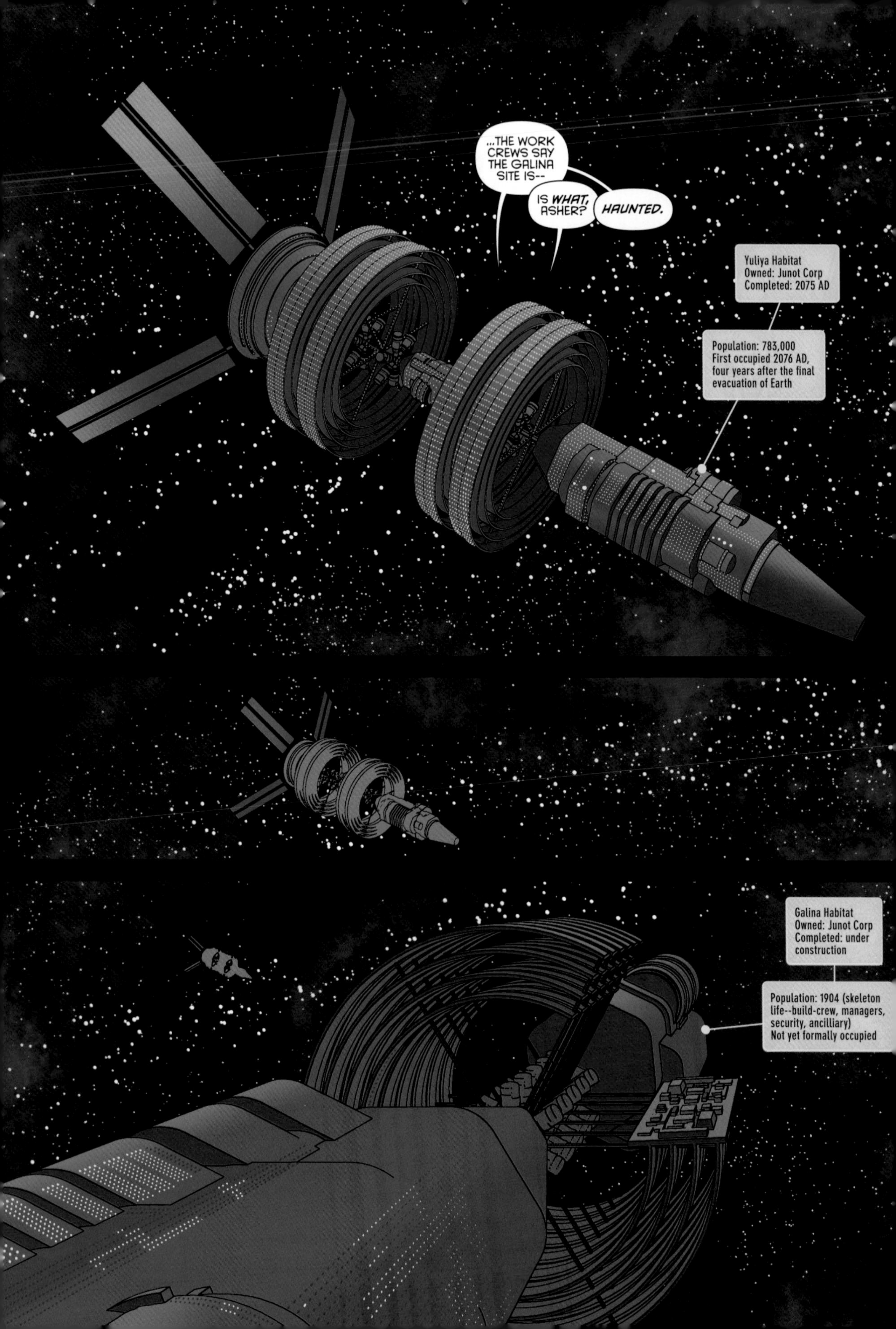

...THE WORK CREWS SAY THE GALINA SITE IS--
IS WHAT, ASHER?
HAUNTED.
Yuliya Habitat
Owned: Junot Corp
Completed: 2075 AD
Population: 783,000
First occupied 2076 AD, four years after the final evacuation of Earth
Galina Habitat
Owned: Junot Corp
Completed: under construction
Population: 1904 (skeleton life--build-crew, managers, security, ancilliary)
Not yet formally occupied

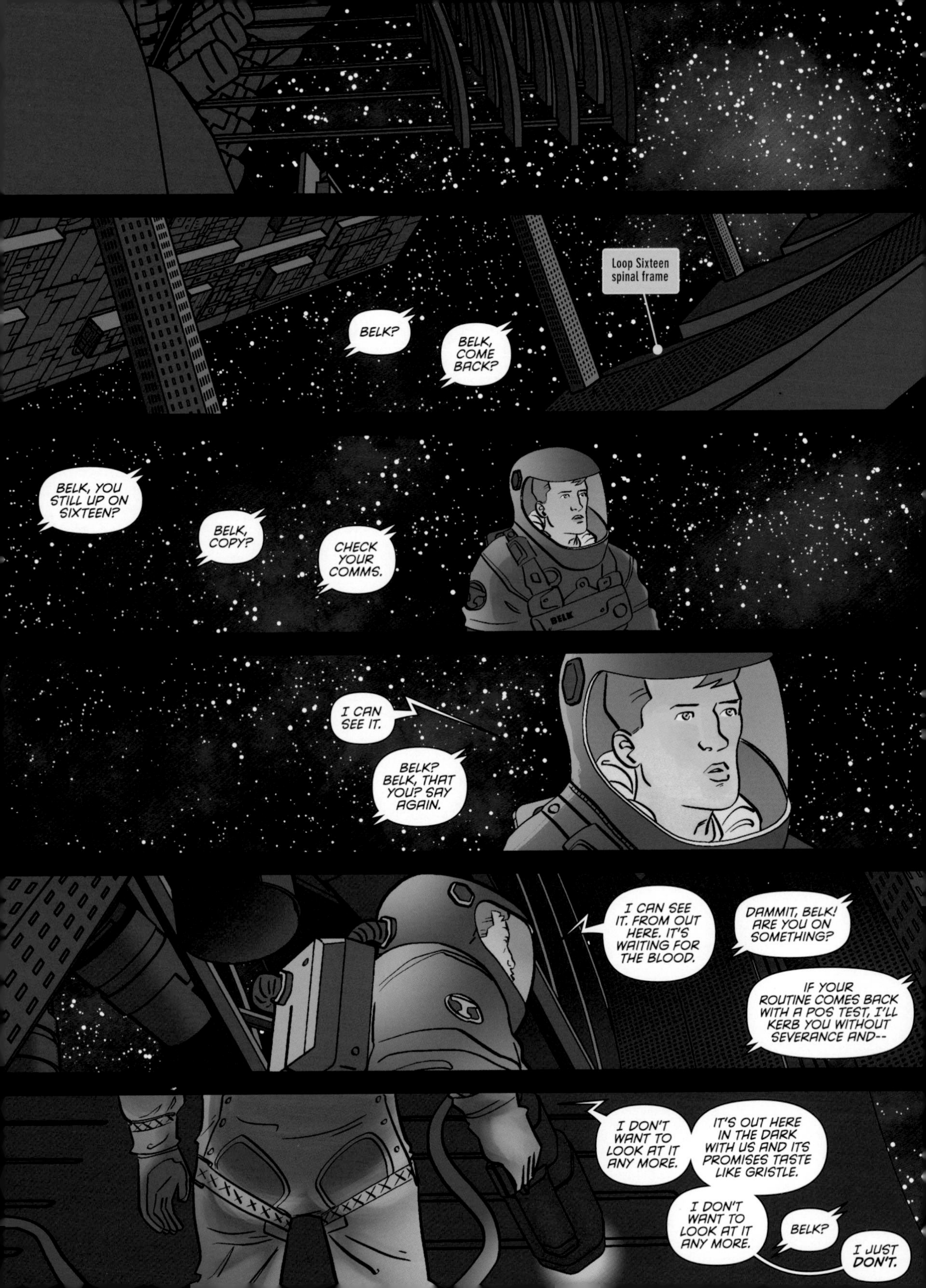
Loop Sixteen spinal frame
BELK?
BELK, COME BACK?
BELK, YOU STILL UP ON SIXTEEN?
BELK, COPY?
CHECK YOUR COMMS.
BELK
I CAN SEE IT.
BELK? BELK, THAT YOU? SAY AGAIN.
I CAN SEE IT. FROM OUT HERE. IT'S WAITING FOR THE BLOOD.
DAMMIT, BELK! ARE YOU ON SOMETHING?
IF YOUR ROUTINE COMES BACK WITH A POS TEST, I'LL KERB YOU WITHOUT SEVERANCE AND--
I DON'T WANT TO LOOK AT IT ANY MORE.
IT'S OUT HERE IN THE DARK WITH US AND ITS PROMISES TASTE LIKE GRISTLE.
I DON'T WANT TO LOOK AT IT ANY MORE.
BELK?
I JUST DON'T.

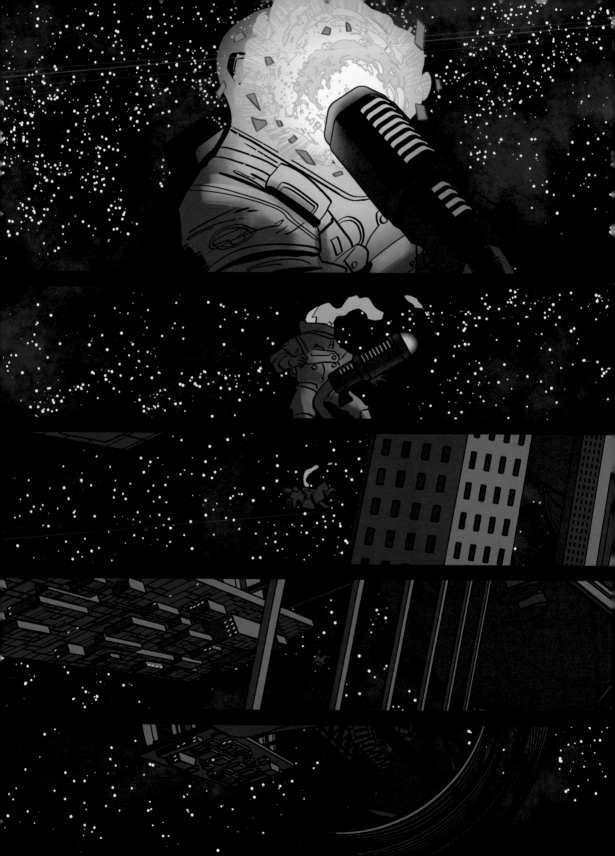

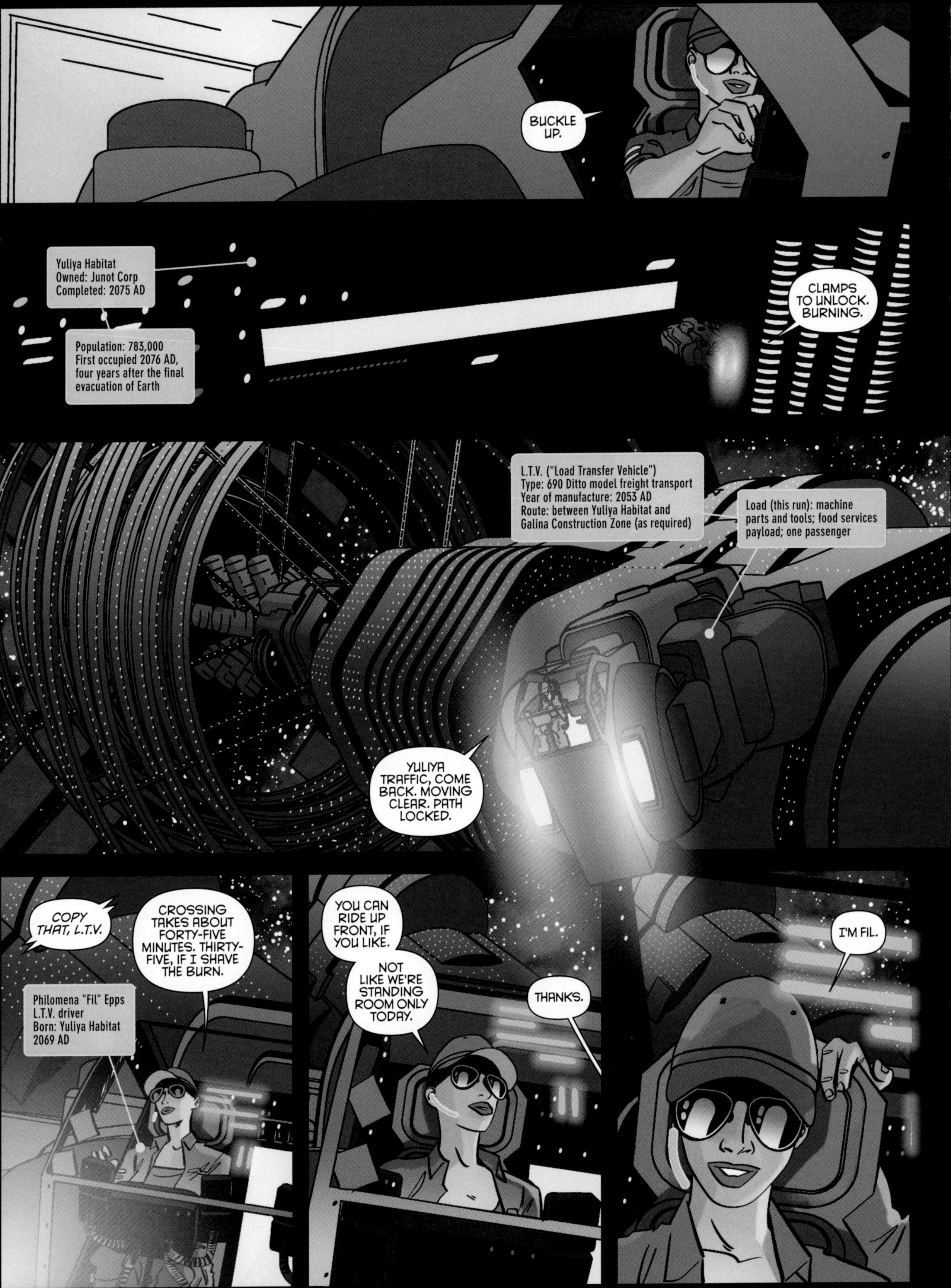

BUCKLE UP.
Yuliya Habitat
Owned: Junot Corp
Completed: 2075 AD
Population: 783,000
First occupied 2076 AD, four years after the final evacuation of Earth
CLAMPS TO UNLOCK. BURNING.
L.T.V. ("Load Transfer Vehicle")
Type: 690 Ditto model freight transport
Year of manufacture: 2053 AD
Route: between Yuliya Habitat and Galina Construction Zone (as required)
Load (this run): machine parts and tools; food services payload; one passenger
YULIYA TRAFFIC, COME BACK. MOVING CLEAR. PATH LOCKED.
COPY THAT, L.T.V.
CROSSING TAKES ABOUT FORTY-FIVE MINUTES. THIRTY-FIVE, IF I SHAVE THE BURN.
Philomena "Fil" Epps
L.T.V. driver
Born: Yuliya Habitat
2069 AD
YOU CAN RIDE UP FRONT, IF YOU LIKE.
NOT LIKE WE'RE STANDING ROOM ONLY TODAY.
THANKS.
I'M FIL.

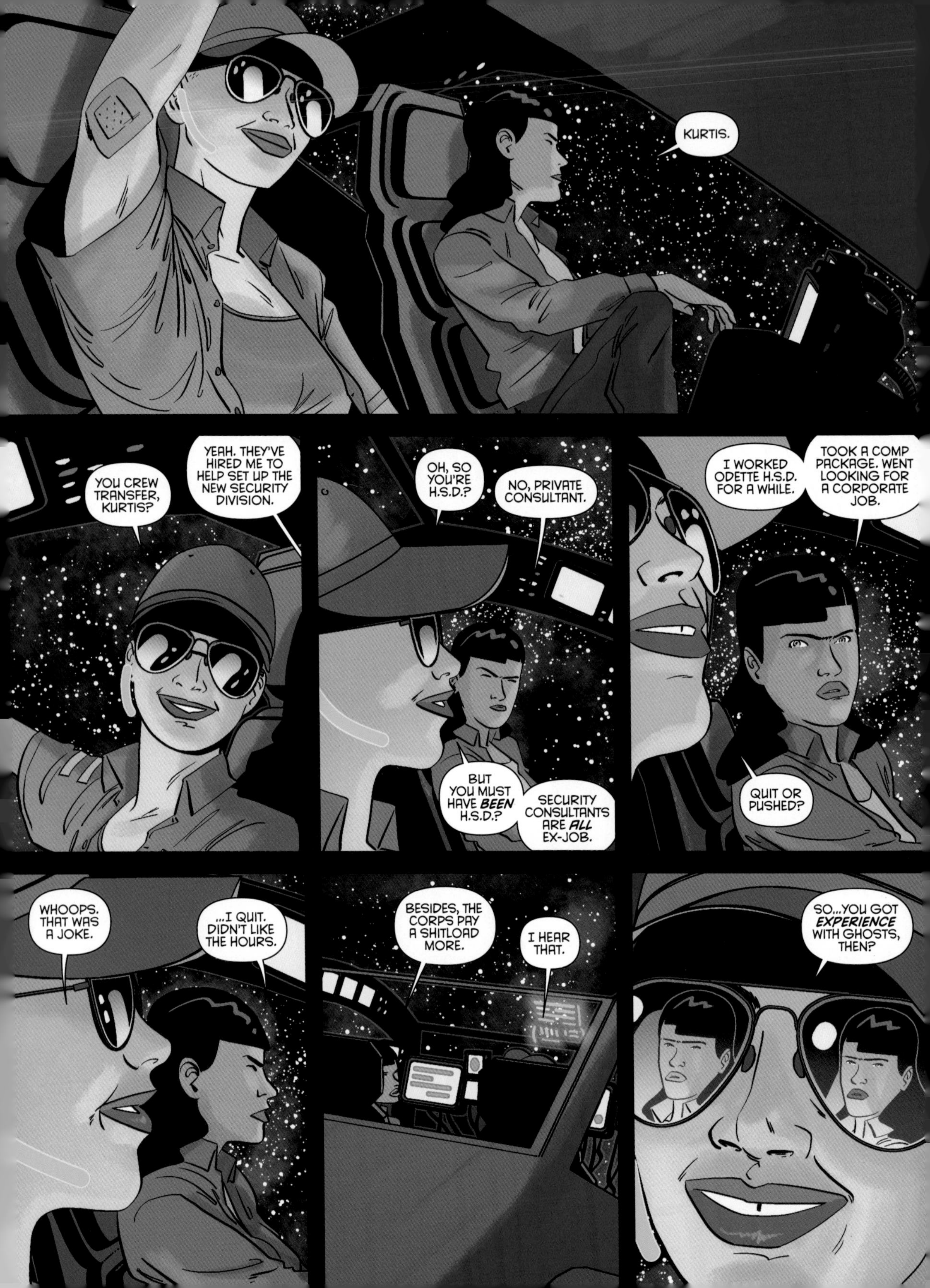
KURTIS.
YOU CREW TRANSFER, KURTIS?
YEAH. THEY'VE HIRED ME TO HELP SET UP THE NEW SECURITY DIVISION.
OH, SO YOU'RE H.S.D.?
NO, PRIVATE CONSULTANT.
BUT YOU MUST HAVE *BEEN* H.S.D.?
SECURITY CONSULTANTS ARE *ALL* EX-JOB.
I WORKED ODETTE H.S.D. FOR A WHILE.
TOOK A COMP PACKAGE. WENT LOOKING FOR A CORPORATE JOB.
QUIT OR PUSHED?
WHOOPS. THAT WAS A JOKE.
...I QUIT. DIDN'T LIKE THE HOURS.
BESIDES, THE CORPS PAY A SHITLOAD MORE.
I HEAR THAT.
SO...YOU GOT *EXPERIENCE* WITH GHOSTS, THEN?

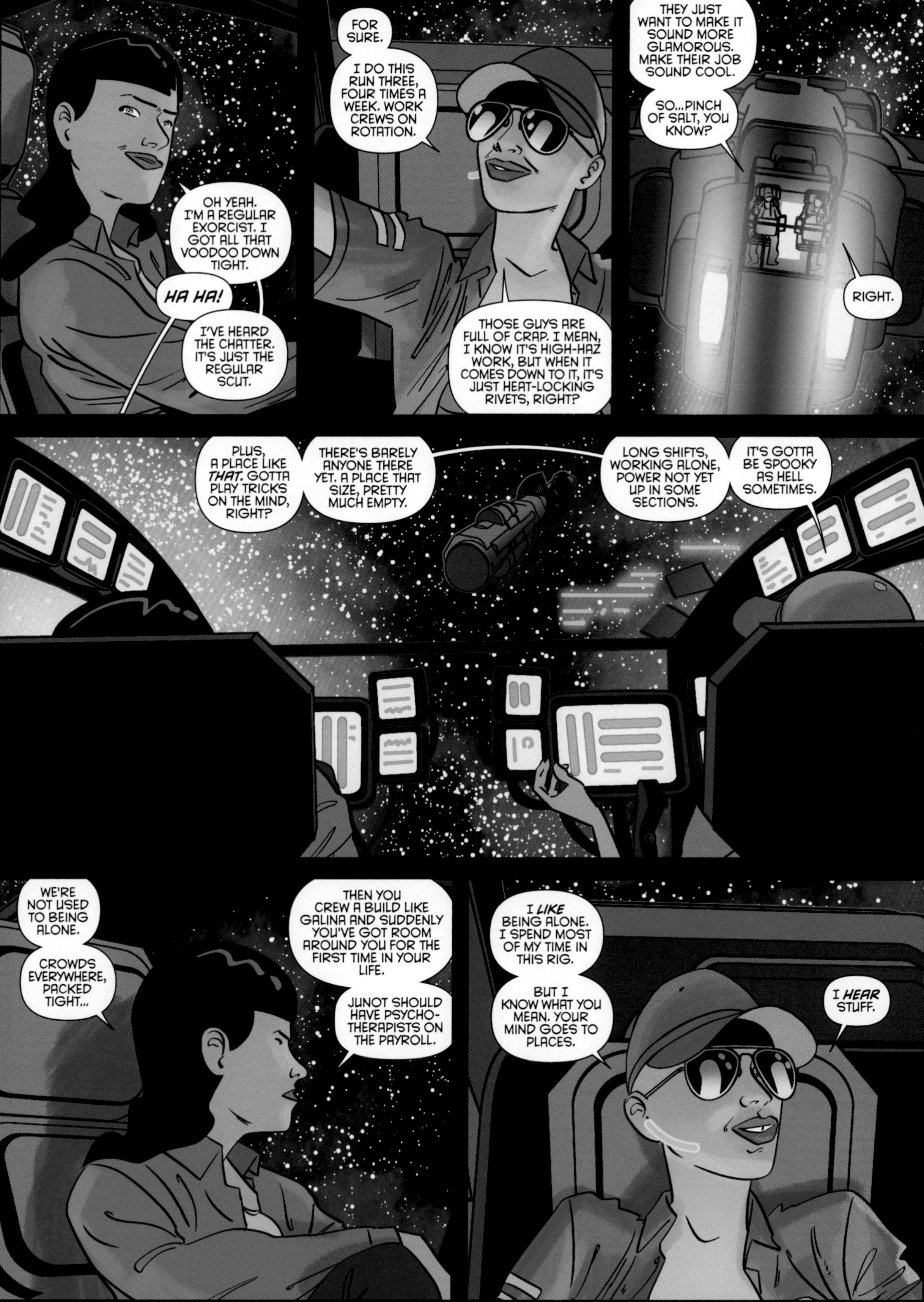
OH YEAH. I'M A REGULAR EXORCIST. I GOT ALL THAT VOODOO DOWN TIGHT.
HA HA!
I'VE HEARD THE CHATTER. IT'S JUST THE REGULAR SCUT.
FOR SURE.
I DO THIS RUN THREE, FOUR TIMES A WEEK. WORK CREWS ON ROTATION.
THOSE GUYS ARE FULL OF CRAP. I MEAN, I KNOW IT'S HIGH-HAZ WORK, BUT WHEN IT COMES DOWN TO IT, IT'S JUST HEAT-LOCKING RIVETS, RIGHT?
THEY JUST WANT TO MAKE IT SOUND MORE GLAMOROUS. MAKE THEIR JOB SOUND COOL.
SO...PINCH OF SALT, YOU KNOW?
RIGHT.
PLUS, A PLACE LIKE THAT. GOTTA PLAY TRICKS ON THE MIND, RIGHT?
THERE'S BARELY ANYONE THERE YET. A PLACE THAT SIZE, PRETTY MUCH EMPTY.
LONG SHIFTS, WORKING ALONE, POWER NOT YET UP IN SOME SECTIONS.
IT'S GOTTA BE SPOOKY AS HELL SOMETIMES.
WE'RE NOT USED TO BEING ALONE.
CROWDS EVERYWHERE, PACKED TIGHT...
THEN YOU CREW A BUILD LIKE GALINA AND SUDDENLY YOU'VE GOT ROOM AROUND YOU FOR THE FIRST TIME IN YOUR LIFE.
JUNOT SHOULD HAVE PSYCHO-THERAPISTS ON THE PAYROLL.
I LIKE BEING ALONE. I SPEND MOST OF MY TIME IN THIS RIG.
BUT I KNOW WHAT YOU MEAN. YOUR MIND GOES TO PLACES.
I HEAR STUFF.

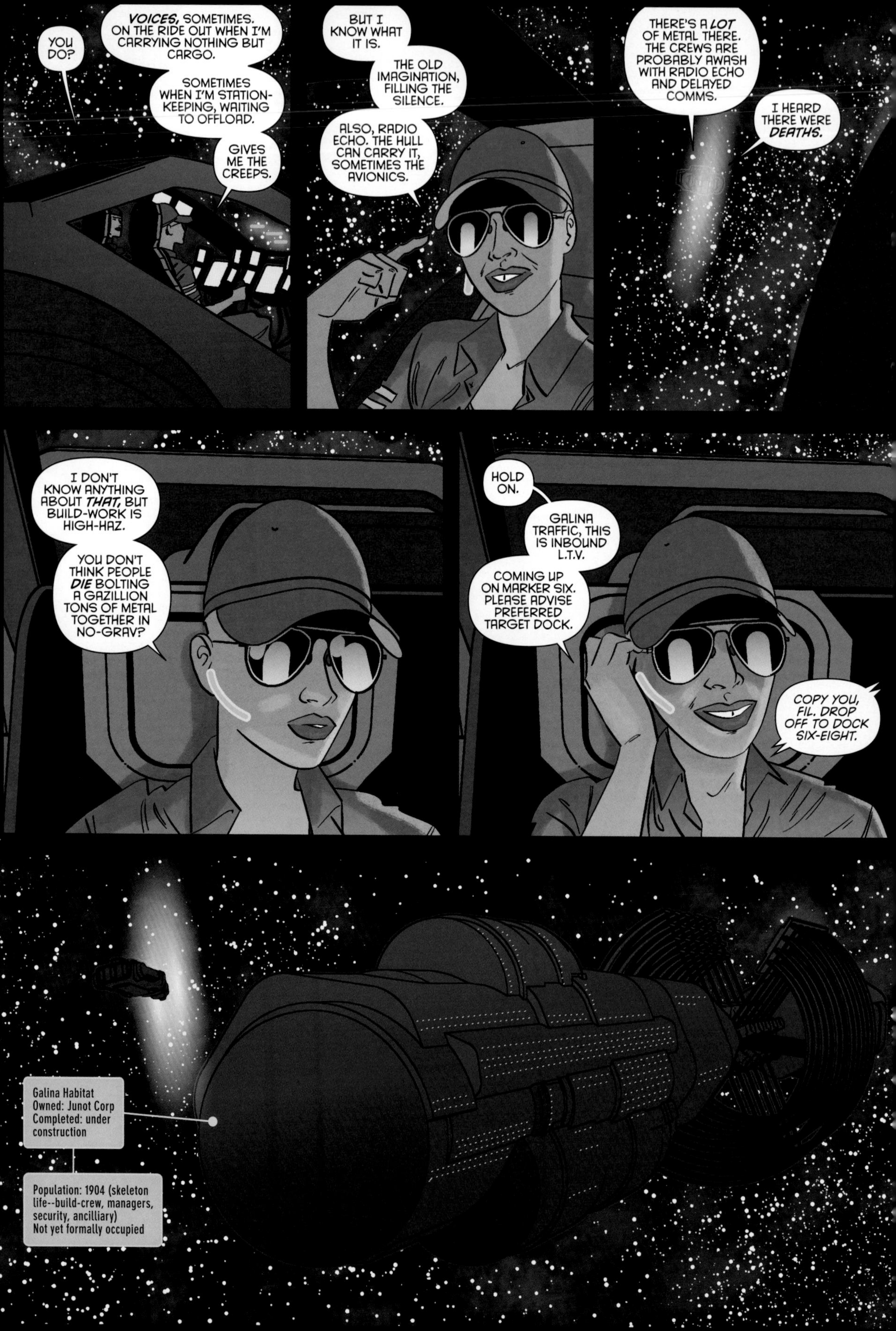
YOU DO?
VOICES, SOMETIMES. ON THE RIDE OUT WHEN I'M CARRYING NOTHING BUT CARGO.
SOMETIMES WHEN I'M STATION-KEEPING, WAITING TO OFFLOAD.
GIVES ME THE CREEPS.
BUT I KNOW WHAT IT IS.
THE OLD IMAGINATION, FILLING THE SILENCE.
ALSO, RADIO ECHO. THE HULL CAN CARRY IT, SOMETIMES THE AVIONICS.
THERE'S A LOT OF METAL THERE. THE CREWS ARE PROBABLY AWASH WITH RADIO ECHO AND DELAYED COMMS.
I HEARD THERE WERE DEATHS.
I DON'T KNOW ANYTHING ABOUT THAT, BUT BUILD-WORK IS HIGH-HAZ.
YOU DON'T THINK PEOPLE DIE BOLTING A GAZILLION TONS OF METAL TOGETHER IN NO-GRAV?
HOLD ON.
GALINA TRAFFIC, THIS IS INBOUND L.T.V.
COMING UP ON MARKER SIX. PLEASE ADVISE PREFERRED TARGET DOCK.
COPY YOU, FIL. DROP OFF TO DOCK SIX-EIGHT.
Galina Habitat
Owned: Junot Corp
Completed: under construction
Population: 1904 (skeleton life--build-crew, managers, security, ancilliary)
Not yet formally occupied

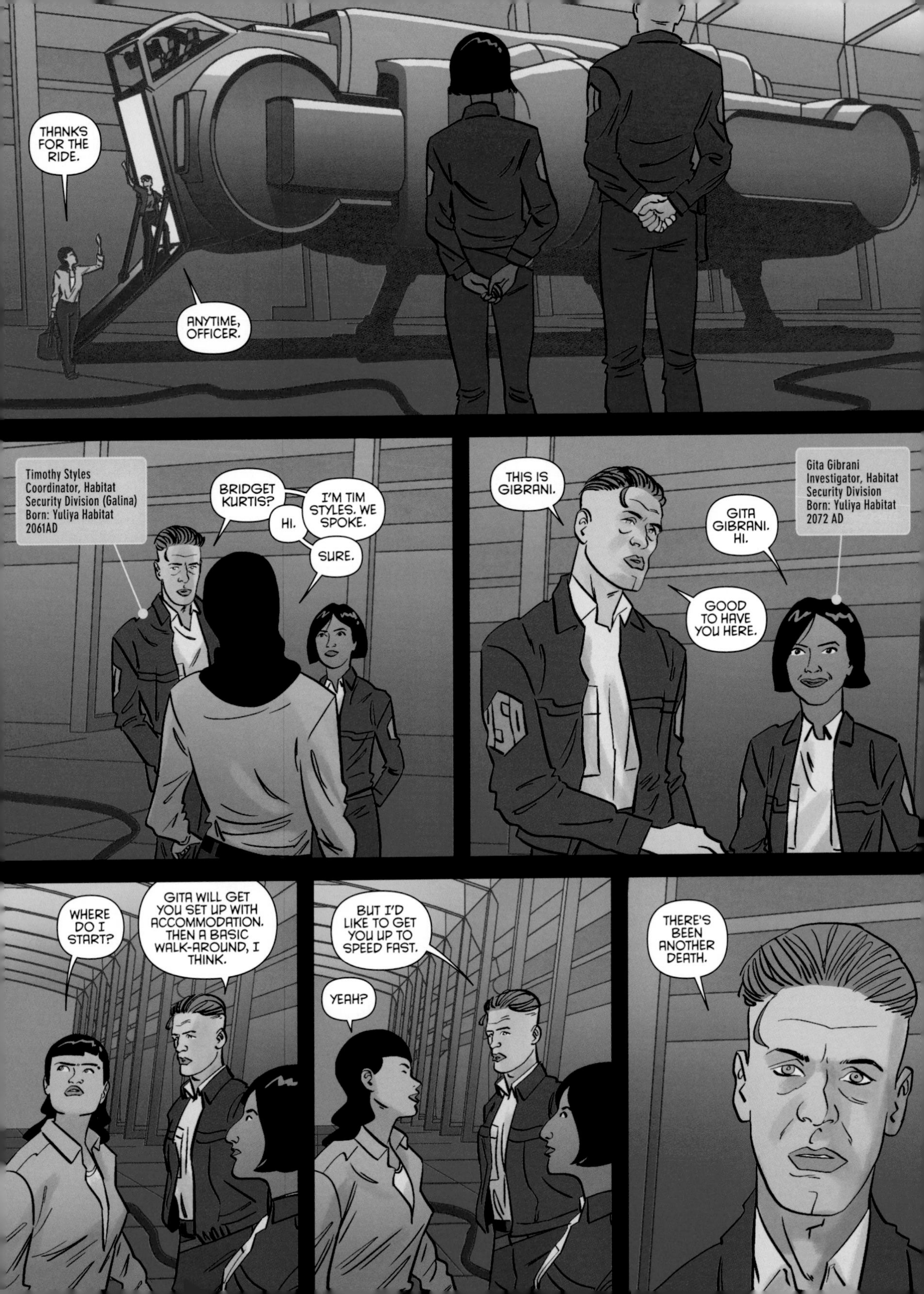
THANKS FOR THE RIDE.
ANYTIME, OFFICER.
Timothy Styles
Coordinator, Habitat
Security Division (Galina)
Born: Yuliya Habitat
2061AD
BRIDGET KURTIS?
HI.
I'M TIM STYLES. WE SPOKE.
SURE.
THIS IS GIBRANI.
GITA GIBRANI. HI.
Gita Gibrani
Investigator, Habitat
Security Division
Born: Yuliya Habitat
2072 AD
GOOD TO HAVE YOU HERE.
WHERE DO I START?
GITA WILL GET YOU SET UP WITH ACCOMMODATION. THEN A BASIC WALK-AROUND, I THINK.
BUT I'D LIKE TO GET YOU UP TO SPEED FAST.
YEAH?
THERE'S BEEN ANOTHER DEATH.

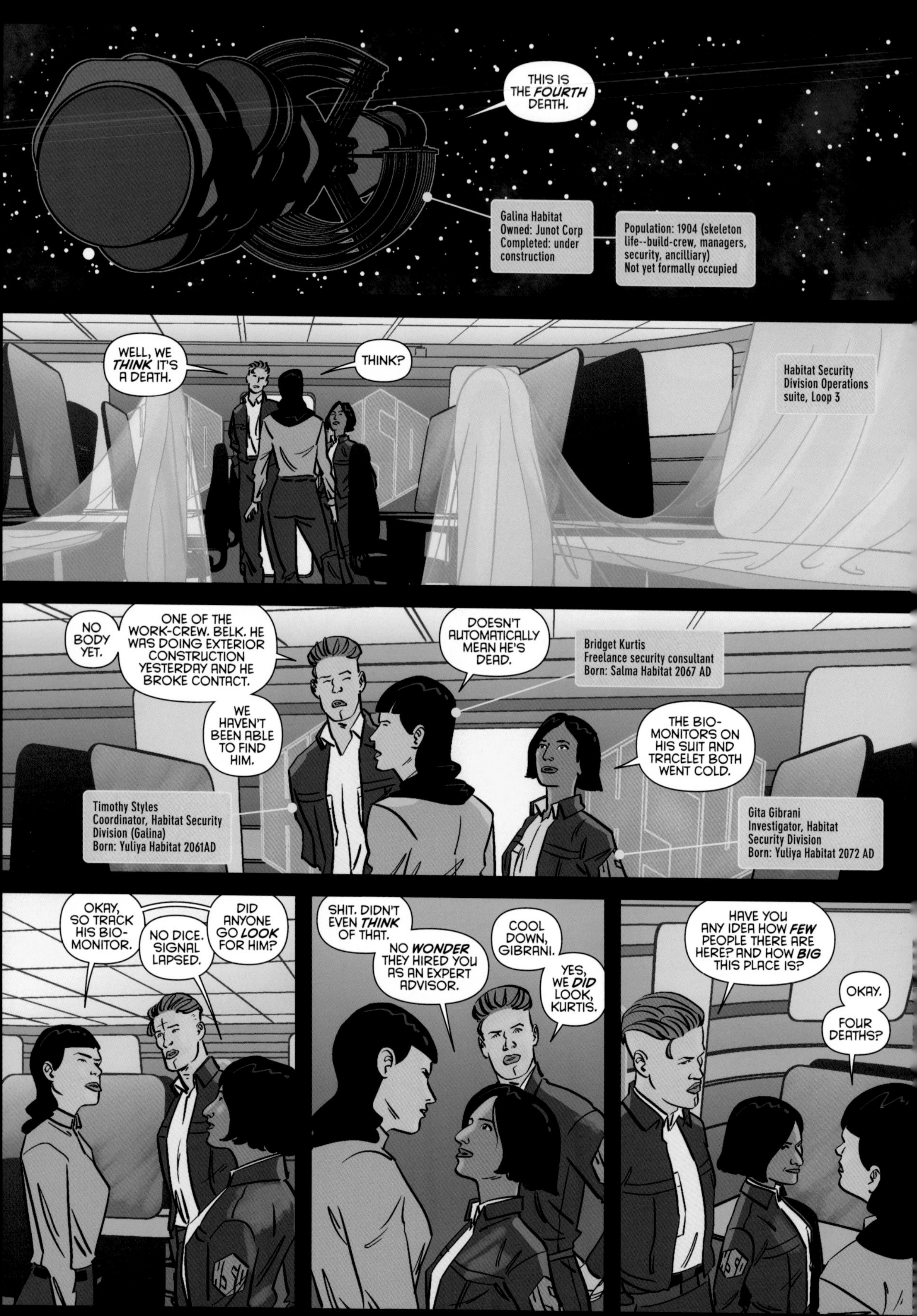

THIS IS THE FOURTH DEATH.
Galina Habitat
Owned: Junot Corp
Completed: under construction
Population: 1904 (skeleton life--build-crew, managers, security, ancilliary)
Not yet formally occupied
Habitat Security Division Operations suite, Loop 3
WELL, WE THINK IT'S A DEATH.
THINK?
NO BODY YET.
ONE OF THE WORK-CREW. BELK. HE WAS DOING EXTERIOR CONSTRUCTION YESTERDAY AND HE BROKE CONTACT.
WE HAVEN'T BEEN ABLE TO FIND HIM.
DOESN'T AUTOMATICALLY MEAN HE'S DEAD.
Bridget Kurtis
Freelance security consultant
Born: Salma Habitat 2067 AD
THE BIO-MONITORS ON HIS SUIT AND TRACELET BOTH WENT COLD.
Timothy Styles
Coordinator, Habitat Security Division (Galina)
Born: Yuliya Habitat 2061AD
Gita Gibrani
Investigator, Habitat Security Division
Born: Yuliya Habitat 2072 AD
OKAY, SO TRACK HIS BIO-MONITOR.
NO DICE. SIGNAL LAPSED.
DID ANYONE GO LOOK FOR HIM?
SHIT. DIDN'T EVEN THINK OF THAT.
NO WONDER THEY HIRED YOU AS AN EXPERT ADVISOR.
COOL DOWN, GIBRANI.
YES, WE DID LOOK, KURTIS.
HAVE YOU ANY IDEA HOW FEW PEOPLE THERE ARE HERE? AND HOW BIG THIS PLACE IS?
OKAY.
FOUR DEATHS?

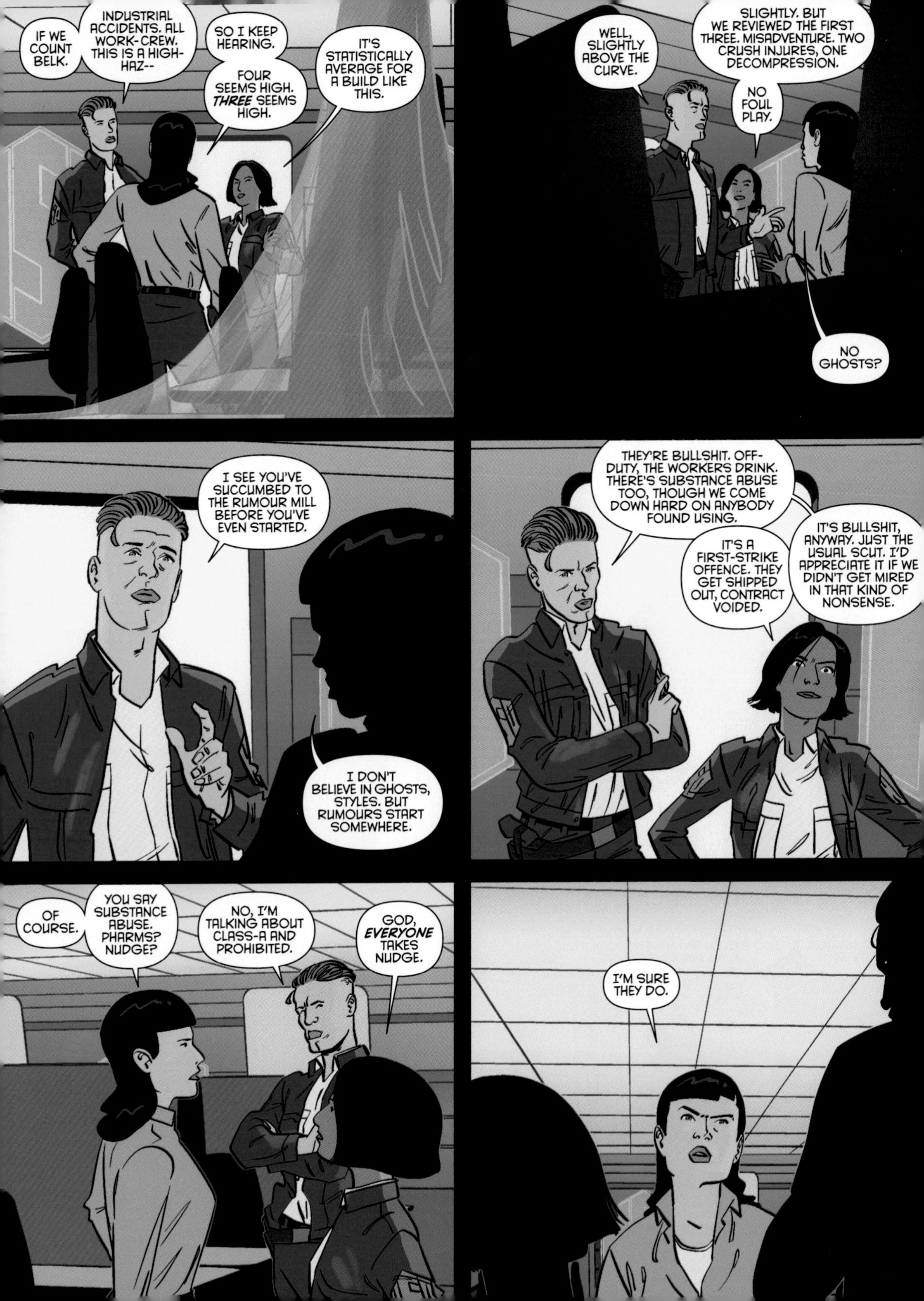
IF WE COUNT BELK.
INDUSTRIAL ACCIDENTS. ALL WORK-CREW. THIS IS A HIGH-HAZ--
SO I KEEP HEARING.
FOUR SEEMS HIGH. *THREE* SEEMS HIGH.
IT'S STATISTICALLY AVERAGE FOR A BUILD LIKE THIS.
WELL, SLIGHTLY ABOVE THE CURVE.
SLIGHTLY. BUT WE REVIEWED THE FIRST THREE. MISADVENTURE. TWO CRUSH INJURES, ONE DECOMPRESSION.
NO FOUL PLAY.
NO GHOSTS?
I SEE YOU'VE SUCCUMBED TO THE RUMOUR MILL BEFORE YOU'VE EVEN STARTED.
I DON'T BELIEVE IN GHOSTS, STYLES. BUT RUMOURS START SOMEWHERE.
THEY'RE BULLSHIT. OFF-DUTY, THE WORKERS DRINK. THERE'S SUBSTANCE ABUSE TOO, THOUGH WE COME DOWN HARD ON ANYBODY FOUND USING.
IT'S A FIRST-STRIKE OFFENCE. THEY GET SHIPPED OUT, CONTRACT VOIDED.
IT'S BULLSHIT, ANYWAY. JUST THE USUAL SCUT. I'D APPRECIATE IT IF WE DIDN'T GET MIRED IN THAT KIND OF NONSENSE.
OF COURSE.
YOU SAY SUBSTANCE ABUSE. PHARMS? NUDGE?
NO, I'M TALKING ABOUT CLASS-A AND PROHIBITED.
GOD, *EVERYONE* TAKES NUDGE.
I'M SURE THEY DO.

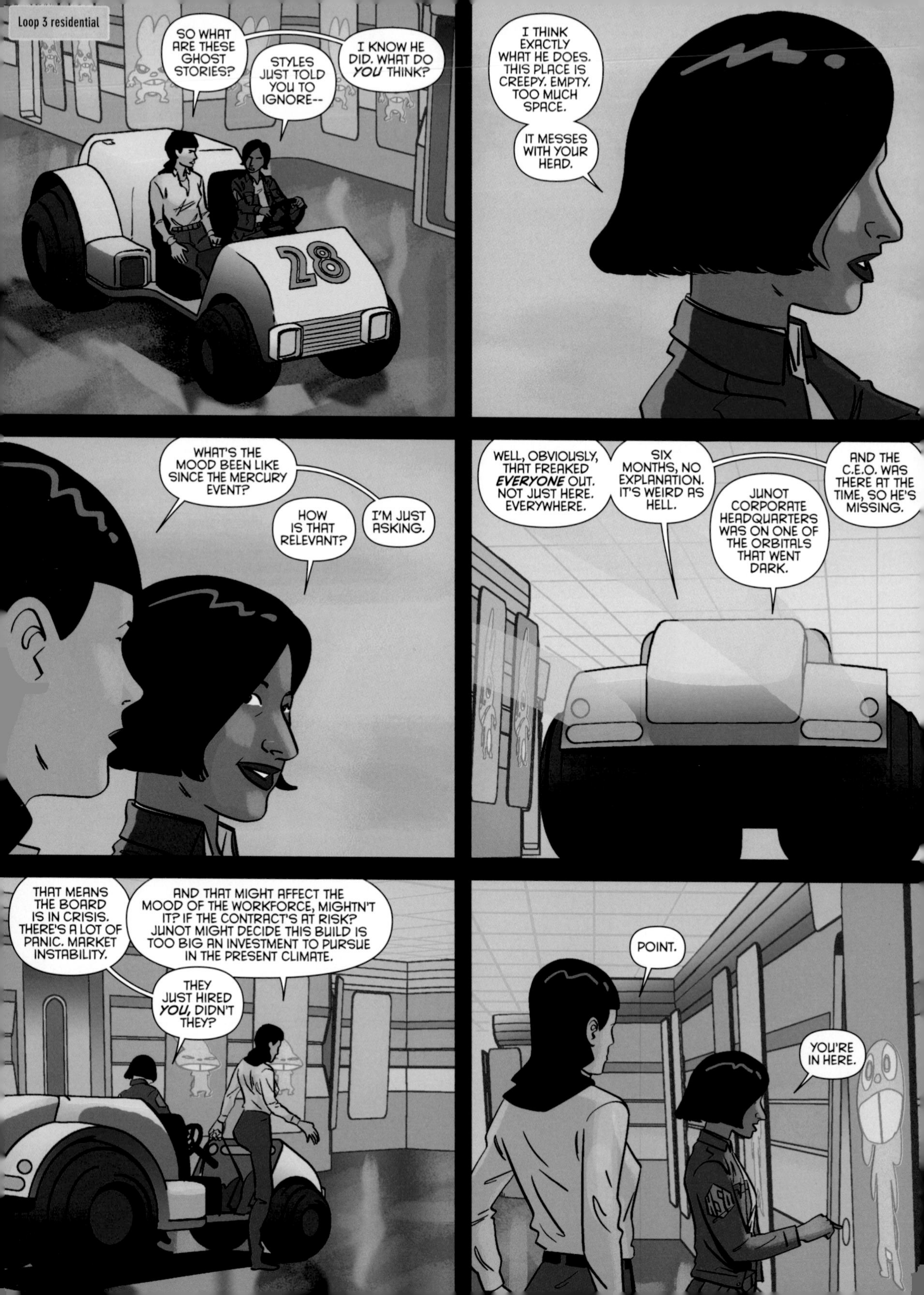
Loop 3 residential
SO WHAT ARE THESE GHOST STORIES?
STYLES JUST TOLD YOU TO IGNORE--
I KNOW HE DID. WHAT DO *YOU* THINK?
I THINK EXACTLY WHAT HE DOES. THIS PLACE IS CREEPY. EMPTY. TOO MUCH SPACE.
IT MESSES WITH YOUR HEAD.
WHAT'S THE MOOD BEEN LIKE SINCE THE MERCURY EVENT?
HOW IS THAT RELEVANT?
I'M JUST ASKING.
WELL, OBVIOUSLY, THAT FREAKED *EVERYONE* OUT. NOT JUST HERE. EVERYWHERE.
SIX MONTHS, NO EXPLANATION. IT'S WEIRD AS HELL.
JUNOT CORPORATE HEADQUARTERS WAS ON ONE OF THE ORBITALS THAT WENT DARK.
AND THE C.E.O. WAS THERE AT THE TIME, SO HE'S MISSING.
THAT MEANS THE BOARD IS IN CRISIS. THERE'S A LOT OF PANIC. MARKET INSTABILITY.
AND THAT MIGHT AFFECT THE MOOD OF THE WORKFORCE, MIGHTN'T IT? IF THE CONTRACT'S AT RISK? JUNOT MIGHT DECIDE THIS BUILD IS TOO BIG AN INVESTMENT TO PURSUE IN THE PRESENT CLIMATE.
THEY JUST HIRED *YOU*, DIDN'T THEY?
POINT.
YOU'RE IN HERE.

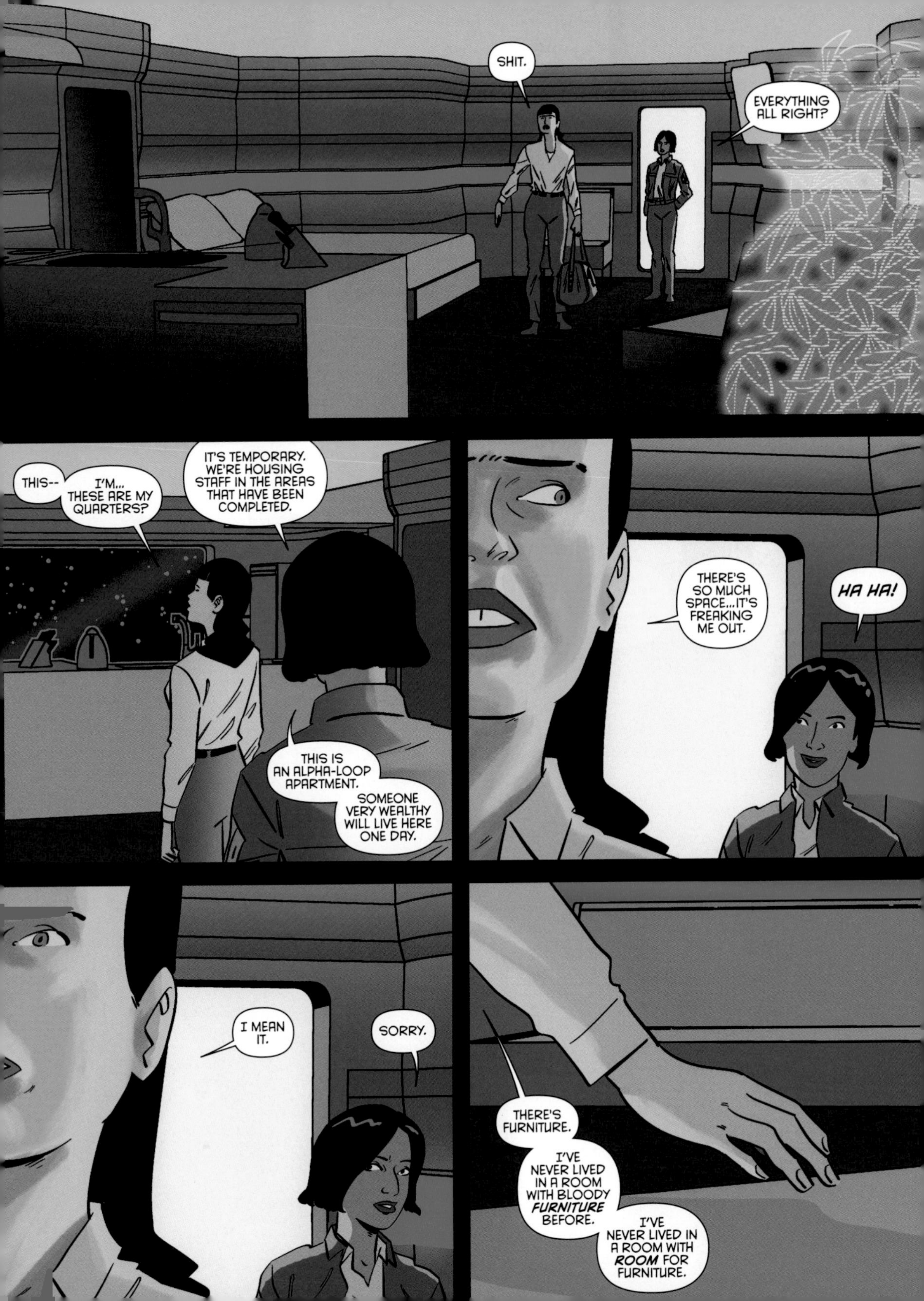
SHIT.
EVERYTHING ALL RIGHT?
THIS--
I'M... THESE ARE MY QUARTERS?
IT'S TEMPORARY. WE'RE HOUSING STAFF IN THE AREAS THAT HAVE BEEN COMPLETED.
THIS IS AN ALPHA-LOOP APARTMENT.
SOMEONE VERY WEALTHY WILL LIVE HERE ONE DAY.
THERE'S SO MUCH SPACE...IT'S FREAKING ME OUT.
HA HA!
I MEAN IT.
SORRY.
THERE'S FURNITURE.
I'VE NEVER LIVED IN A ROOM WITH BLOODY FURNITURE BEFORE.
I'VE NEVER LIVED IN A ROOM WITH ROOM FOR FURNITURE.

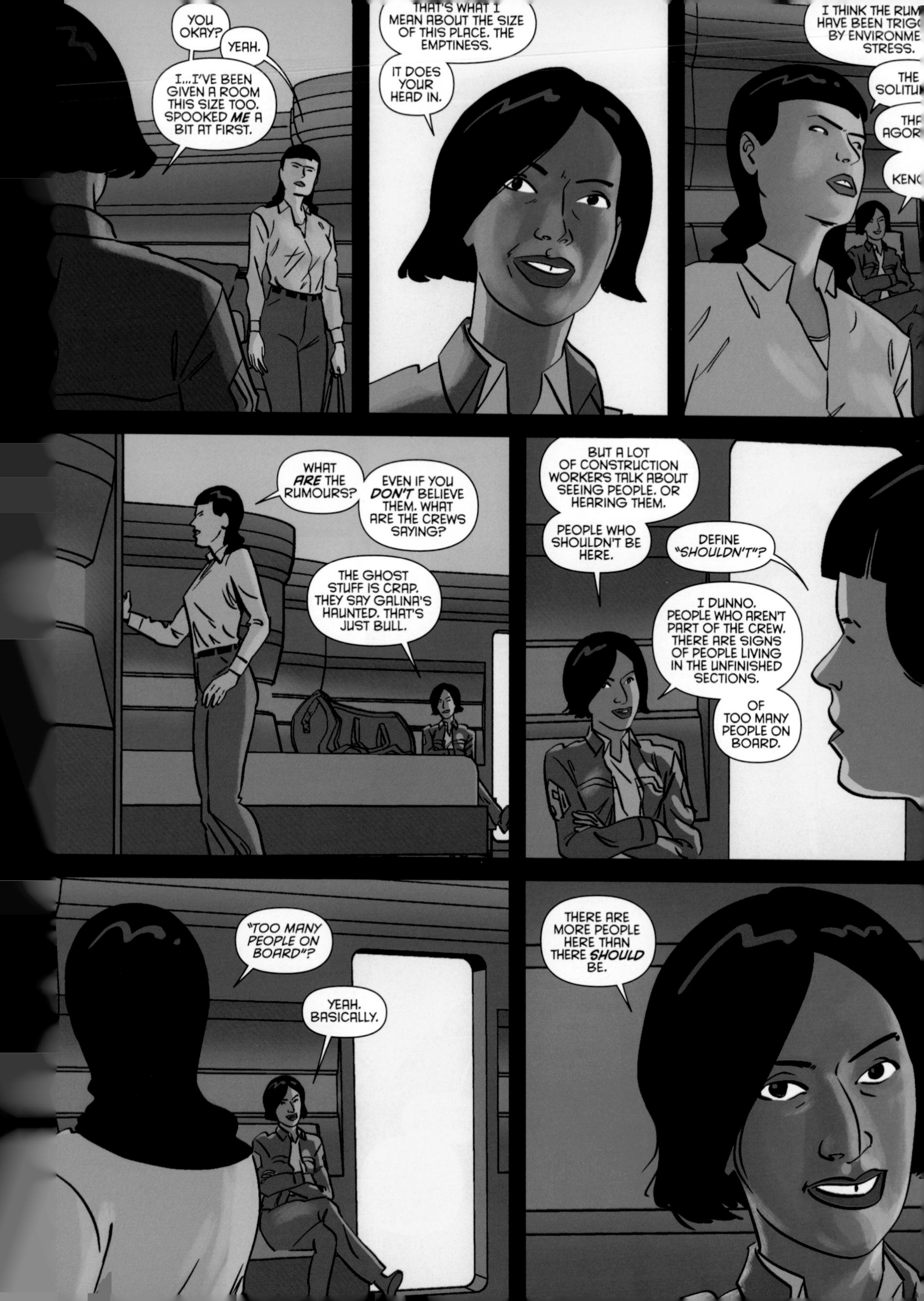
YOU OKAY?
YEAH.
I...I'VE BEEN GIVEN A ROOM THIS SIZE TOO. SPOOKED ME A BIT AT FIRST.
THAT'S WHAT I MEAN ABOUT THE SIZE OF THIS PLACE. THE EMPTINESS.
IT DOES YOUR HEAD IN.
I THINK THE RUM
HAVE BEEN TRIG
BY ENVIRONME
STRESS.
THE
SOLITU
THE
AGOR
KEN
WHAT ARE THE RUMOURS?
EVEN IF YOU DON'T BELIEVE THEM. WHAT ARE THE CREWS SAYING?
THE GHOST STUFF IS CRAP. THEY SAY GALINA'S HAUNTED. THAT'S JUST BULL.
BUT A LOT OF CONSTRUCTION WORKERS TALK ABOUT SEEING PEOPLE. OR HEARING THEM.
PEOPLE WHO SHOULDN'T BE HERE.
DEFINE "SHOULDN'T"?
I DUNNO. PEOPLE WHO AREN'T PART OF THE CREW. THERE ARE SIGNS OF PEOPLE LIVING IN THE UNFINISHED SECTIONS.
OF TOO MANY PEOPLE ON BOARD.
"TOO MANY PEOPLE ON BOARD"?
YEAH. BASICALLY.
THERE ARE MORE PEOPLE HERE THAN THERE SHOULD BE.

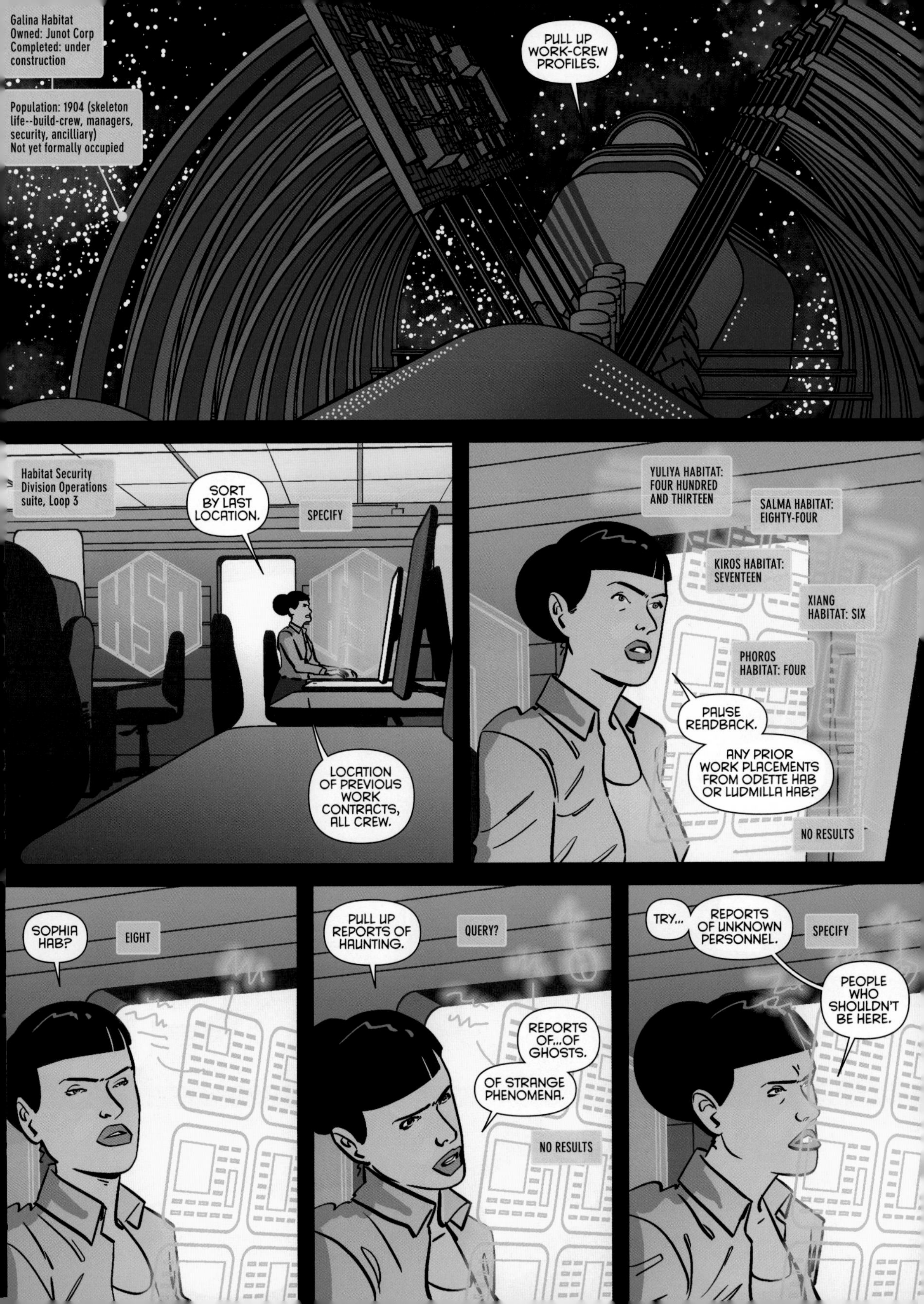

Galina Habitat
Owned: Junot Corp
Completed: under construction
Population: 1904 (skeleton life--build-crew, managers, security, ancilliary)
Not yet formally occupied
PULL UP WORK-CREW PROFILES.
Habitat Security Division Operations suite, Loop 3
SORT BY LAST LOCATION.
SPECIFY
LOCATION OF PREVIOUS WORK CONTRACTS, ALL CREW.
YULIYA HABITAT: FOUR HUNDRED AND THIRTEEN
SALMA HABITAT: EIGHTY-FOUR
KIROS HABITAT: SEVENTEEN
XIANG HABITAT: SIX
PHOROS HABITAT: FOUR
PAUSE READBACK.
ANY PRIOR WORK PLACEMENTS FROM ODETTE HAB OR LUDMILLA HAB?
NO RESULTS
SOPHIA HAB?
EIGHT
PULL UP REPORTS OF HAUNTING.
QUERY?
REPORTS OF...OF GHOSTS.
OF STRANGE PHENOMENA.
NO RESULTS
TRY...
REPORTS OF UNKNOWN PERSONNEL.
SPECIFY
PEOPLE WHO SHOULDN'T BE HERE.

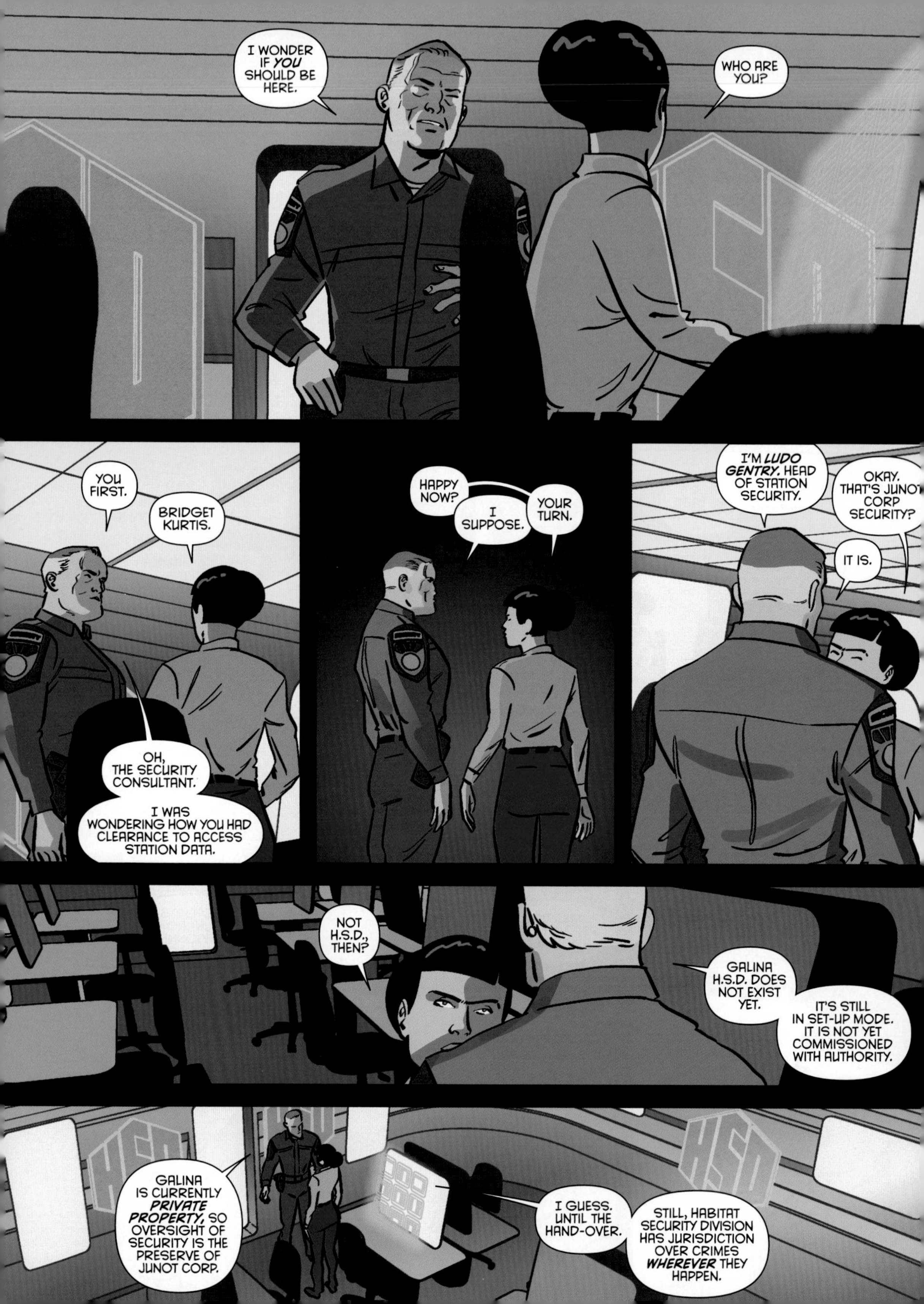
I WONDER IF *YOU* SHOULD BE HERE.
WHO ARE YOU?
YOU FIRST.
BRIDGET KURTIS.
OH, THE SECURITY CONSULTANT.
I WAS WONDERING HOW YOU HAD CLEARANCE TO ACCESS STATION DATA.
HAPPY NOW?
I SUPPOSE.
YOUR TURN.
I'M *LUDO GENTRY.* HEAD OF STATION SECURITY.
OKAY. THAT'S JUNOT CORP SECURITY?
IT IS.
NOT H.S.D., THEN?
GALINA H.S.D. DOES NOT EXIST YET.
IT'S STILL IN SET-UP MODE. IT IS NOT YET COMMISSIONED WITH AUTHORITY.
GALINA IS CURRENTLY *PRIVATE PROPERTY,* SO OVERSIGHT OF SECURITY IS THE PRESERVE OF JUNOT CORP.
I GUESS. UNTIL THE HAND-OVER.
STILL, HABITAT SECURITY DIVISION HAS JURISDICTION OVER CRIMES *WHEREVER* THEY HAPPEN.

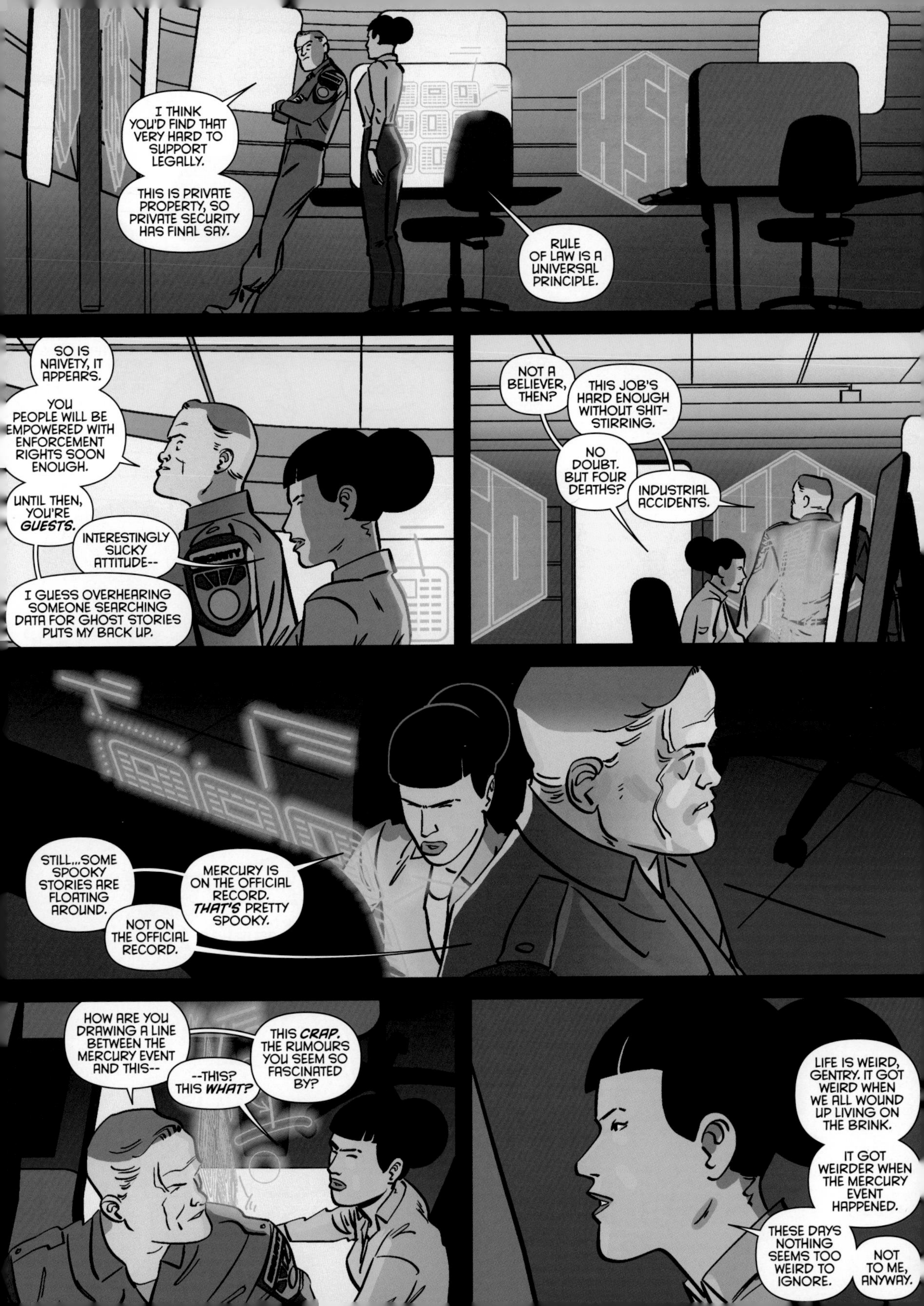
I THINK YOU'D FIND THAT VERY HARD TO SUPPORT LEGALLY.
THIS IS PRIVATE PROPERTY, SO PRIVATE SECURITY HAS FINAL SAY.
RULE OF LAW IS A UNIVERSAL PRINCIPLE.
SO IS NAIVETY, IT APPEARS.
YOU PEOPLE WILL BE EMPOWERED WITH ENFORCEMENT RIGHTS SOON ENOUGH.
UNTIL THEN, YOU'RE *GUESTS.*
INTERESTINGLY SUCKY ATTITUDE--
I GUESS OVERHEARING SOMEONE SEARCHING DATA FOR GHOST STORIES PUTS MY BACK UP.
NOT A BELIEVER, THEN?
THIS JOB'S HARD ENOUGH WITHOUT SHIT-STIRRING.
NO DOUBT. BUT FOUR DEATHS?
INDUSTRIAL ACCIDENTS.
STILL...SOME SPOOKY STORIES ARE FLOATING AROUND.
MERCURY IS ON THE OFFICIAL RECORD. *THAT'S* PRETTY SPOOKY.
NOT ON THE OFFICIAL RECORD.
HOW ARE YOU DRAWING A LINE BETWEEN THE MERCURY EVENT AND THIS--
--THIS? THIS *WHAT?*
THIS *CRAP.* THE RUMOURS YOU SEEM SO FASCINATED BY?
LIFE IS WEIRD, GENTRY. IT GOT WEIRD WHEN WE ALL WOUND UP LIVING ON THE BRINK.
IT GOT WEIRDER WHEN THE MERCURY EVENT HAPPENED.
THESE DAYS NOTHING SEEMS TOO WEIRD TO IGNORE.
NOT TO ME, ANYWAY.

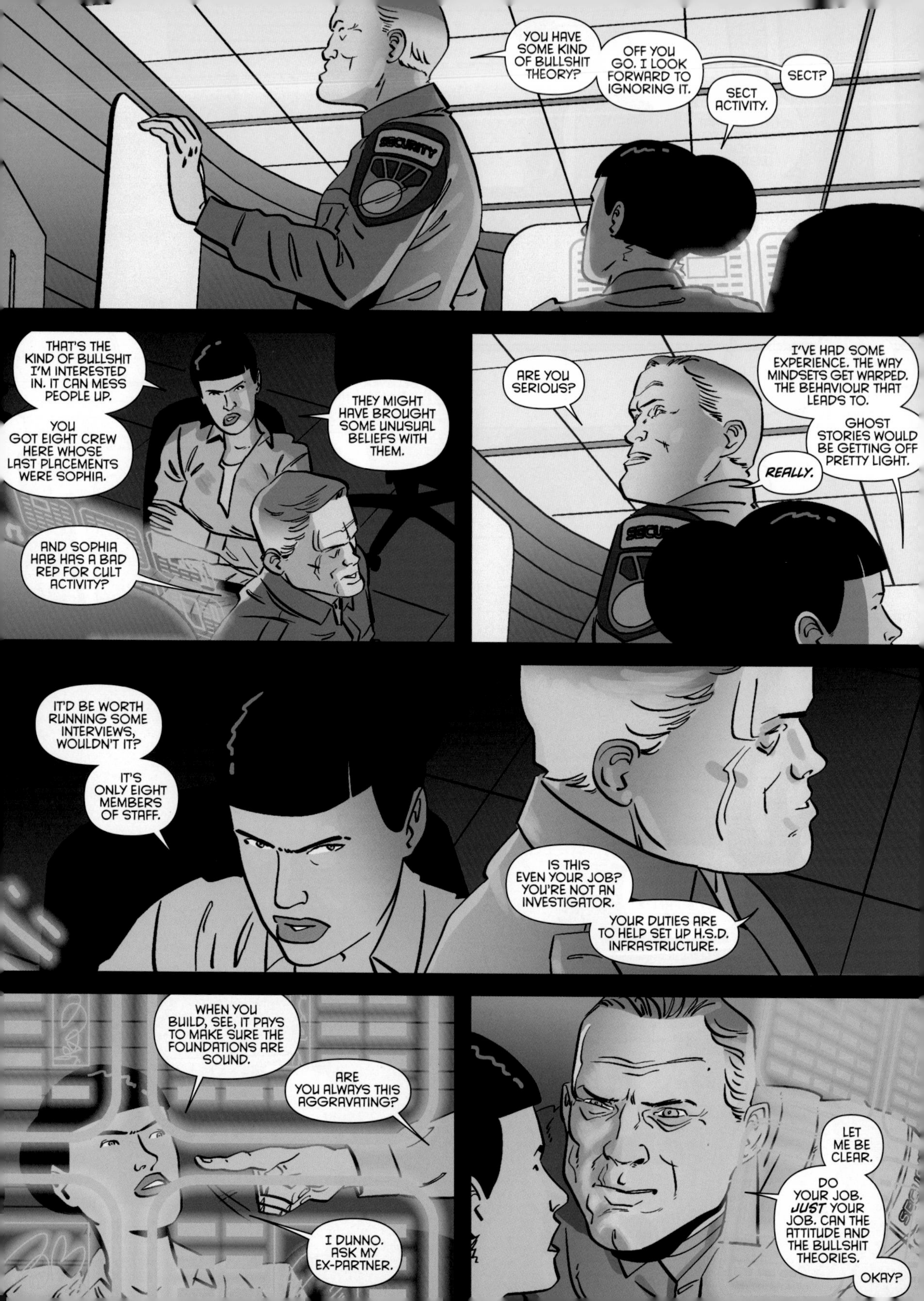
YOU HAVE SOME KIND OF BULLSHIT THEORY?
OFF YOU GO. I LOOK FORWARD TO IGNORING IT.
SECT ACTIVITY.
SECT?
THAT'S THE KIND OF BULLSHIT I'M INTERESTED IN. IT CAN MESS PEOPLE UP.
YOU GOT EIGHT CREW HERE WHOSE LAST PLACEMENTS WERE SOPHIA.
THEY MIGHT HAVE BROUGHT SOME UNUSUAL BELIEFS WITH THEM.
AND SOPHIA HAB HAS A BAD REP FOR CULT ACTIVITY?
ARE YOU SERIOUS?
I'VE HAD SOME EXPERIENCE. THE WAY MINDSETS GET WARPED. THE BEHAVIOUR THAT LEADS TO.
GHOST STORIES WOULD BE GETTING OFF PRETTY LIGHT.
REALLY.
IT'D BE WORTH RUNNING SOME INTERVIEWS, WOULDN'T IT?
IT'S ONLY EIGHT MEMBERS OF STAFF.
IS THIS EVEN YOUR JOB? YOU'RE NOT AN INVESTIGATOR.
YOUR DUTIES ARE TO HELP SET UP H.S.D. INFRASTRUCTURE.
WHEN YOU BUILD, SEE, IT PAYS TO MAKE SURE THE FOUNDATIONS ARE SOUND.
ARE YOU ALWAYS THIS AGGRAVATING?
I DUNNO. ASK MY EX-PARTNER.
LET ME BE CLEAR.
DO YOUR JOB. JUST YOUR JOB. CAN THE ATTITUDE AND THE BULLSHIT THEORIES.
OKAY?

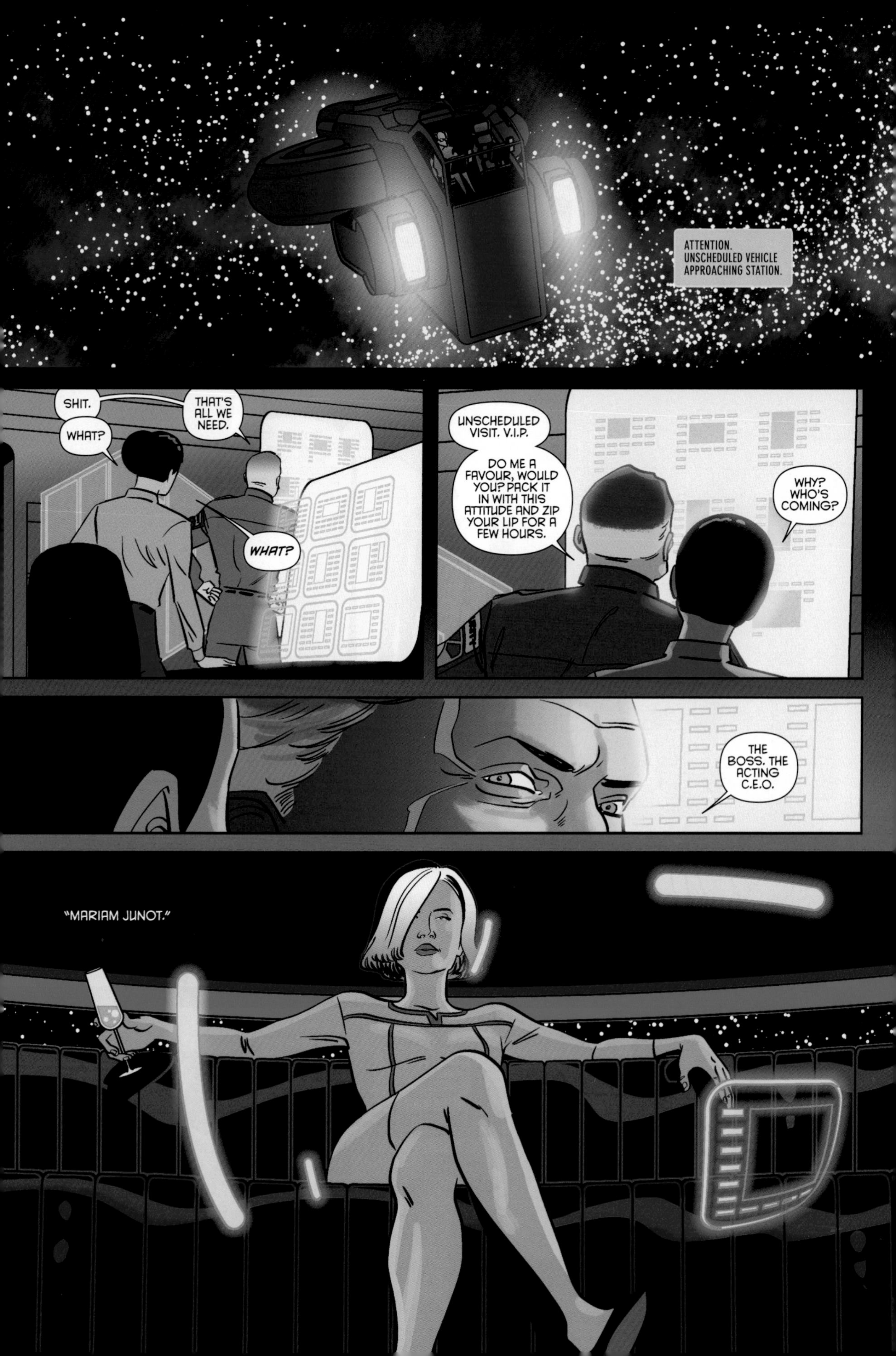
ATTENTION. UNSCHEDULED VEHICLE APPROACHING STATION.
SHIT.
THAT'S ALL WE NEED.
WHAT?
WHAT?
UNSCHEDULED VISIT. V.I.P.
DO ME A FAVOUR, WOULD YOU? PACK IT IN WITH THIS ATTITUDE AND ZIP YOUR LIP FOR A FEW HOURS.
WHY? WHO'S COMING?
THE BOSS. THE ACTING C.E.O.
"MARIAM JUNOT."

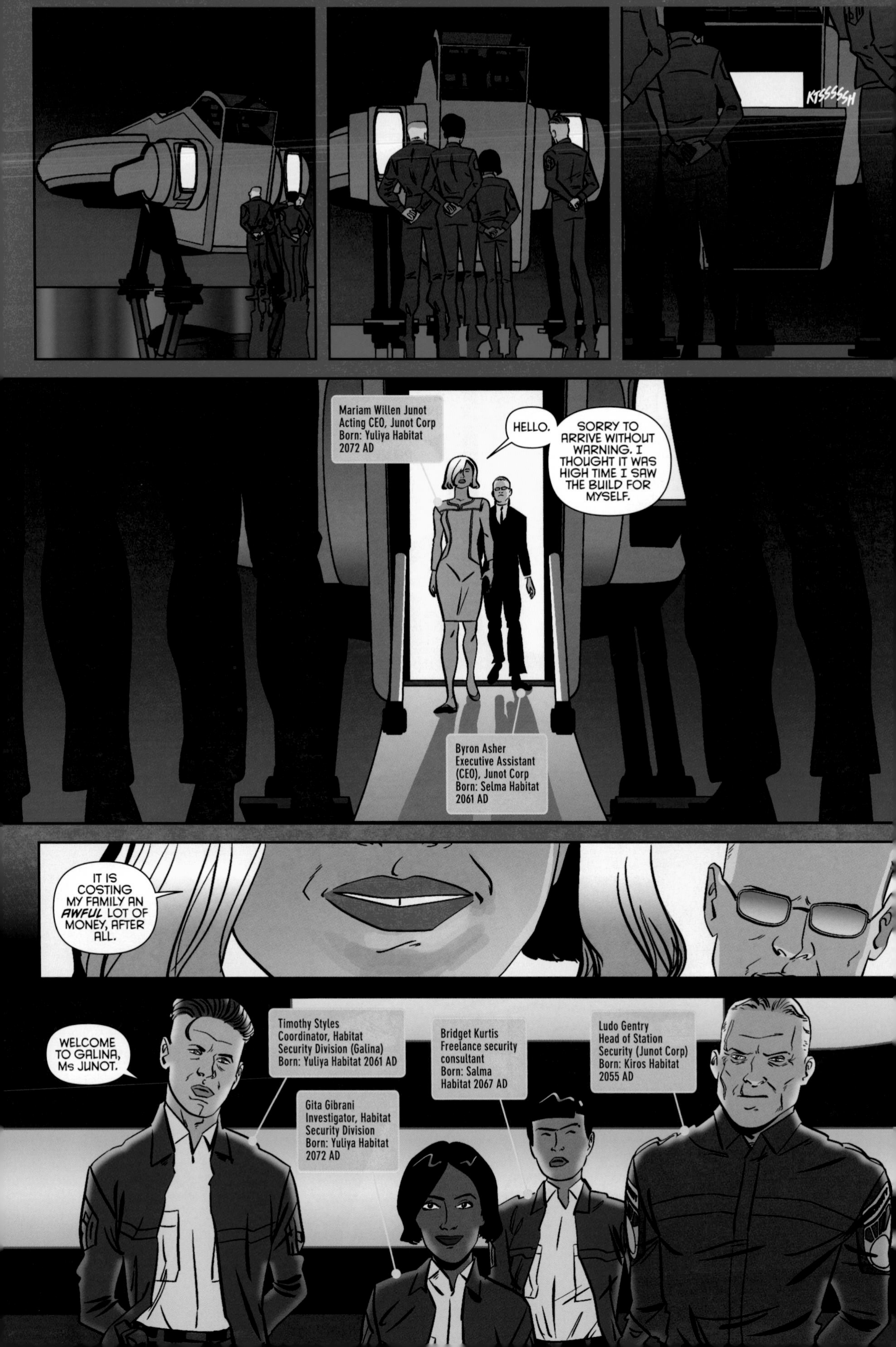
KTSSSSSH
Mariam Willen Junot
Acting CEO, Junot Corp
Born: Yuliya Habitat
2072 AD
HELLO.
SORRY TO ARRIVE WITHOUT WARNING. I THOUGHT IT WAS HIGH TIME I SAW THE BUILD FOR MYSELF.
Byron Asher
Executive Assistant
(CEO), Junot Corp
Born: Selma Habitat
2061 AD
IT IS COSTING MY FAMILY AN AWFUL LOT OF MONEY, AFTER ALL.
WELCOME TO GALINA, Ms JUNOT.
Timothy Styles
Coordinator, Habitat
Security Division (Galina)
Born: Yuliya Habitat 2061 AD
Gita Gibrani
Investigator, Habitat
Security Division
Born: Yuliya Habitat
2072 AD
Bridget Kurtis
Freelance security
consultant
Born: Salma
Habitat 2067 AD
Ludo Gentry
Head of Station
Security (Junot Corp)
Born: Kiros Habitat
2055 AD

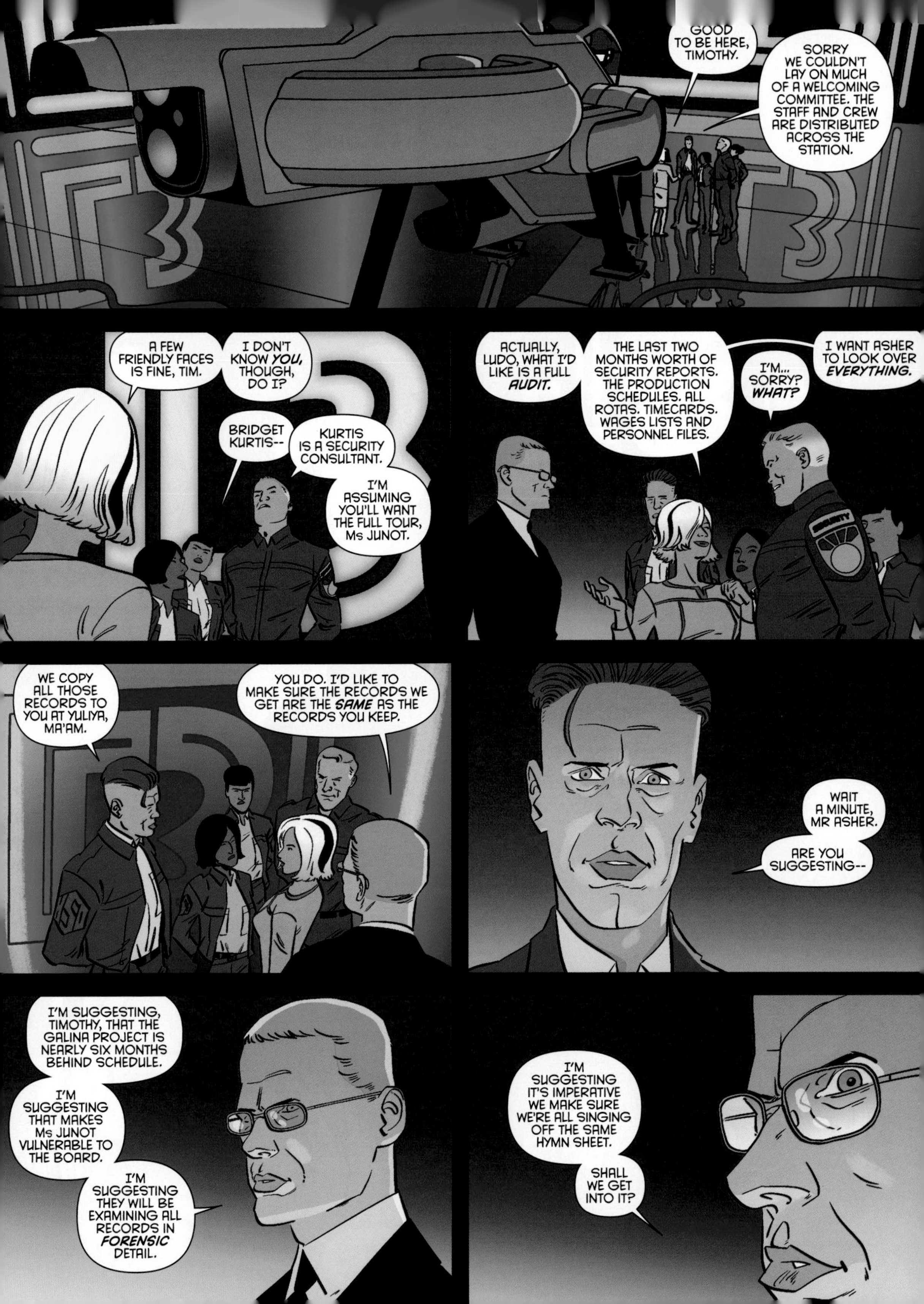
GOOD TO BE HERE, TIMOTHY.
SORRY WE COULDN'T LAY ON MUCH OF A WELCOMING COMMITTEE. THE STAFF AND CREW ARE DISTRIBUTED ACROSS THE STATION.
A FEW FRIENDLY FACES IS FINE, TIM.
I DON'T KNOW *YOU,* THOUGH, DO I?
BRIDGET KURTIS--
KURTIS IS A SECURITY CONSULTANT.
I'M ASSUMING YOU'LL WANT THE FULL TOUR, Ms JUNOT.
ACTUALLY, LUDO, WHAT I'D LIKE IS A FULL *AUDIT.*
THE LAST TWO MONTHS WORTH OF SECURITY REPORTS. THE PRODUCTION SCHEDULES. ALL ROTAS. TIMECARDS. WAGES LISTS AND PERSONNEL FILES.
I WANT ASHER TO LOOK OVER *EVERYTHING.*
I'M... SORRY? *WHAT?*
WE COPY ALL THOSE RECORDS TO YOU AT YULIYA, MA'AM.
YOU DO. I'D LIKE TO MAKE SURE THE RECORDS WE GET ARE THE *SAME* AS THE RECORDS YOU KEEP.
WAIT A MINUTE, MR ASHER.
ARE YOU SUGGESTING--
I'M SUGGESTING, TIMOTHY, THAT THE GALINA PROJECT IS NEARLY SIX MONTHS BEHIND SCHEDULE.
I'M SUGGESTING THAT MAKES Ms JUNOT VULNERABLE TO THE BOARD.
I'M SUGGESTING THEY WILL BE EXAMINING ALL RECORDS IN *FORENSIC* DETAIL.
I'M SUGGESTING IT'S IMPERATIVE WE MAKE SURE WE'RE ALL SINGING OFF THE SAME HYMN SHEET.
SHALL WE GET INTO IT?

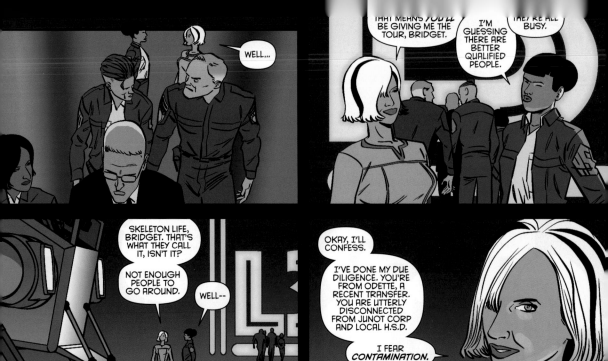

WELL...

THAT MEANS *YOU'LL* BE GIVING ME THE TOUR, BRIDGET.

I'M GUESSING THERE ARE BETTER QUALIFIED PEOPLE.

THEY'RE ALL BUSY.

SKELETON LIFE, BRIDGET. THAT'S WHAT THEY CALL IT, ISN'T IT?

NOT ENOUGH PEOPLE TO GO AROUND.

WELL--

OKAY, I'LL CONFESS.

I'VE DONE MY DUE DILIGENCE. YOU'RE FROM ODETTE, A RECENT TRANSFER. YOU ARE UTTERLY DISCONNECTED FROM JUNOT CORP AND LOCAL H.S.D.

I FEAR *CONTAMINATION.*

CONTAMINATION?

THE BOARD IS TRYING TO OUST ME. A BUY-OUT FROM FONTAG CORP, PERHAPS.

I DON'T TRUST GENTRY AND THE OTHER SENIORS. I DON'T TRUST *ANYONE* WITH LINKS TO THE BOARD.

YOU TRUST ME BECAUSE I'M AN UNKNOWN?

INTERESTING PSYCHOLOGY.

THIS IS ME GIVING YOU FULL--AND *PRIVATE*--SECURITY CLEARANCE.

TO INVESTIGATE.

INVESTIGATE WHAT?

THE HAUNTING, BRIDGET, THE *HAUNTING.*

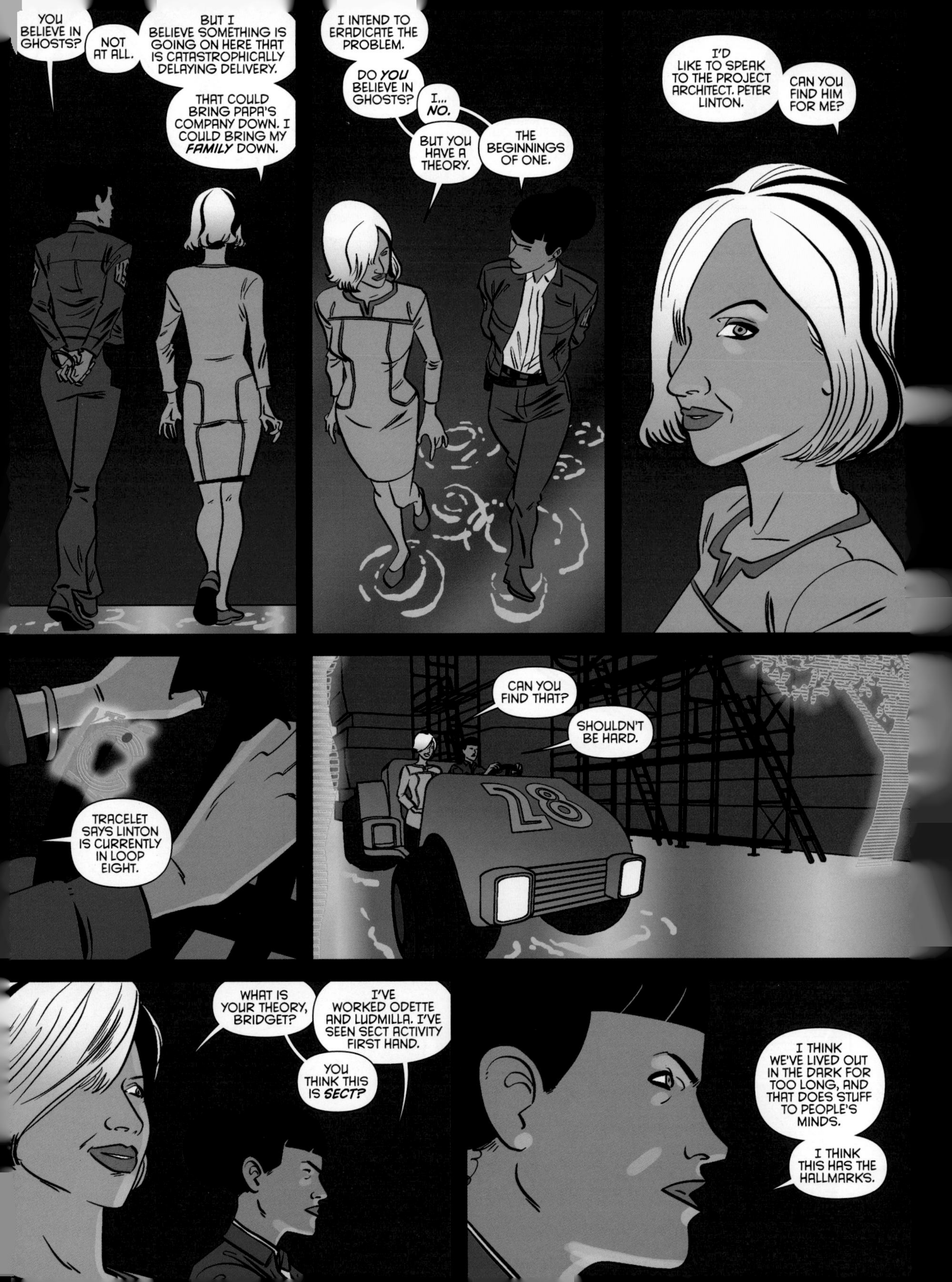
YOU BELIEVE IN GHOSTS?
NOT AT ALL.
BUT I BELIEVE SOMETHING IS GOING ON HERE THAT IS CATASTROPHICALLY DELAYING DELIVERY.
THAT COULD BRING PAPA'S COMPANY DOWN. I COULD BRING MY *FAMILY* DOWN.
I INTEND TO ERADICATE THE PROBLEM.
DO *YOU* BELIEVE IN GHOSTS?
I... *NO.*
BUT YOU HAVE A THEORY.
THE BEGINNINGS OF ONE.
I'D LIKE TO SPEAK TO THE PROJECT ARCHITECT. PETER LINTON.
CAN YOU FIND HIM FOR ME?
TRACELET SAYS LINTON IS CURRENTLY IN LOOP EIGHT.
CAN YOU FIND THAT?
SHOULDN'T BE HARD.
28
WHAT IS YOUR THEORY, BRIDGET?
I'VE WORKED ODETTE AND LUDMILLA. I'VE SEEN SECT ACTIVITY FIRST HAND.
YOU THINK THIS IS *SECT?*
I THINK WE'VE LIVED OUT IN THE DARK FOR TOO LONG, AND THAT DOES STUFF TO PEOPLE'S MINDS.
I THINK THIS HAS THE HALLMARKS.

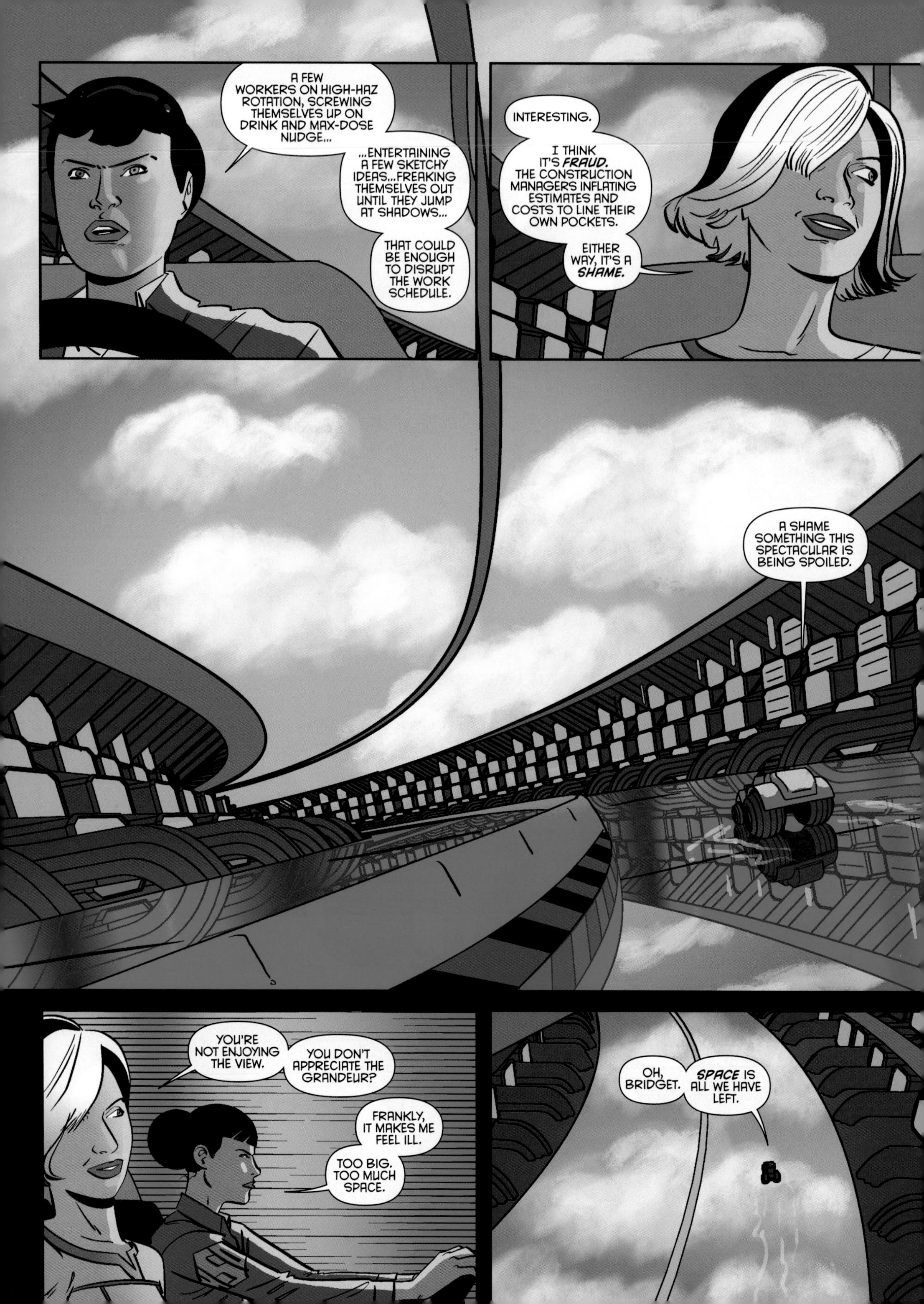
A FEW WORKERS ON HIGH-HAZ ROTATION, SCREWING THEMSELVES UP ON DRINK AND MAX-DOSE NUDGE...
...ENTERTAINING A FEW SKETCHY IDEAS...FREAKING THEMSELVES OUT UNTIL THEY JUMP AT SHADOWS...
THAT COULD BE ENOUGH TO DISRUPT THE WORK SCHEDULE.
INTERESTING.
I THINK IT'S FRAUD. THE CONSTRUCTION MANAGERS INFLATING ESTIMATES AND COSTS TO LINE THEIR OWN POCKETS.
EITHER WAY, IT'S A SHAME.
A SHAME SOMETHING THIS SPECTACULAR IS BEING SPOILED.
YOU'RE NOT ENJOYING THE VIEW.
YOU DON'T APPRECIATE THE GRANDEUR?
FRANKLY, IT MAKES ME FEEL ILL.
TOO BIG. TOO MUCH SPACE.
OH, BRIDGET.
SPACE IS ALL WE HAVE LEFT.

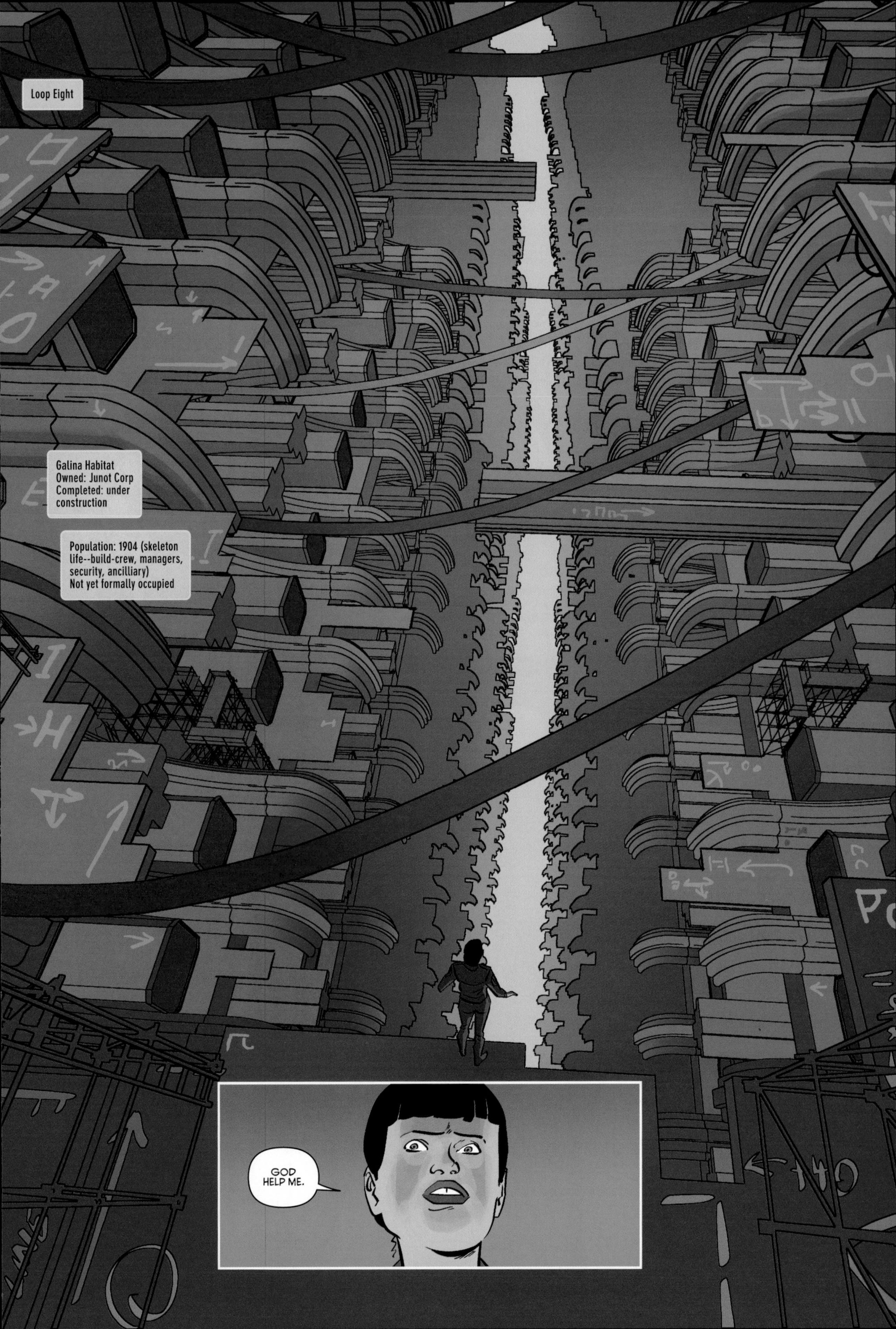

Loop Eight
Galina Habitat
Owned: Junot Corp
Completed: under construction
Population: 1904 (skeleton life--build-crew, managers, security, ancilliary)
Not yet formally occupied
GOD HELP ME.

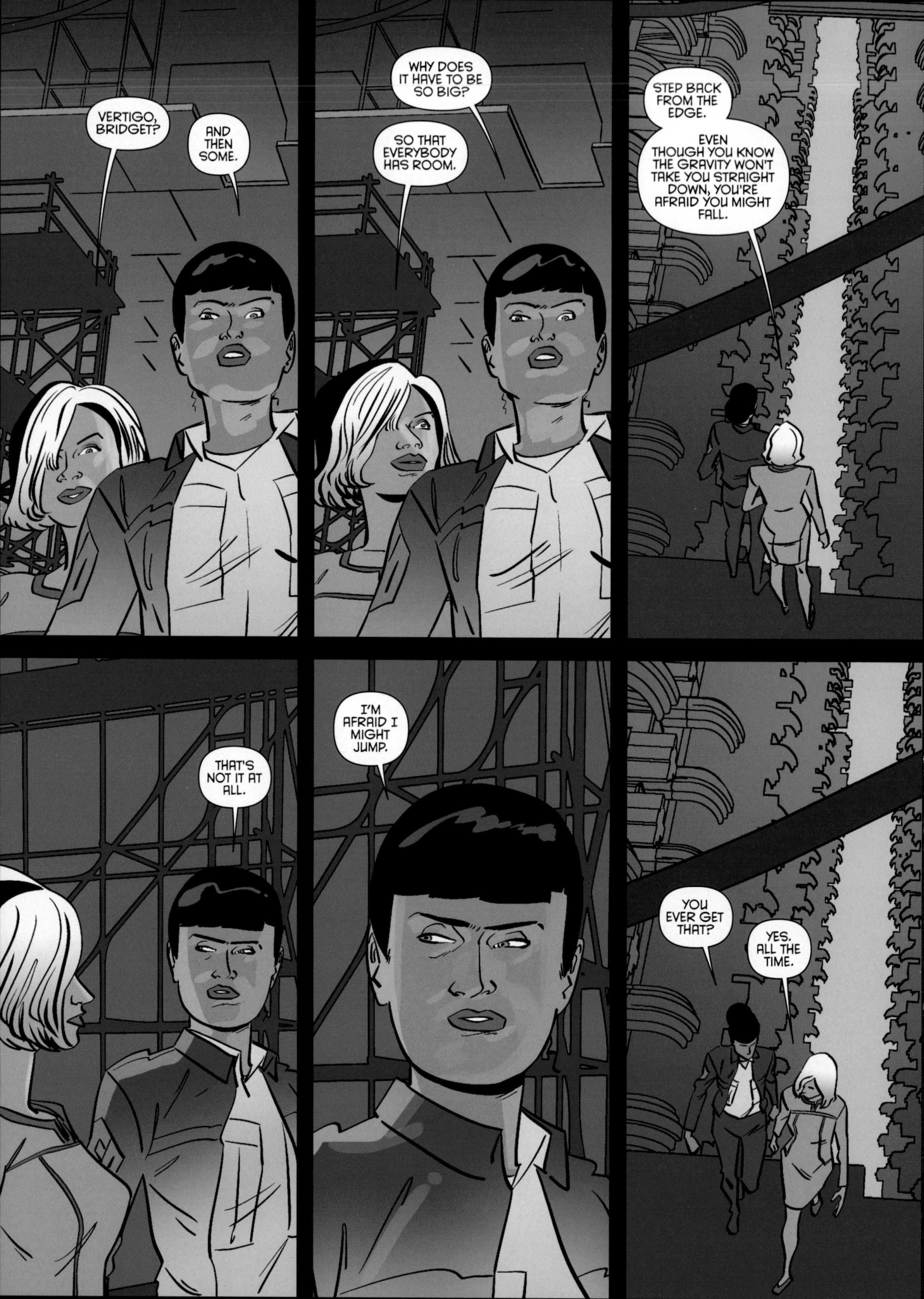
VERTIGO, BRIDGET?
AND THEN SOME.
WHY DOES IT HAVE TO BE SO BIG?
SO THAT EVERYBODY HAS ROOM.
STEP BACK FROM THE EDGE.
EVEN THOUGH YOU KNOW THE GRAVITY WON'T TAKE YOU STRAIGHT DOWN, YOU'RE AFRAID YOU MIGHT FALL.
THAT'S NOT IT AT ALL.
I'M AFRAID I MIGHT JUMP.
YOU EVER GET THAT?
YES. ALL THE TIME.

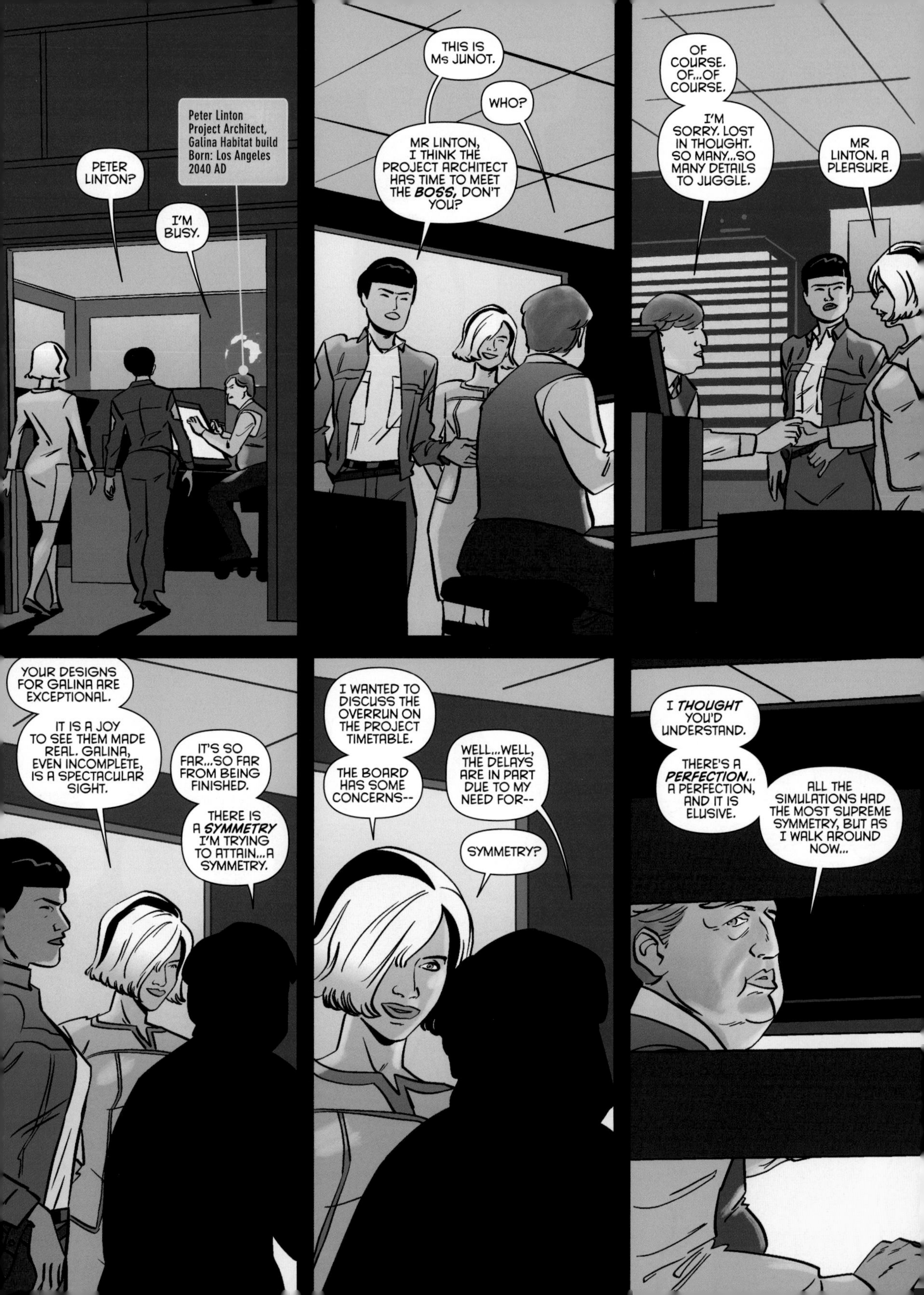
Peter Linton Project Architect, Galina Habitat build Born: Los Angeles 2040 AD
PETER LINTON?
I'M BUSY.
THIS IS Ms JUNOT.
WHO?
MR LINTON, I THINK THE PROJECT ARCHITECT HAS TIME TO MEET THE *BOSS,* DON'T YOU?
OF COURSE. OF...OF COURSE.
I'M SORRY. LOST IN THOUGHT. SO MANY...SO MANY DETAILS TO JUGGLE.
MR LINTON. A PLEASURE.
YOUR DESIGNS FOR GALINA ARE EXCEPTIONAL.
IT IS A JOY TO SEE THEM MADE REAL. GALINA, EVEN INCOMPLETE, IS A SPECTACULAR SIGHT.
IT'S SO FAR...SO FAR FROM BEING FINISHED.
THERE IS A *SYMMETRY* I'M TRYING TO ATTAIN...A SYMMETRY.
I WANTED TO DISCUSS THE OVERRUN ON THE PROJECT TIMETABLE.
THE BOARD HAS SOME CONCERNS--
WELL...WELL, THE DELAYS ARE IN PART DUE TO MY NEED FOR--
SYMMETRY?
I *THOUGHT* YOU'D UNDERSTAND.
THERE'S A *PERFECTION*... A PERFECTION, AND IT IS ELUSIVE.
ALL THE SIMULATIONS HAD THE MOST SUPREME SYMMETRY, BUT AS I WALK AROUND NOW...

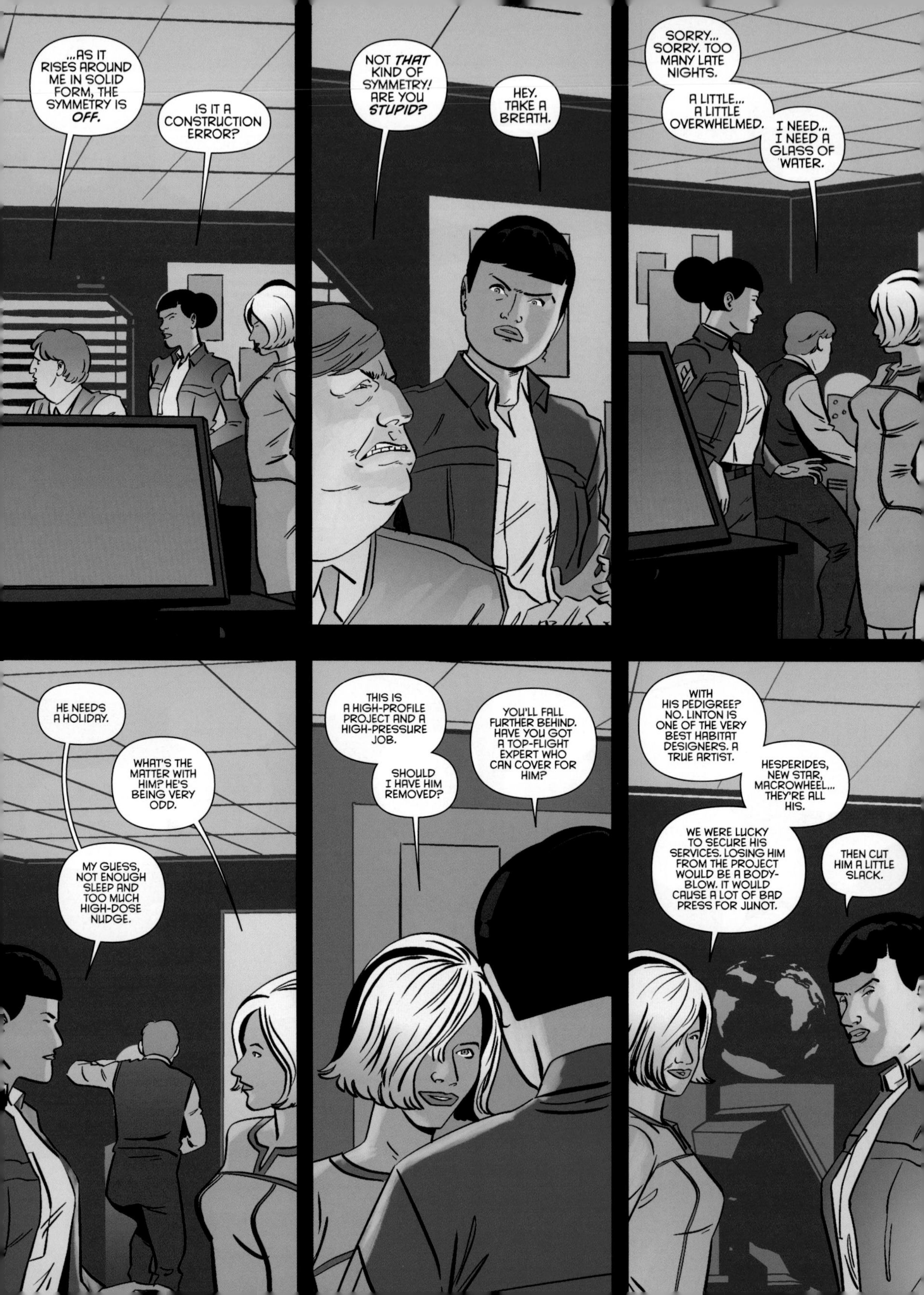
...AS IT RISES AROUND ME IN SOLID FORM, THE SYMMETRY IS *OFF.*
IS IT A CONSTRUCTION ERROR?
NOT *THAT* KIND OF SYMMETRY! ARE YOU *STUPID?*
HEY. TAKE A BREATH.
SORRY... SORRY. TOO MANY LATE NIGHTS.
A LITTLE... A LITTLE OVERWHELMED.
I NEED... I NEED A GLASS OF WATER.
HE NEEDS A HOLIDAY.
WHAT'S THE MATTER WITH HIM? HE'S BEING VERY ODD.
MY GUESS, NOT ENOUGH SLEEP AND TOO MUCH HIGH-DOSE NUDGE.
THIS IS A HIGH-PROFILE PROJECT AND A HIGH-PRESSURE JOB.
SHOULD I HAVE HIM REMOVED?
YOU'LL FALL FURTHER BEHIND. HAVE YOU GOT A TOP-FLIGHT EXPERT WHO CAN COVER FOR HIM?
WITH HIS PEDIGREE? NO. LINTON IS ONE OF THE VERY BEST HABITAT DESIGNERS. A TRUE ARTIST.
HESPERIDES, NEW STAR, MACROWHEEL... THEY'RE ALL HIS.
WE WERE LUCKY TO SECURE HIS SERVICES. LOSING HIM FROM THE PROJECT WOULD BE A BODY-BLOW. IT WOULD CAUSE A LOT OF BAD PRESS FOR JUNOT.
THEN CUT HIM A LITTLE SLACK.

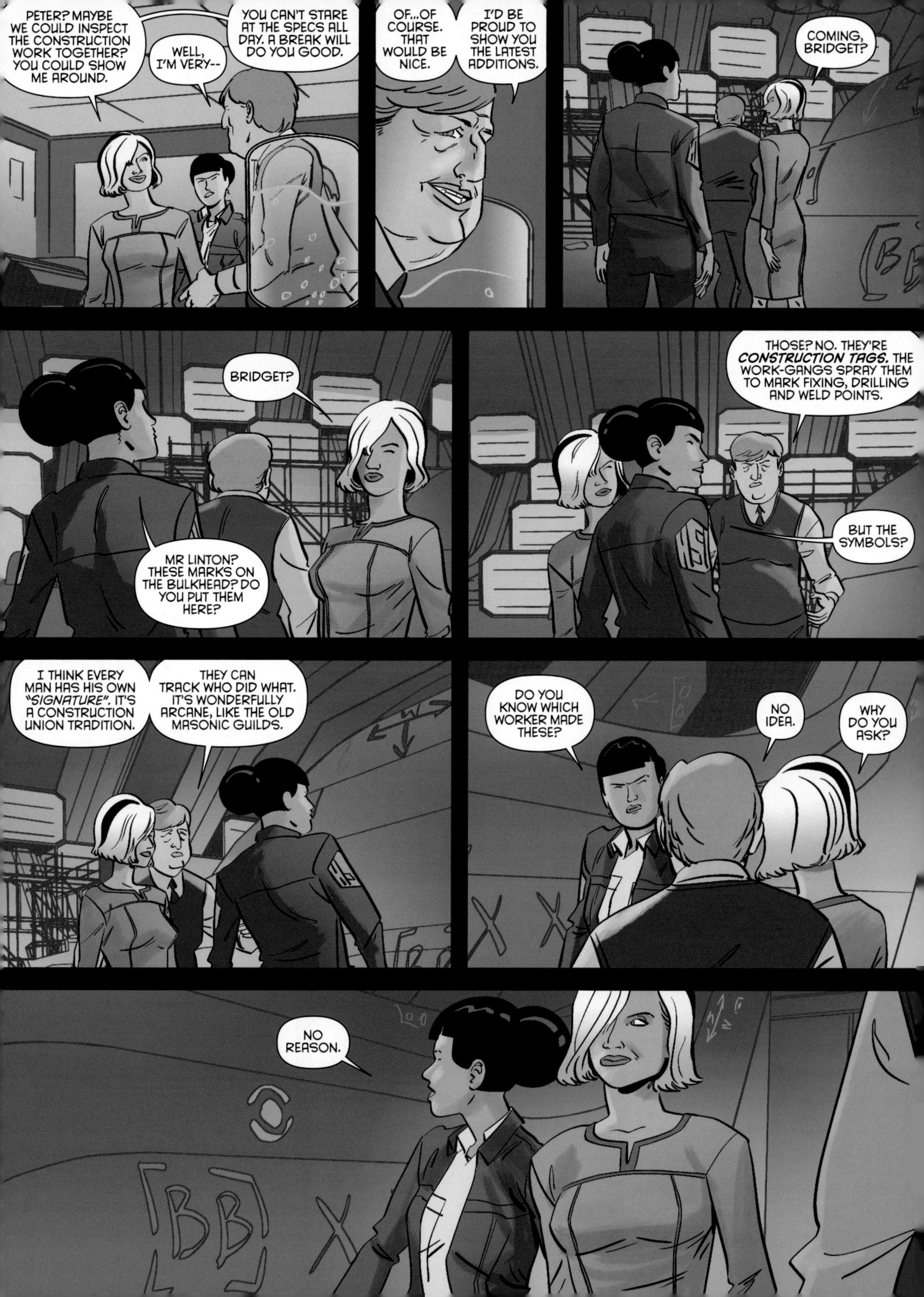
PETER? MAYBE WE COULD INSPECT THE CONSTRUCTION WORK TOGETHER? YOU COULD SHOW ME AROUND.
WELL, I'M VERY--
YOU CAN'T STARE AT THE SPECS ALL DAY. A BREAK WILL DO YOU GOOD.
OF...OF COURSE. THAT WOULD BE NICE.
I'D BE PROUD TO SHOW YOU THE LATEST ADDITIONS.
COMING, BRIDGET?
BRIDGET?
MR LINTON? THESE MARKS ON THE BULKHEAD? DO YOU PUT THEM HERE?
THOSE? NO. THEY'RE *CONSTRUCTION TAGS.* THE WORK-GANGS SPRAY THEM TO MARK FIXING, DRILLING AND WELD POINTS.
BUT THE SYMBOLS?
I THINK EVERY MAN HAS HIS OWN "*SIGNATURE*". IT'S A CONSTRUCTION UNION TRADITION.
THEY CAN TRACK WHO DID WHAT. IT'S WONDERFULLY ARCANE, LIKE THE OLD MASONIC GUILDS.
DO YOU KNOW WHICH WORKER MADE THESE?
NO IDEA.
WHY DO YOU ASK?
NO REASON.

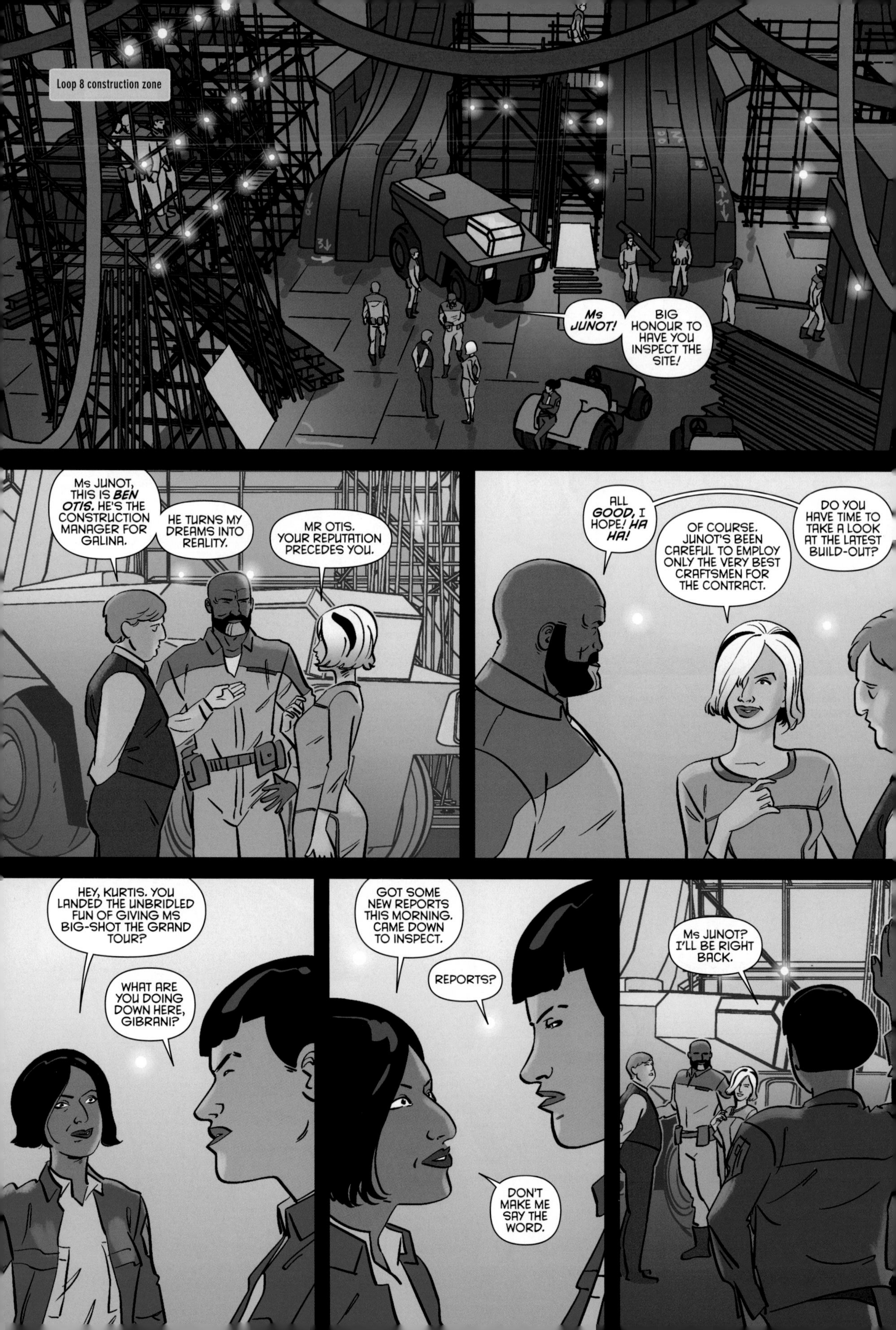
Loop 8 construction zone
Ms JUNOT!
BIG HONOUR TO HAVE YOU INSPECT THE SITE!
Ms JUNOT, THIS IS BEN OTIS. HE'S THE CONSTRUCTION MANAGER FOR GALINA.
HE TURNS MY DREAMS INTO REALITY.
MR OTIS. YOUR REPUTATION PRECEDES YOU.
ALL GOOD, I HOPE! HA HA!
OF COURSE. JUNOT'S BEEN CAREFUL TO EMPLOY ONLY THE VERY BEST CRAFTSMEN FOR THE CONTRACT.
DO YOU HAVE TIME TO TAKE A LOOK AT THE LATEST BUILD-OUT?
HEY, KURTIS. YOU LANDED THE UNBRIDLED FUN OF GIVING MS BIG-SHOT THE GRAND TOUR?
WHAT ARE YOU DOING DOWN HERE, GIBRANI?
GOT SOME NEW REPORTS THIS MORNING. CAME DOWN TO INSPECT.
REPORTS?
DON'T MAKE ME SAY THE WORD.
Ms JUNOT? I'LL BE RIGHT BACK.

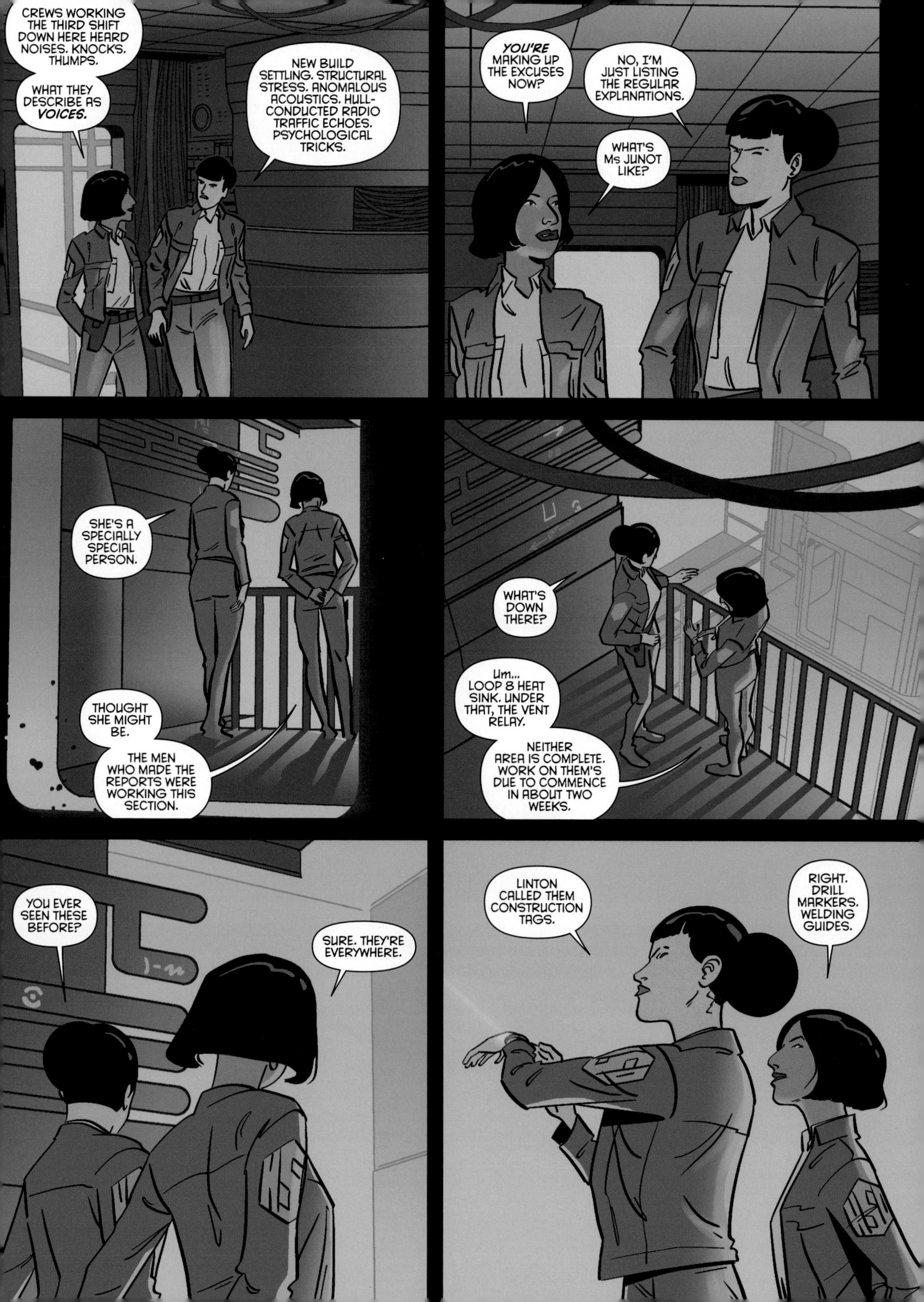
CREWS WORKING THE THIRD SHIFT DOWN HERE HEARD NOISES. KNOCKS. THUMPS.
WHAT THEY DESCRIBE AS *VOICES.*
NEW BUILD SETTLING. STRUCTURAL STRESS. ANOMALOUS ACOUSTICS. HULL-CONDUCTED RADIO TRAFFIC ECHOES. PSYCHOLOGICAL TRICKS.
YOU'RE MAKING UP THE EXCUSES NOW?
NO, I'M JUST LISTING THE REGULAR EXPLANATIONS.
WHAT'S Ms JUNOT LIKE?
SHE'S A SPECIALLY SPECIAL PERSON.
THOUGHT SHE MIGHT BE.
THE MEN WHO MADE THE REPORTS WERE WORKING THIS SECTION.
WHAT'S DOWN THERE?
Um... LOOP 8 HEAT SINK. UNDER THAT, THE VENT RELAY.
NEITHER AREA IS COMPLETE. WORK ON THEM'S DUE TO COMMENCE IN ABOUT TWO WEEKS.
YOU EVER SEEN THESE BEFORE?
SURE. THEY'RE EVERYWHERE.
LINTON CALLED THEM CONSTRUCTION TAGS.
RIGHT. DRILL MARKERS. WELDING GUIDES.

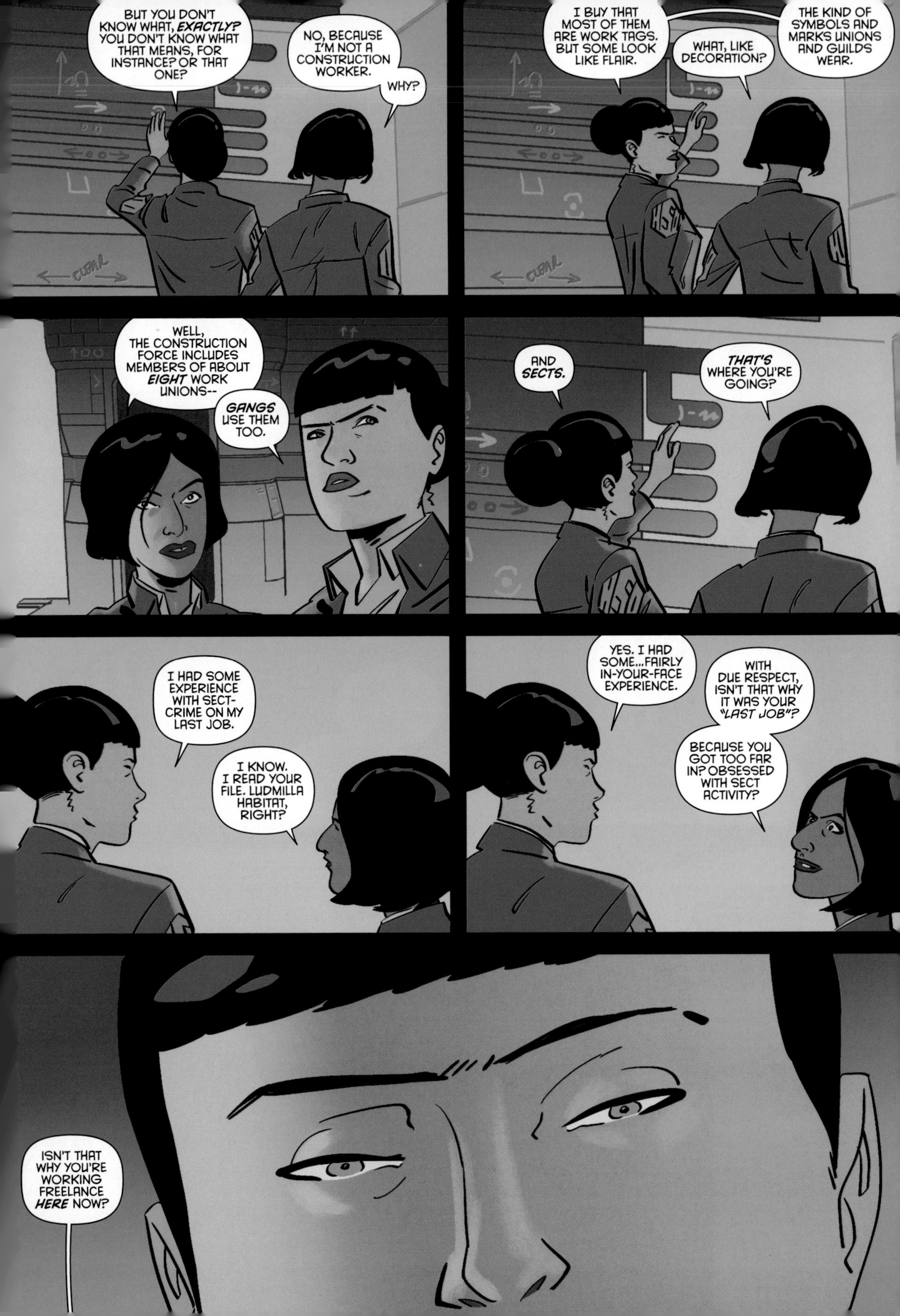
BUT YOU DON'T KNOW WHAT, *EXACTLY?* YOU DON'T KNOW WHAT THAT MEANS, FOR INSTANCE? OR THAT ONE?
NO, BECAUSE I'M NOT A CONSTRUCTION WORKER.
WHY?
I BUY THAT MOST OF THEM ARE WORK TAGS. BUT SOME LOOK LIKE FLAIR.
WHAT, LIKE DECORATION?
THE KIND OF SYMBOLS AND MARKS UNIONS AND GUILDS WEAR.
WELL, THE CONSTRUCTION FORCE INCLUDES MEMBERS OF ABOUT *EIGHT* WORK UNIONS--
GANGS USE THEM TOO.
AND *SECTS.*
THAT'S WHERE YOU'RE GOING?
I HAD SOME EXPERIENCE WITH SECT-CRIME ON MY LAST JOB.
I KNOW. I READ YOUR FILE. LUDMILLA HABITAT, RIGHT?
YES. I HAD SOME...FAIRLY IN-YOUR-FACE EXPERIENCE.
WITH DUE RESPECT, ISN'T THAT WHY IT WAS YOUR *"LAST JOB"?*
BECAUSE YOU GOT TOO FAR IN? OBSESSED WITH SECT ACTIVITY?
ISN'T THAT WHY YOU'RE WORKING FREELANCE *HERE* NOW?

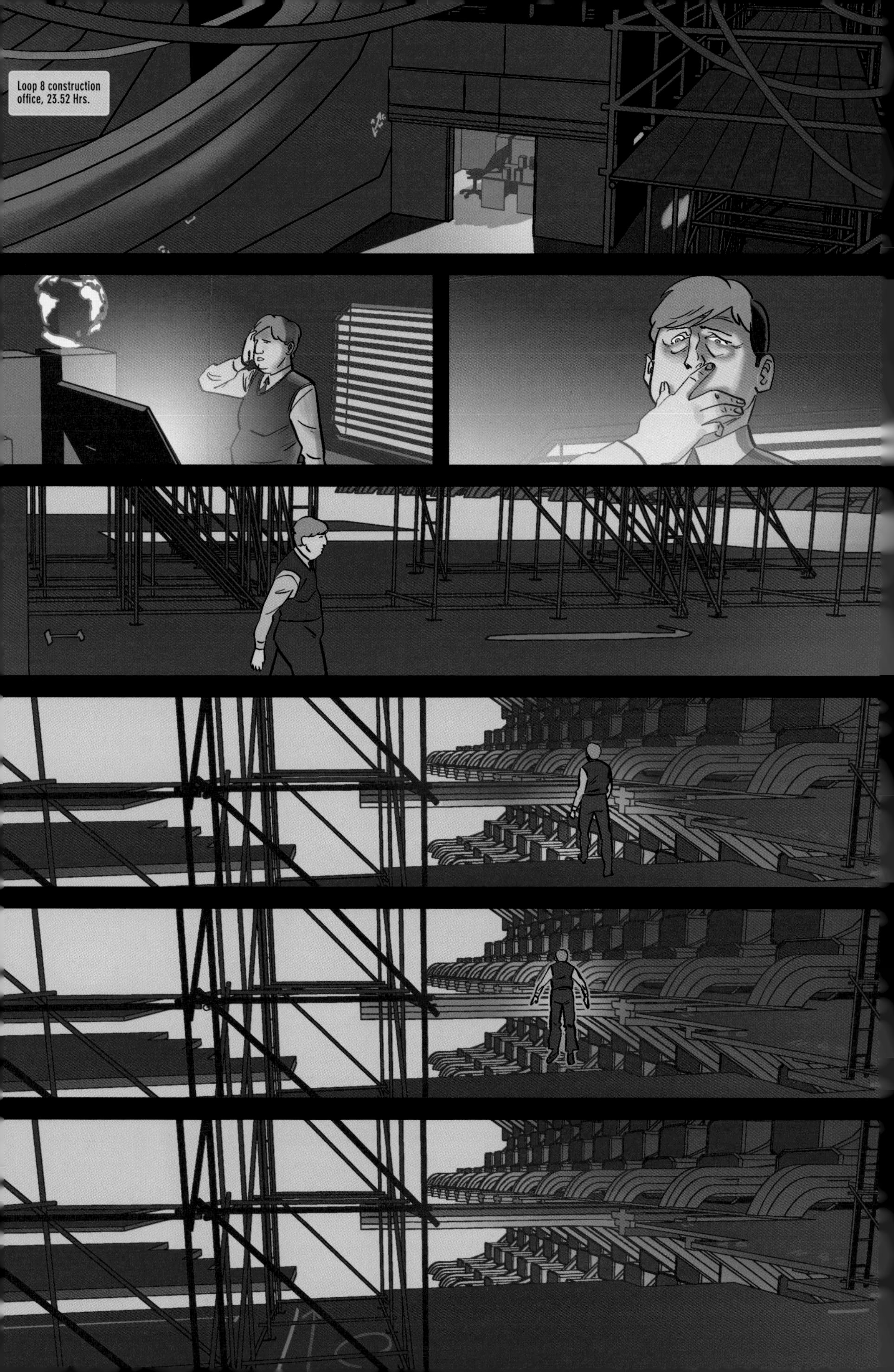
Loop 8 construction office, 23.52 Hrs.

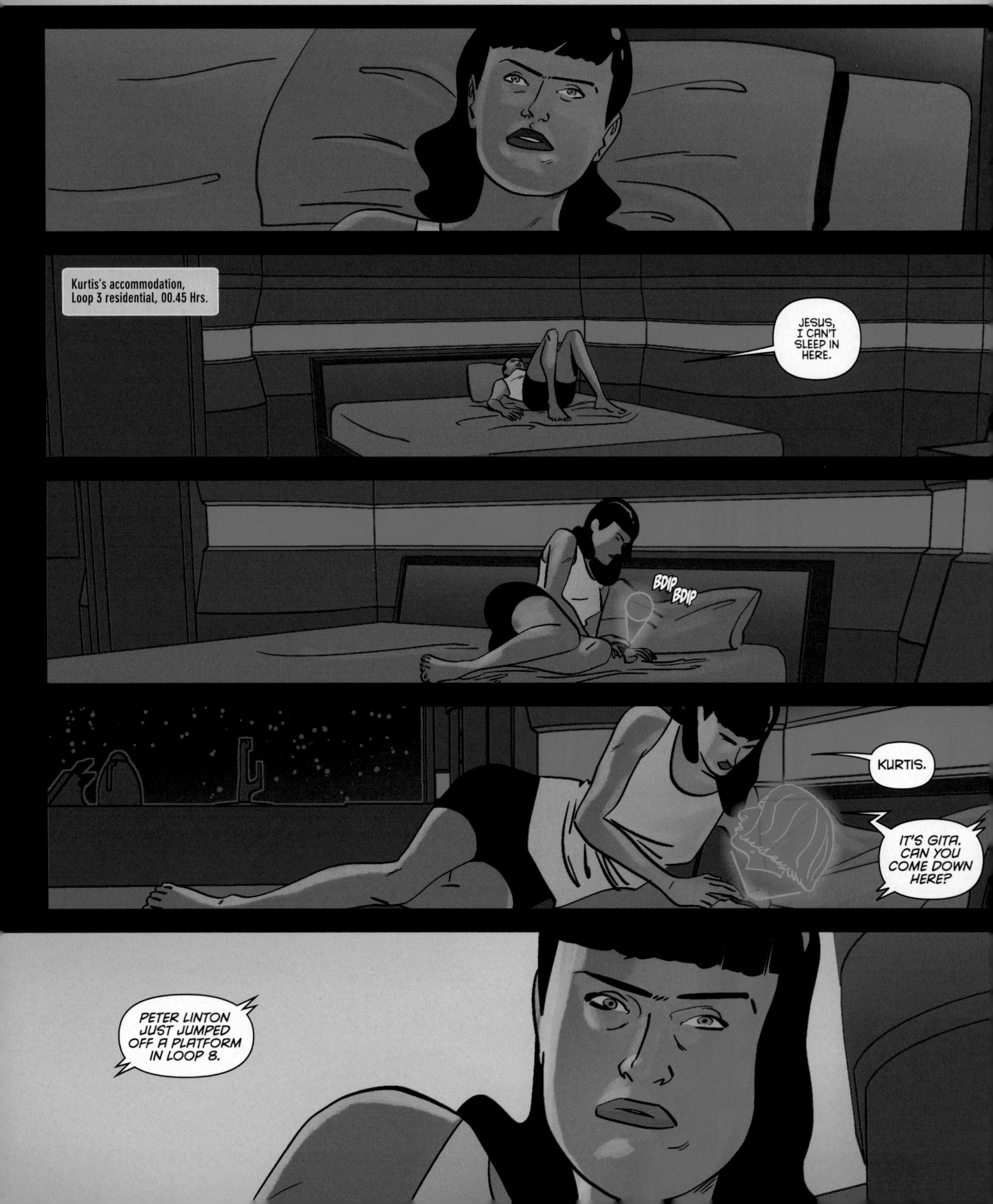

Kurtis's accommodation, Loop 3 residential, 00.45 Hrs.
JESUS, I CAN'T SLEEP IN HERE.
BDIP BDIP
KURTIS.
IT'S GITA. CAN YOU COME DOWN HERE?
PETER LINTON JUST JUMPED OFF A PLATFORM IN LOOP 8.

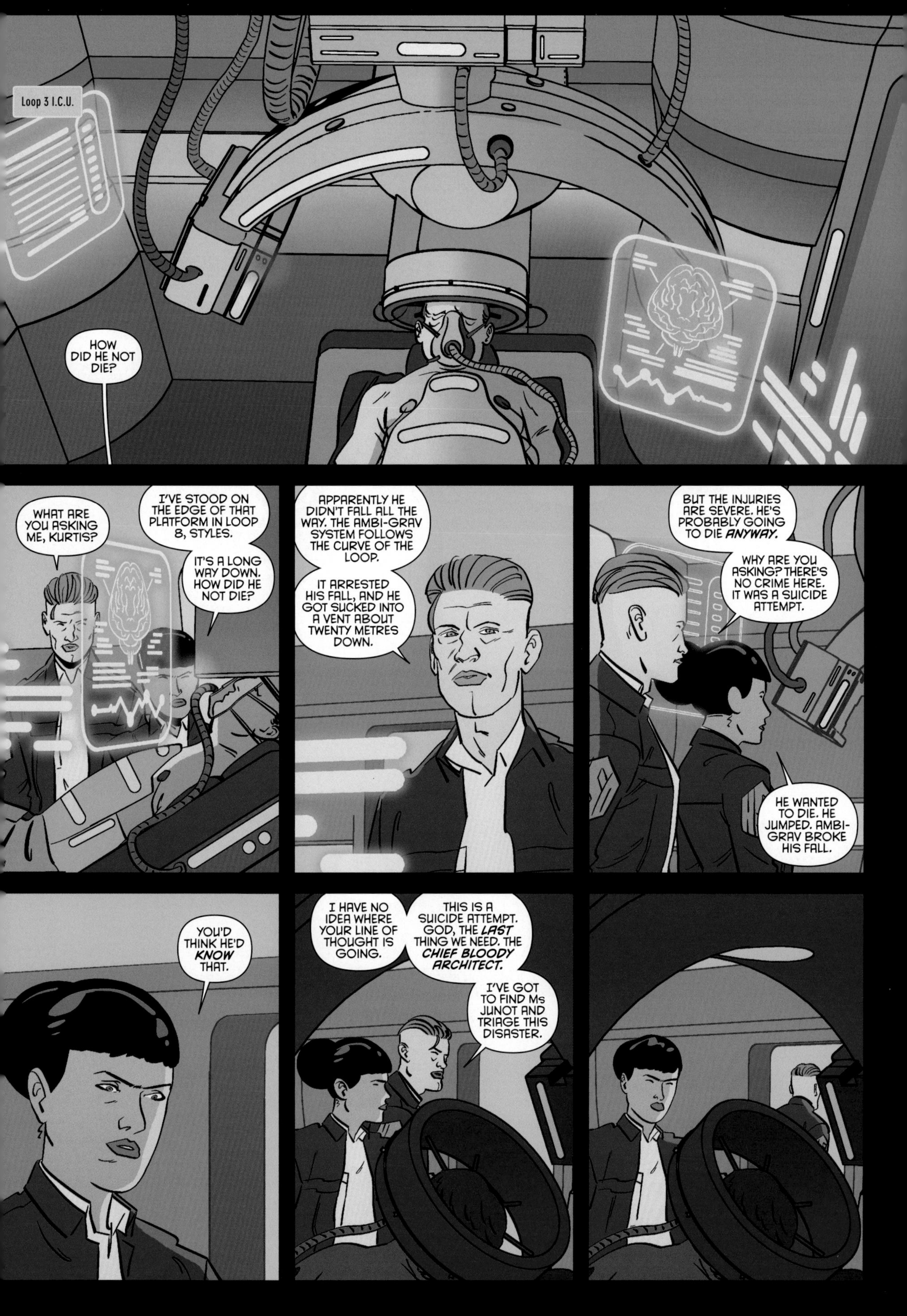
Loop 3 I.C.U.
HOW DID HE NOT DIE?
WHAT ARE YOU ASKING ME, KURTIS?
I'VE STOOD ON THE EDGE OF THAT PLATFORM IN LOOP 8, STYLES.
IT'S A LONG WAY DOWN. HOW DID HE NOT DIE?
APPARENTLY HE DIDN'T FALL ALL THE WAY. THE AMBI-GRAV SYSTEM FOLLOWS THE CURVE OF THE LOOP.
IT ARRESTED HIS FALL, AND HE GOT SUCKED INTO A VENT ABOUT TWENTY METRES DOWN.
BUT THE INJURIES ARE SEVERE. HE'S PROBABLY GOING TO DIE ANYWAY.
WHY ARE YOU ASKING? THERE'S NO CRIME HERE. IT WAS A SUICIDE ATTEMPT.
HE WANTED TO DIE. HE JUMPED. AMBI-GRAV BROKE HIS FALL.
YOU'D THINK HE'D KNOW THAT.
I HAVE NO IDEA WHERE YOUR LINE OF THOUGHT IS GOING.
THIS IS A SUICIDE ATTEMPT. GOD, THE LAST THING WE NEED. THE CHIEF BLOODY ARCHITECT.
I'VE GOT TO FIND Ms JUNOT AND TRIAGE THIS DISASTER.

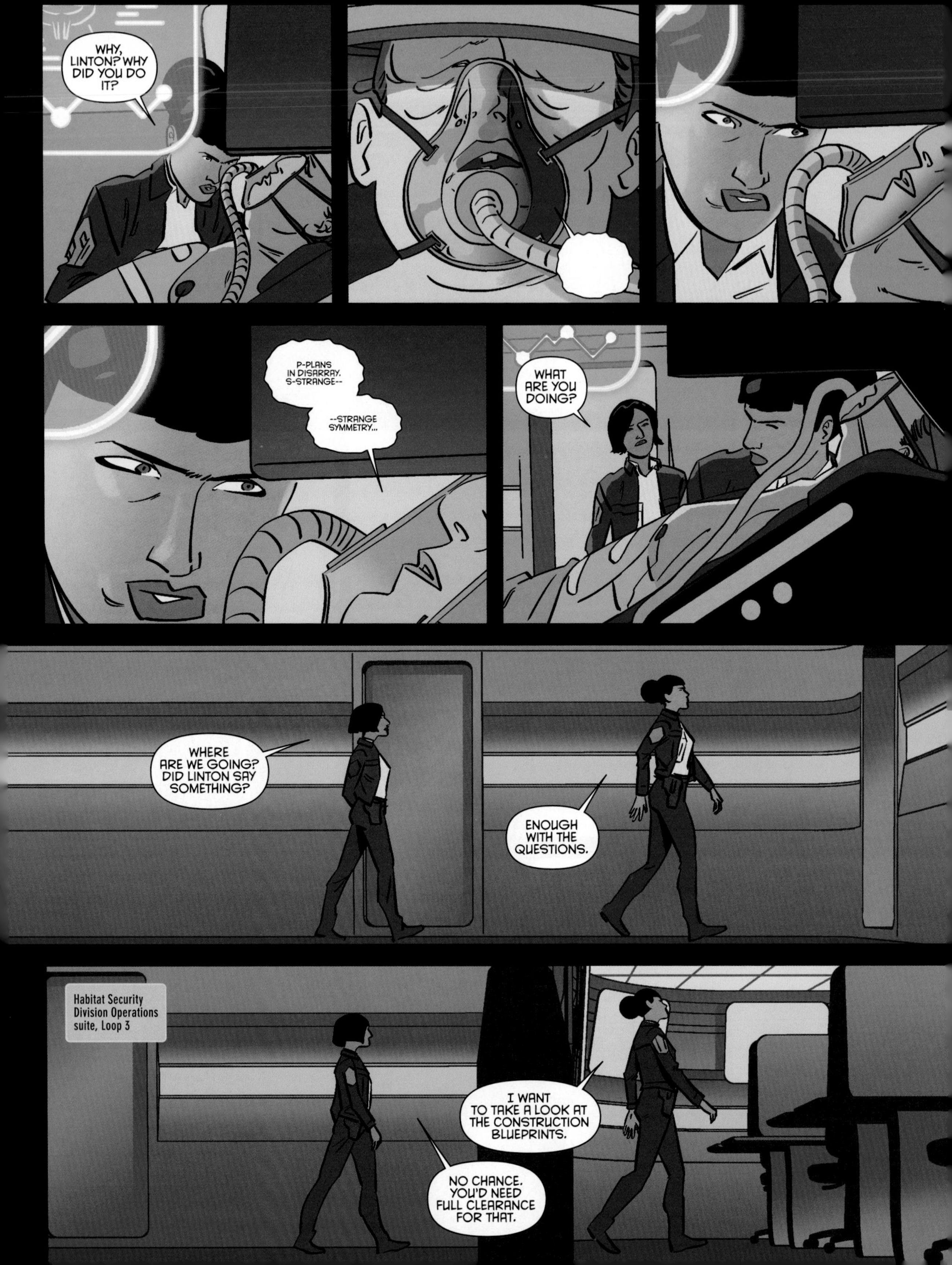
WHY, LINTON? WHY DID YOU DO IT?
P-PLANS IN DISARRAY. S-STRANGE--
--STRANGE SYMMETRY...
WHAT ARE YOU DOING?
WHERE ARE WE GOING? DID LINTON SAY SOMETHING?
ENOUGH WITH THE QUESTIONS.
Habitat Security Division Operations suite, Loop 3
I WANT TO TAKE A LOOK AT THE CONSTRUCTION BLUEPRINTS.
NO CHANCE. YOU'D NEED FULL CLEARANCE FOR THAT.

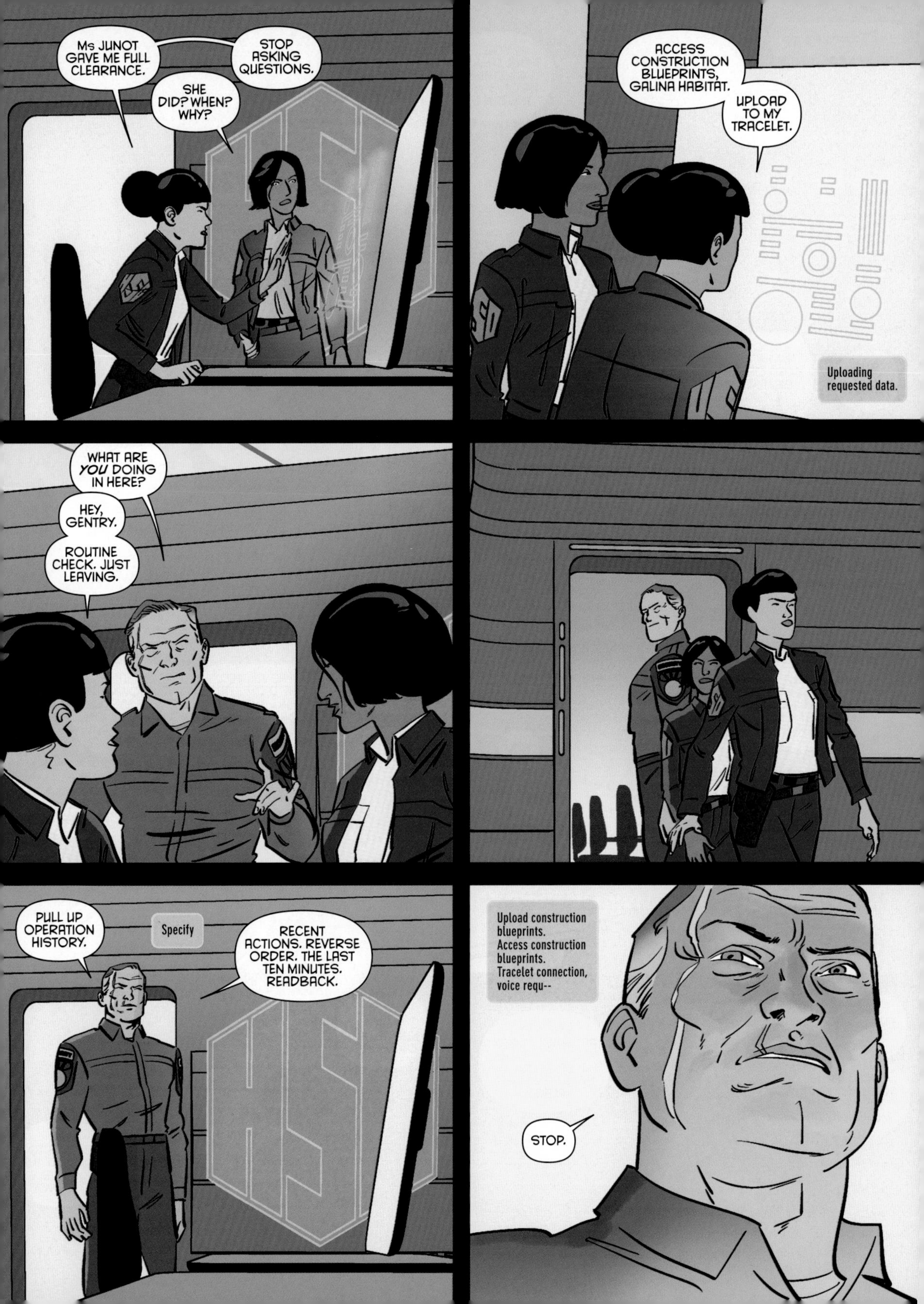

Ms JUNOT GAVE ME FULL CLEARANCE.
STOP ASKING QUESTIONS.
SHE DID? WHEN? WHY?
ACCESS CONSTRUCTION BLUEPRINTS, GALINA HABITAT.
UPLOAD TO MY TRACELET.
Uploading requested data.
WHAT ARE *YOU* DOING IN HERE?
HEY, GENTRY.
ROUTINE CHECK. JUST LEAVING.
PULL UP OPERATION HISTORY.
Specify
RECENT ACTIONS. REVERSE ORDER. THE LAST TEN MINUTES. READBACK.
Upload construction blueprints.
Access construction blueprints.
Tracelet connection, voice requ--
STOP.

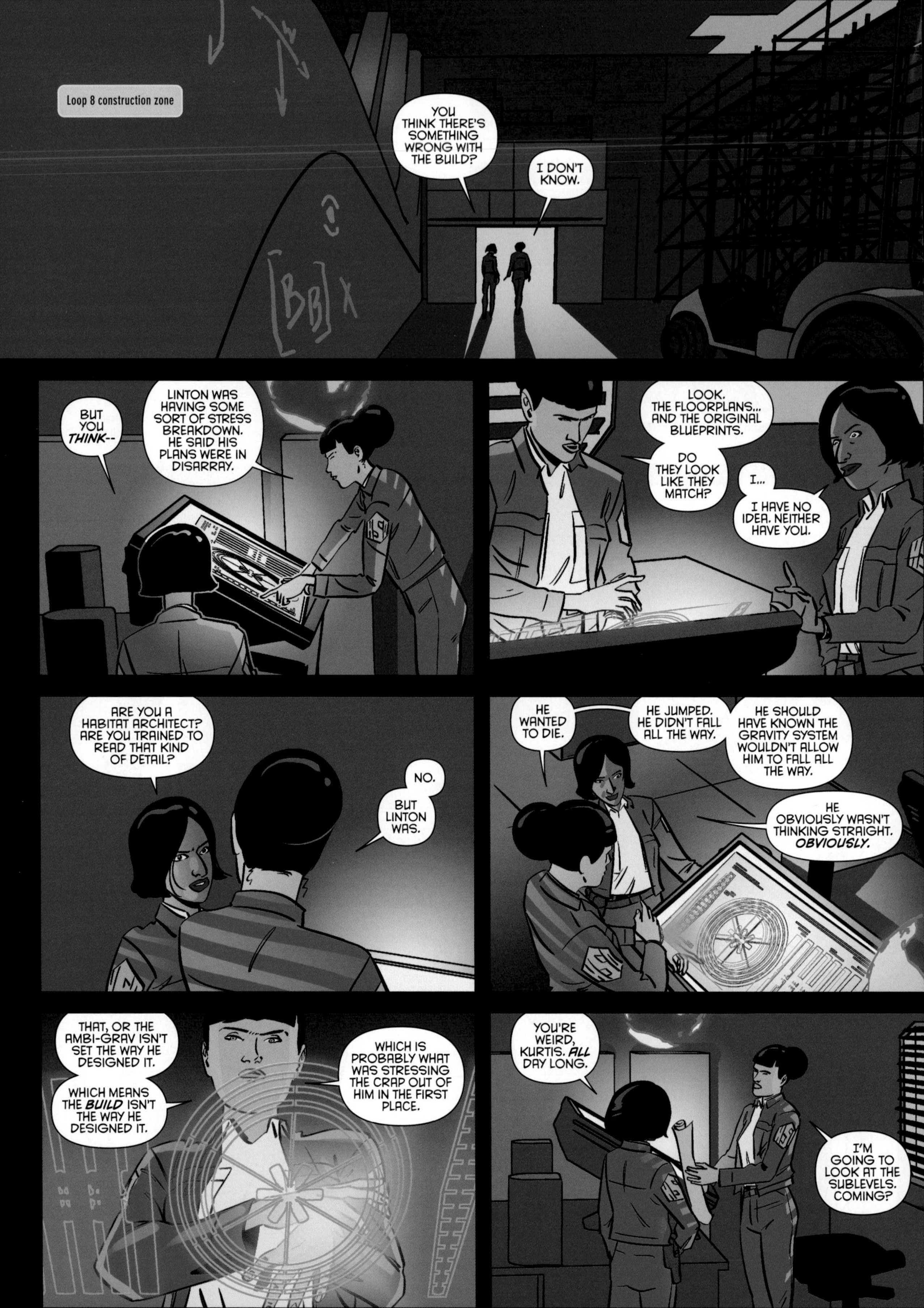

Loop 8 construction zone
YOU THINK THERE'S SOMETHING WRONG WITH THE BUILD?
I DON'T KNOW.
BUT YOU *THINK*--
LINTON WAS HAVING SOME SORT OF STRESS BREAKDOWN. HE SAID HIS PLANS WERE IN DISARRAY.
LOOK. THE FLOORPLANS... AND THE ORIGINAL BLUEPRINTS.
DO THEY LOOK LIKE THEY MATCH?
I...
I HAVE NO IDEA. NEITHER HAVE YOU.
ARE YOU A HABITAT ARCHITECT? ARE YOU TRAINED TO READ THAT KIND OF DETAIL?
NO.
BUT LINTON WAS.
HE WANTED TO DIE.
HE JUMPED. HE DIDN'T FALL ALL THE WAY.
HE SHOULD HAVE KNOWN THE GRAVITY SYSTEM WOULDN'T ALLOW HIM TO FALL ALL THE WAY.
HE OBVIOUSLY WASN'T THINKING STRAIGHT. ***OBVIOUSLY.***
THAT, OR THE AMBI-GRAV ISN'T SET THE WAY HE DESIGNED IT.
WHICH MEANS THE ***BUILD*** ISN'T THE WAY HE DESIGNED IT.
WHICH IS PROBABLY WHAT WAS STRESSING THE CRAP OUT OF HIM IN THE FIRST PLACE.
YOU'RE WEIRD, KURTIS. ***ALL*** DAY LONG.
I'M GOING TO LOOK AT THE SUBLEVELS. COMING?

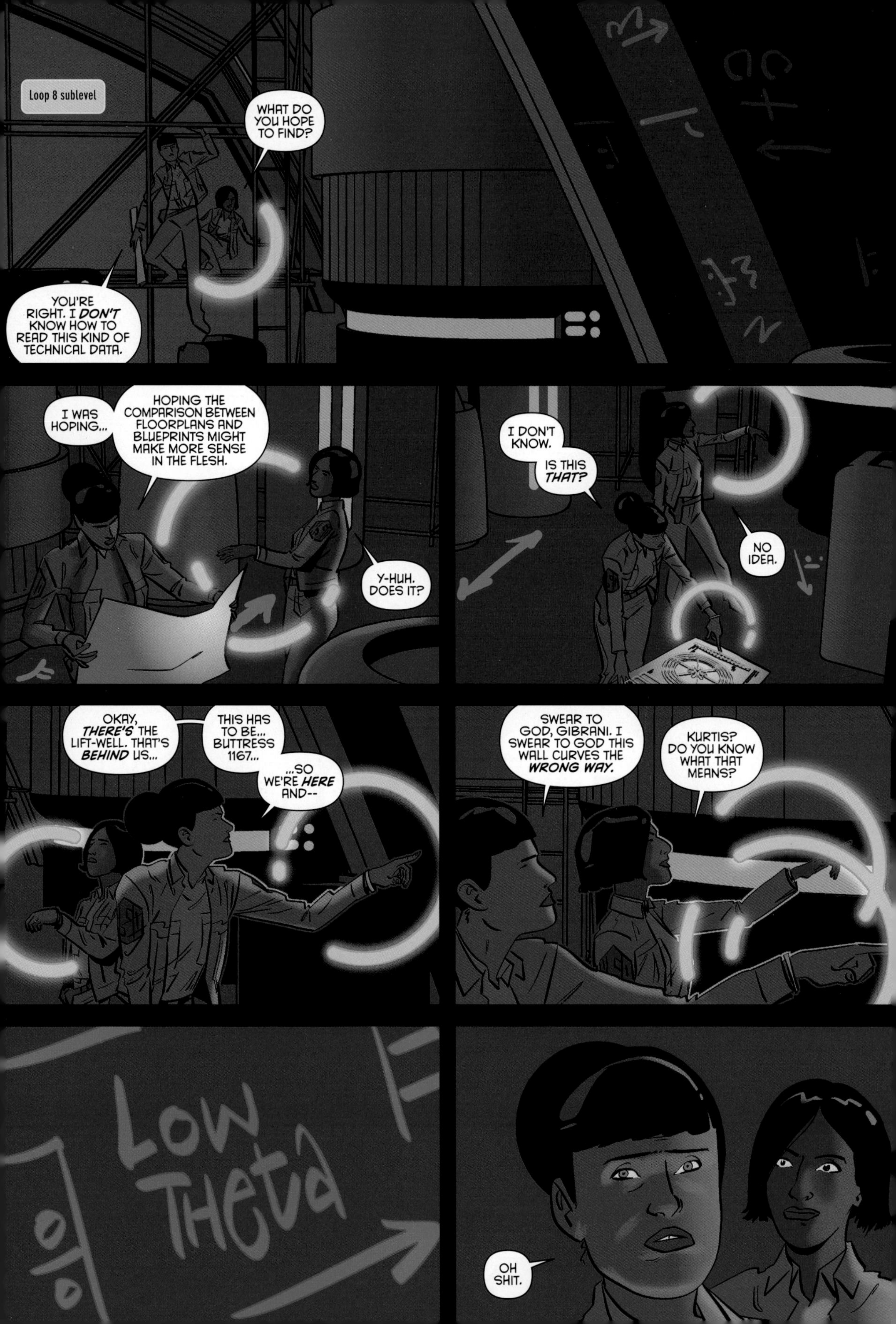
Loop 8 sublevel
WHAT DO YOU HOPE TO FIND?
YOU'RE RIGHT. I DON'T KNOW HOW TO READ THIS KIND OF TECHNICAL DATA.
I WAS HOPING...
HOPING THE COMPARISON BETWEEN FLOORPLANS AND BLUEPRINTS MIGHT MAKE MORE SENSE IN THE FLESH.
Y-HUH. DOES IT?
I DON'T KNOW.
IS THIS THAT?
NO IDEA.
OKAY, THERE'S THE LIFT-WELL. THAT'S BEHIND US...
THIS HAS TO BE... BUTTRESS 1167...
...SO WE'RE HERE AND--
SWEAR TO GOD, GIBRANI. I SWEAR TO GOD THIS WALL CURVES THE WRONG WAY.
KURTIS? DO YOU KNOW WHAT THAT MEANS?
Low Theta
OH SHIT.

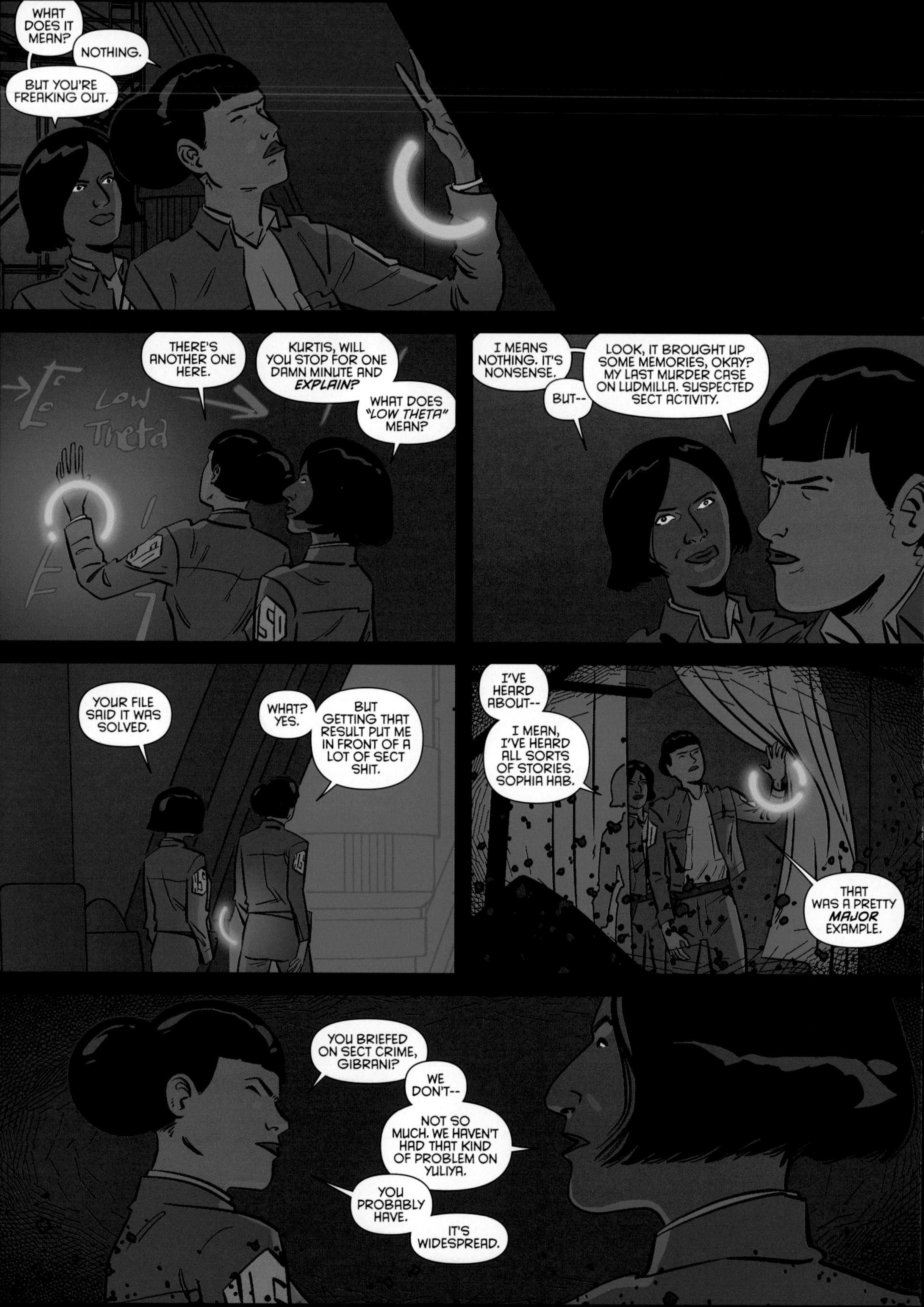
WHAT DOES IT MEAN?
NOTHING.
BUT YOU'RE FREAKING OUT.
THERE'S ANOTHER ONE HERE.
KURTIS, WILL YOU STOP FOR ONE DAMN MINUTE AND *EXPLAIN?*
WHAT DOES *"LOW THETA"* MEAN?
Low Theta
I MEANS NOTHING. IT'S NONSENSE.
BUT--
LOOK, IT BROUGHT UP SOME MEMORIES, OKAY? MY LAST MURDER CASE ON LUDMILLA. SUSPECTED SECT ACTIVITY.
YOUR FILE SAID IT WAS SOLVED.
WHAT? YES.
BUT GETTING THAT RESULT PUT ME IN FRONT OF A LOT OF SECT SHIT.
I'VE HEARD ABOUT--
I MEAN, I'VE HEARD ALL SORTS OF STORIES. SOPHIA HAB.
THAT WAS A PRETTY *MAJOR* EXAMPLE.
YOU BRIEFED ON SECT CRIME, GIBRANI?
WE DON'T--
NOT SO MUCH. WE HAVEN'T HAD THAT KIND OF PROBLEM ON YULIYA.
YOU PROBABLY HAVE.
IT'S WIDESPREAD.

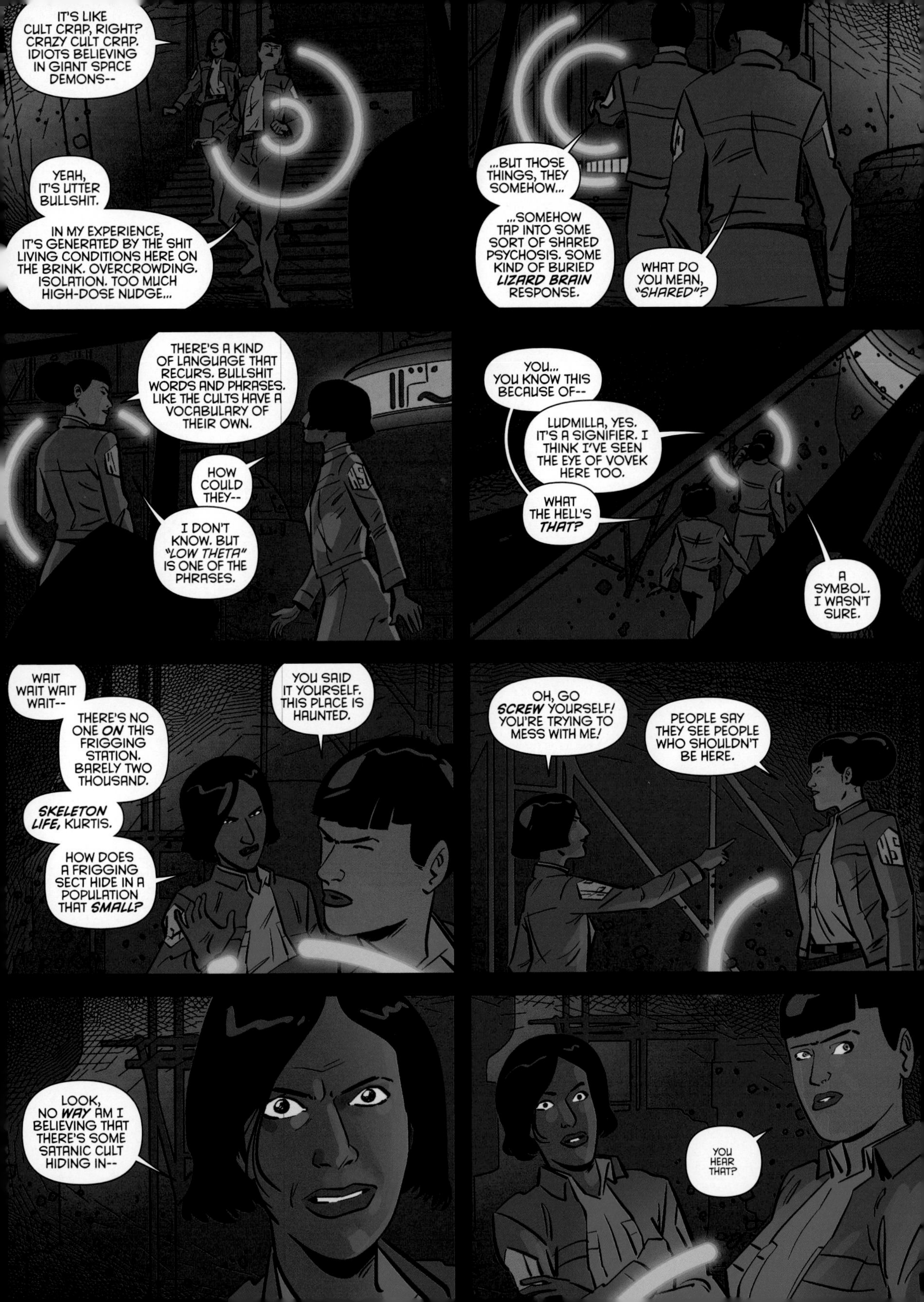
IT'S LIKE CULT CRAP, RIGHT? CRAZY CULT CRAP. IDIOTS BELIEVING IN GIANT SPACE DEMONS--
YEAH, IT'S UTTER BULLSHIT.
IN MY EXPERIENCE, IT'S GENERATED BY THE SHIT LIVING CONDITIONS HERE ON THE BRINK. OVERCROWDING. ISOLATION. TOO MUCH HIGH-DOSE NUDGE...
...BUT THOSE THINGS, THEY SOMEHOW...
...SOMEHOW TAP INTO SOME SORT OF SHARED PSYCHOSIS. SOME KIND OF BURIED LIZARD BRAIN RESPONSE.
WHAT DO YOU MEAN, "SHARED"?
THERE'S A KIND OF LANGUAGE THAT RECURS. BULLSHIT WORDS AND PHRASES. LIKE THE CULTS HAVE A VOCABULARY OF THEIR OWN.
HOW COULD THEY--
I DON'T KNOW. BUT "LOW THETA" IS ONE OF THE PHRASES.
YOU... YOU KNOW THIS BECAUSE OF--
LUDMILLA, YES. IT'S A SIGNIFIER. I THINK I'VE SEEN THE EYE OF VOVEK HERE TOO.
WHAT THE HELL'S THAT?
A SYMBOL. I WASN'T SURE.
WAIT WAIT WAIT WAIT--
THERE'S NO ONE ON THIS FRIGGING STATION. BARELY TWO THOUSAND.
SKELETON LIFE, KURTIS.
HOW DOES A FRIGGING SECT HIDE IN A POPULATION THAT SMALL?
YOU SAID IT YOURSELF. THIS PLACE IS HAUNTED.
OH, GO SCREW YOURSELF! YOU'RE TRYING TO MESS WITH ME!
PEOPLE SAY THEY SEE PEOPLE WHO SHOULDN'T BE HERE.
LOOK, NO WAY AM I BELIEVING THAT THERE'S SOME SATANIC CULT HIDING IN--
YOU HEAR THAT?

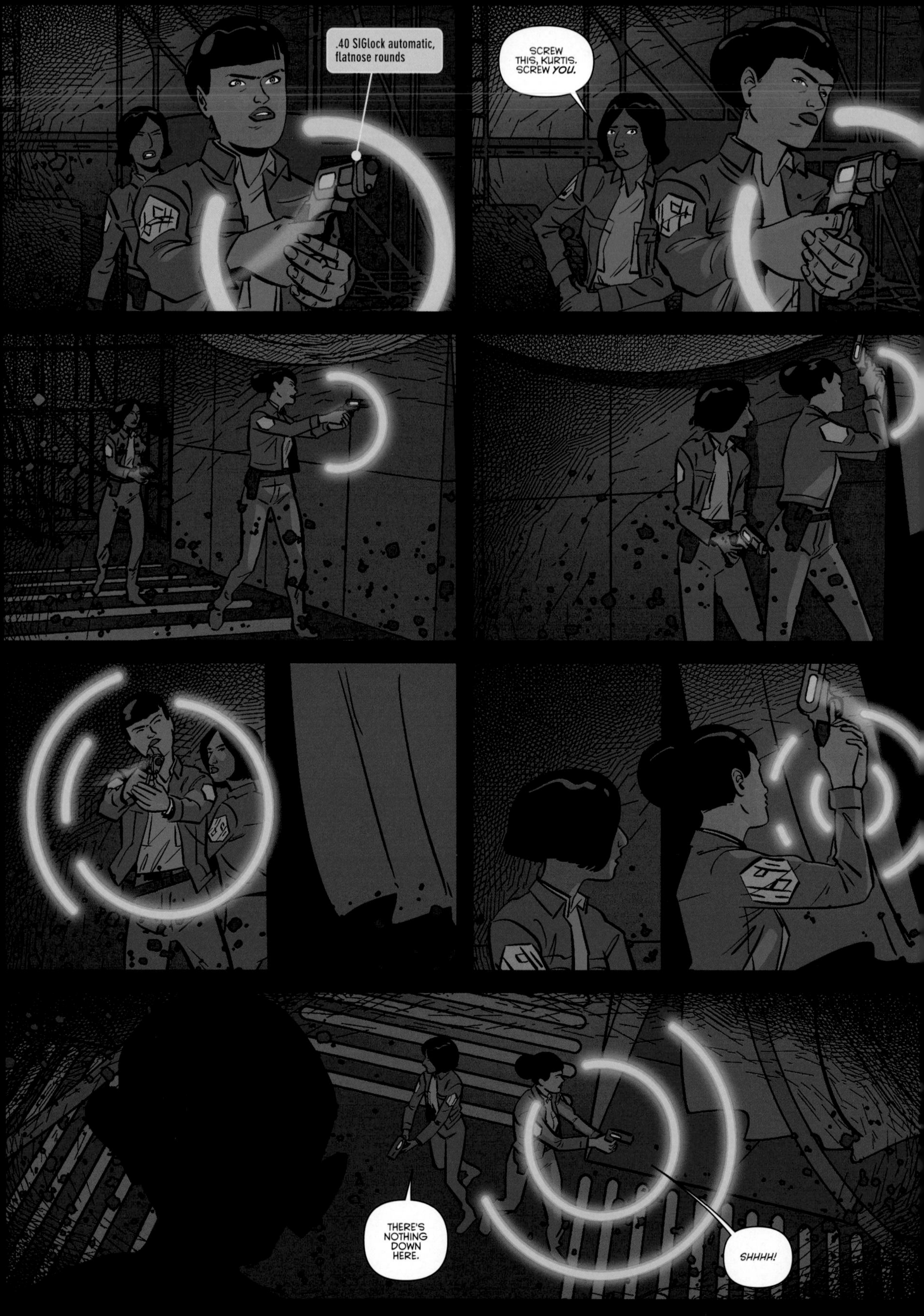
.40 SIGlock automatic, flatnose rounds
SCREW THIS, KURTIS. SCREW *YOU.*
THERE'S NOTHING DOWN HERE.
SHHHH!

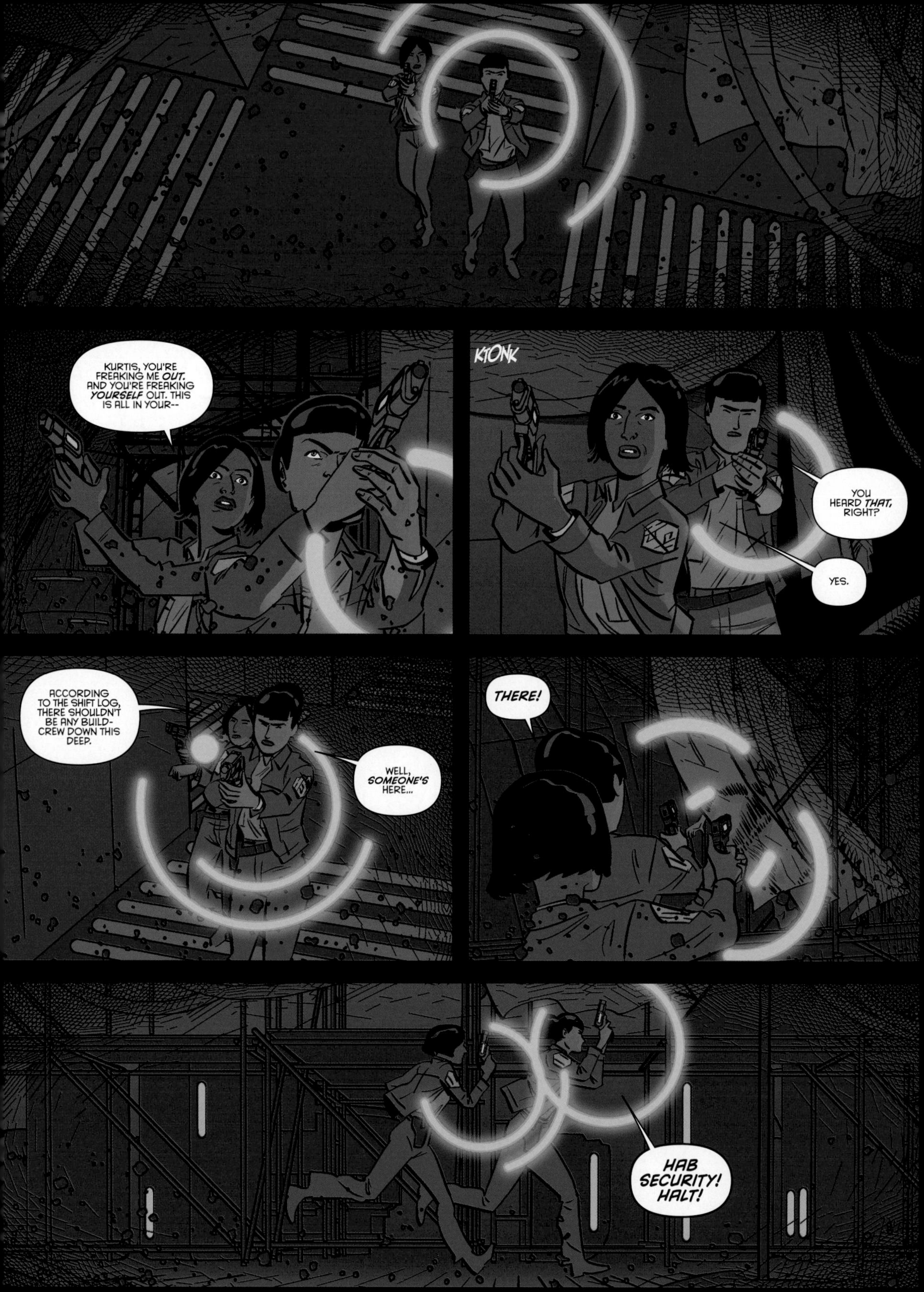
KURTIS, YOU'RE FREAKING ME *OUT.* AND YOU'RE FREAKING *YOURSELF* OUT. THIS IS ALL IN YOUR--
KTONK
YOU HEARD *THAT,* RIGHT?
YES.
ACCORDING TO THE SHIFT LOG, THERE SHOULDN'T BE ANY BUILD-CREW DOWN THIS DEEP.
WELL, *SOMEONE'S* HERE...
THERE!
HAB SECURITY! HALT!

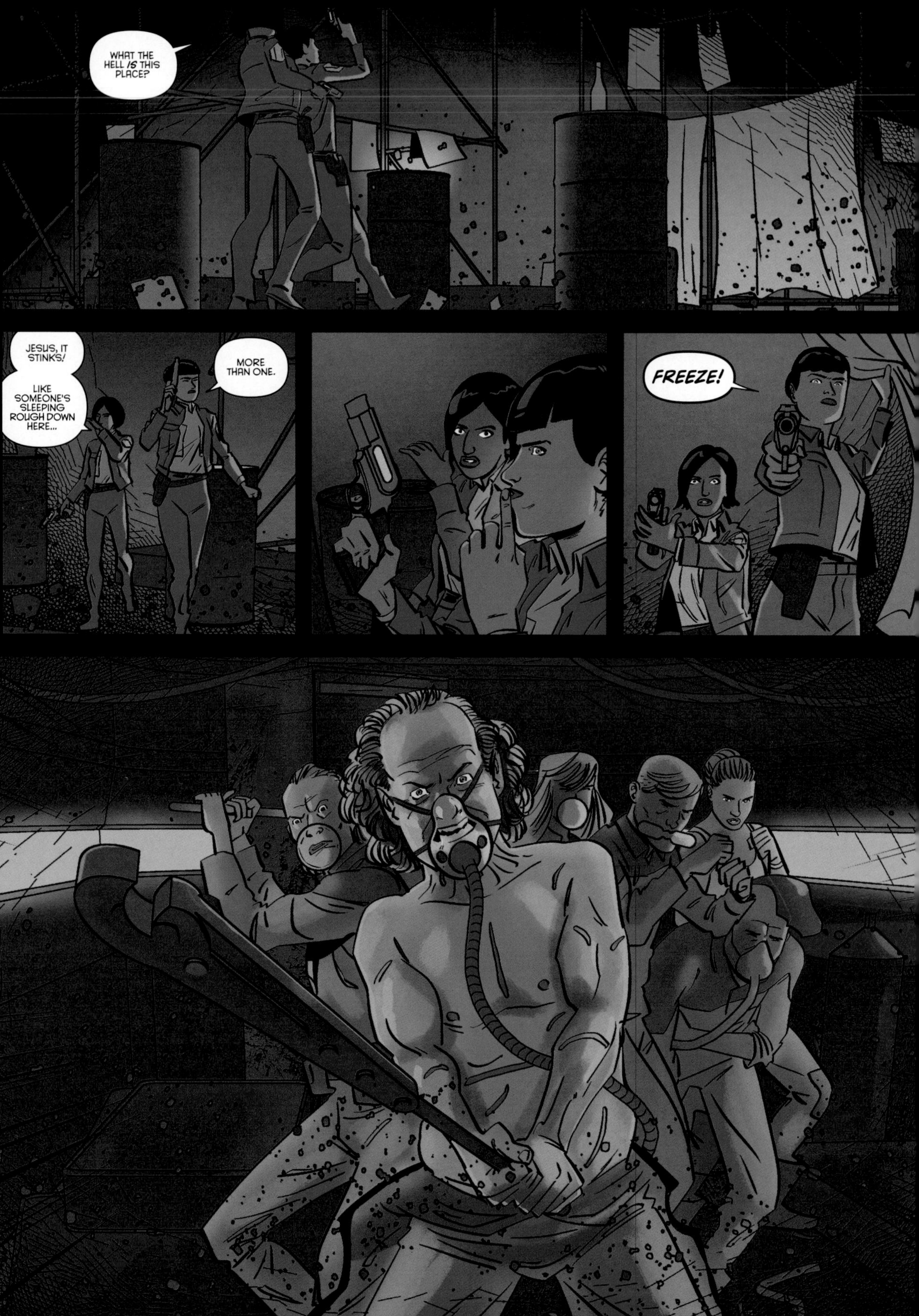
WHAT THE HELL *IS* THIS PLACE?
JESUS, IT STINKS!
LIKE SOMEONE'S SLEEPING ROUGH DOWN HERE...
MORE THAN ONE.
FREEZE!

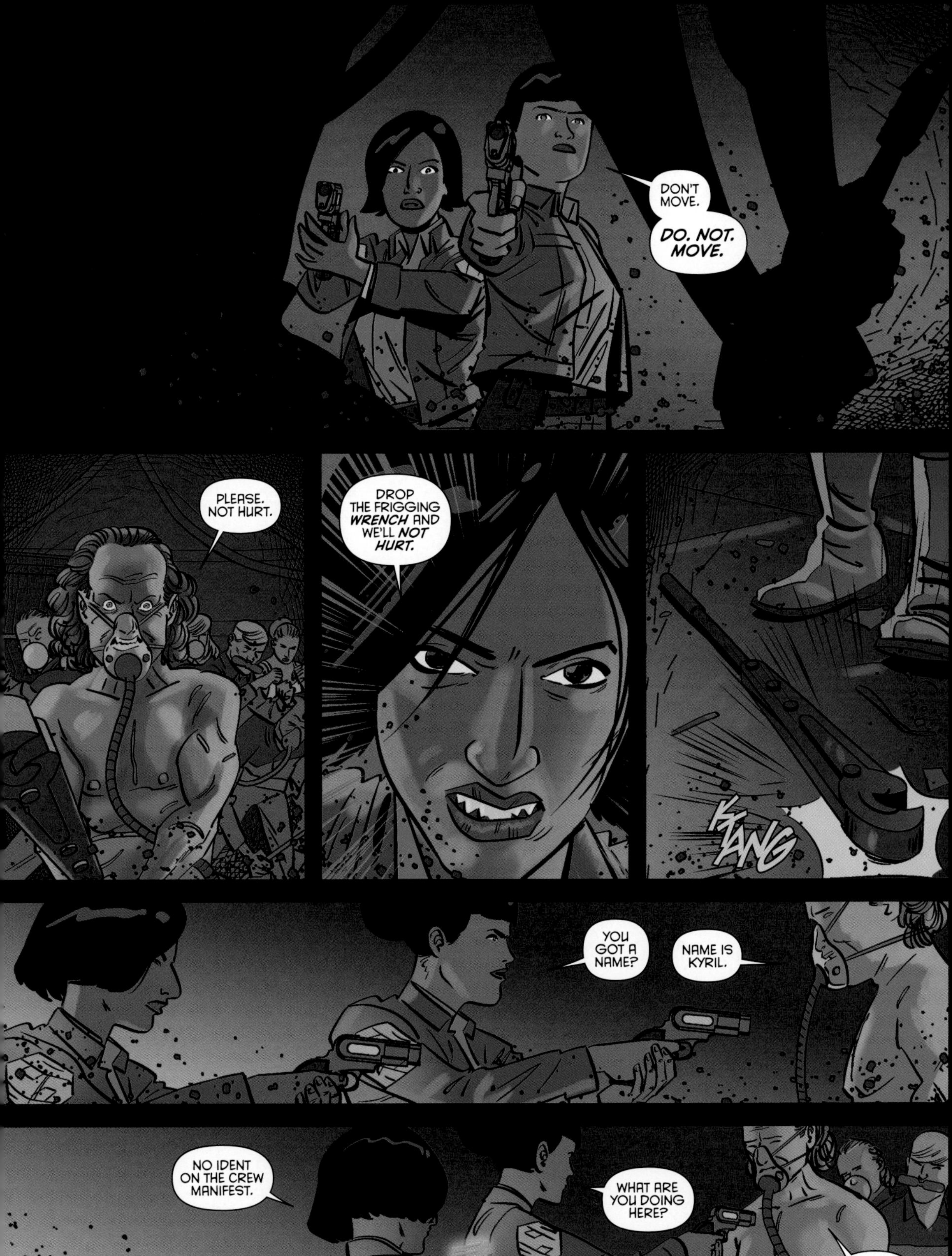

DON'T MOVE.
DO. NOT. MOVE.
PLEASE. NOT HURT.
DROP THE FRIGGING WRENCH AND WE'LL NOT HURT.
KLANG
YOU GOT A NAME?
NAME IS KYRIL.
NO IDENT ON THE CREW MANIFEST.
WHAT ARE YOU DOING HERE?
WE TO WORK. TO BE BUILD.

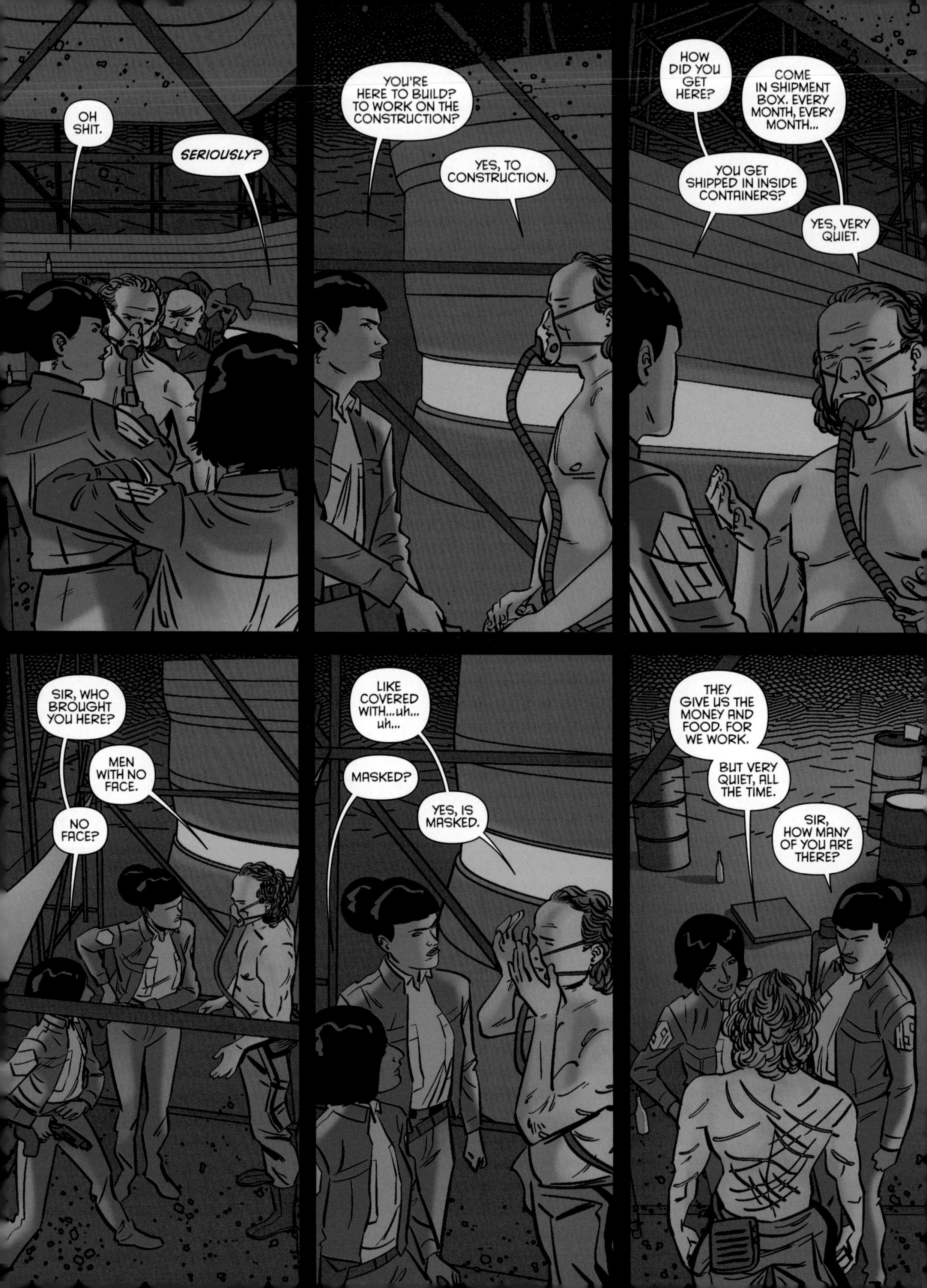

OH SHIT.
SERIOUSLY?
YOU'RE HERE TO BUILD? TO WORK ON THE CONSTRUCTION?
YES, TO CONSTRUCTION.
HOW DID YOU GET HERE?
COME IN SHIPMENT BOX. EVERY MONTH, EVERY MONTH...
YOU GET SHIPPED IN INSIDE CONTAINERS?
YES, VERY QUIET.
SIR, WHO BROUGHT YOU HERE?
MEN WITH NO FACE.
NO FACE?
LIKE COVERED WITH...uh... uh...
MASKED?
YES, IS MASKED.
THEY GIVE US THE MONEY AND FOOD. FOR WE WORK.
BUT VERY QUIET, ALL THE TIME.
SIR, HOW MANY OF YOU ARE THERE?

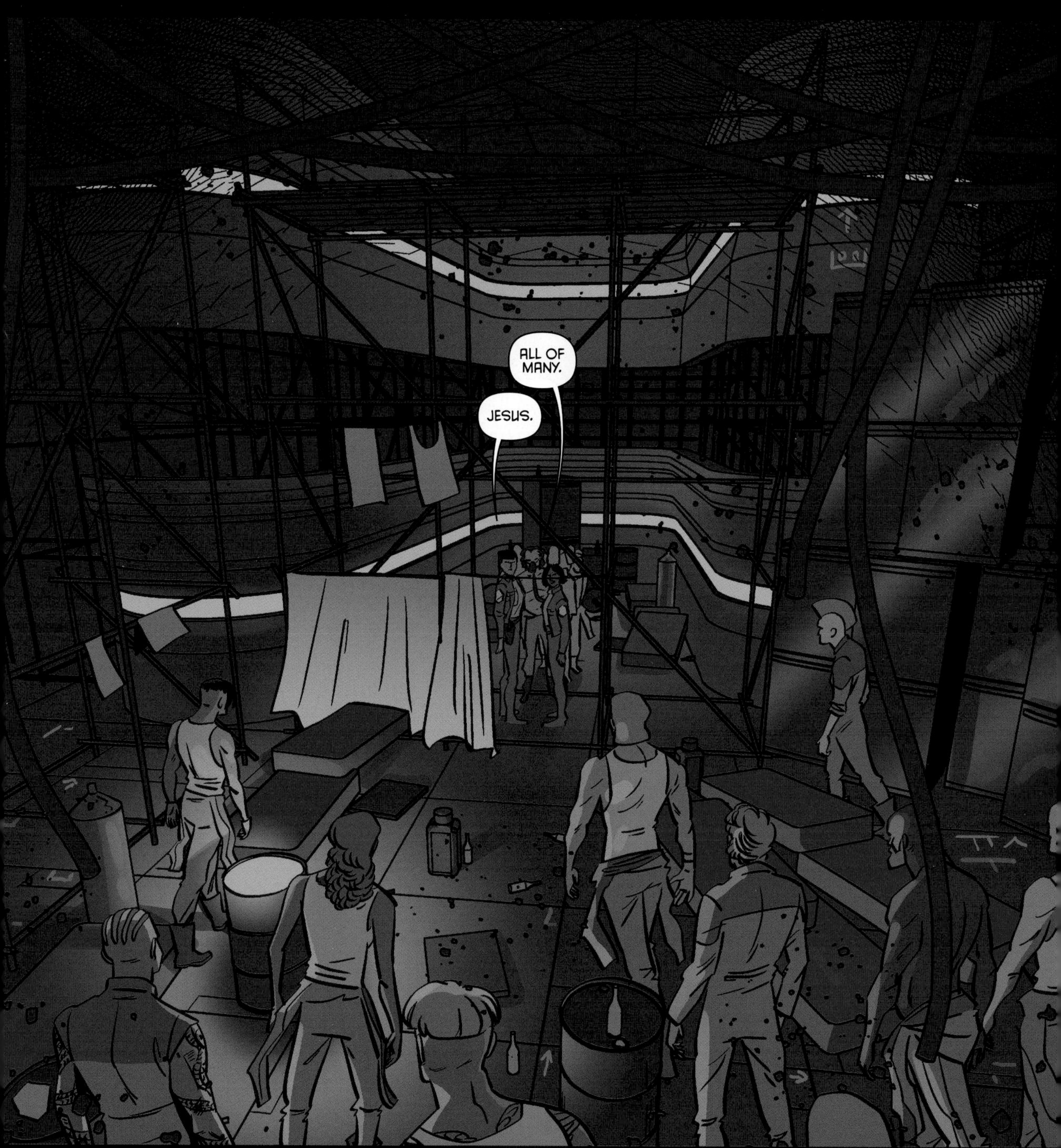
ALL OF MANY.
JESUS.

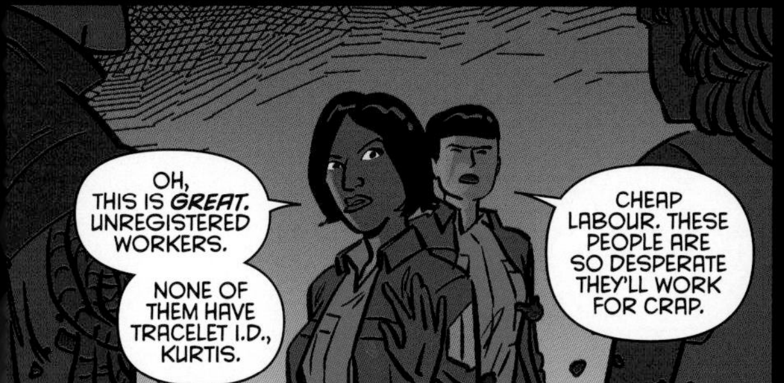
OH, THIS IS *GREAT.* UNREGISTERED WORKERS.
NONE OF THEM HAVE TRACELET I.D., KURTIS.
CHEAP LABOUR. THESE PEOPLE ARE SO DESPERATE THEY'LL WORK FOR CRAP.

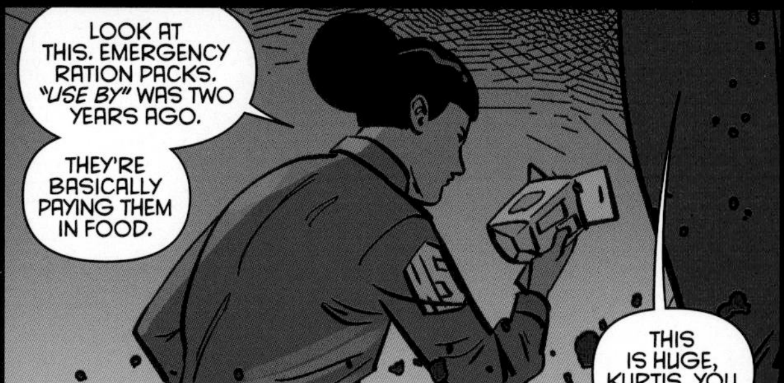
LOOK AT THIS. EMERGENCY RATION PACKS. *"USE BY"* WAS TWO YEARS AGO.
THEY'RE BASICALLY PAYING THEM IN FOOD.
THIS IS HUGE, KURTIS. YOU REALISE?
THE REPORT WILL SCREW JUNOT AND--

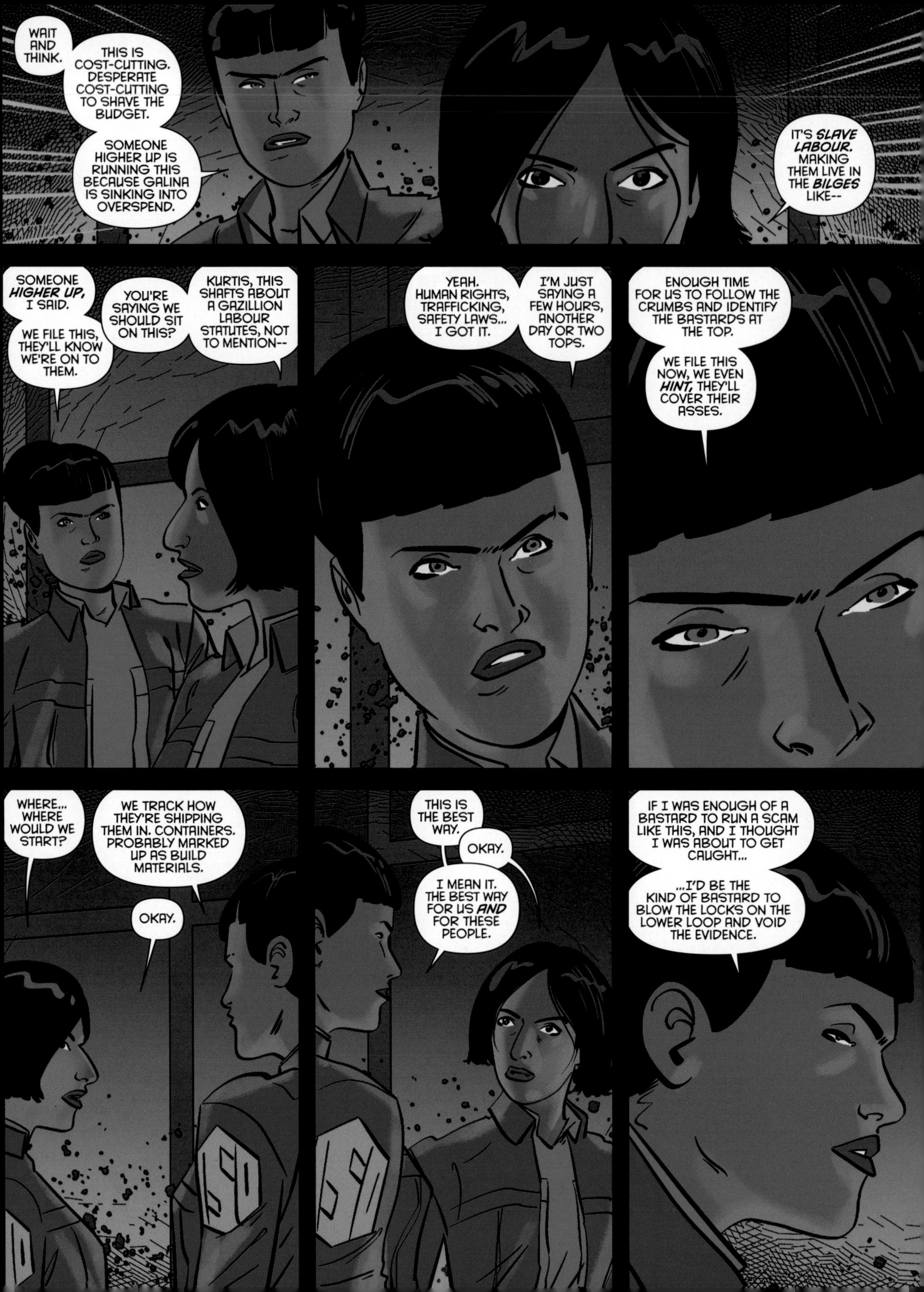
WAIT AND THINK.
THIS IS COST-CUTTING. DESPERATE COST-CUTTING TO SHAVE THE BUDGET.
SOMEONE HIGHER UP IS RUNNING THIS BECAUSE GALINA IS SINKING INTO OVERSPEND.
IT'S SLAVE LABOUR. MAKING THEM LIVE IN THE BILGES LIKE--
SOMEONE HIGHER UP, I SAID.
WE FILE THIS, THEY'LL KNOW WE'RE ON TO THEM.
YOU'RE SAYING WE SHOULD SIT ON THIS?
KURTIS, THIS SHAFTS ABOUT A GAZILLION LABOUR STATUTES, NOT TO MENTION--
YEAH. HUMAN RIGHTS, TRAFFICKING, SAFETY LAWS... I GOT IT.
I'M JUST SAYING A FEW HOURS, ANOTHER DAY OR TWO TOPS.
ENOUGH TIME FOR US TO FOLLOW THE CRUMBS AND IDENTIFY THE BASTARDS AT THE TOP.
WE FILE THIS NOW, WE EVEN HINT, THEY'LL COVER THEIR ASSES.
WHERE... WHERE WOULD WE START?
WE TRACK HOW THEY'RE SHIPPING THEM IN. CONTAINERS. PROBABLY MARKED UP AS BUILD MATERIALS.
OKAY.
THIS IS THE BEST WAY.
OKAY.
I MEAN IT. THE BEST WAY FOR US AND FOR THESE PEOPLE.
IF I WAS ENOUGH OF A BASTARD TO RUN A SCAM LIKE THIS, AND I THOUGHT I WAS ABOUT TO GET CAUGHT...
...I'D BE THE KIND OF BASTARD TO BLOW THE LOCKS ON THE LOWER LOOP AND VOID THE EVIDENCE.

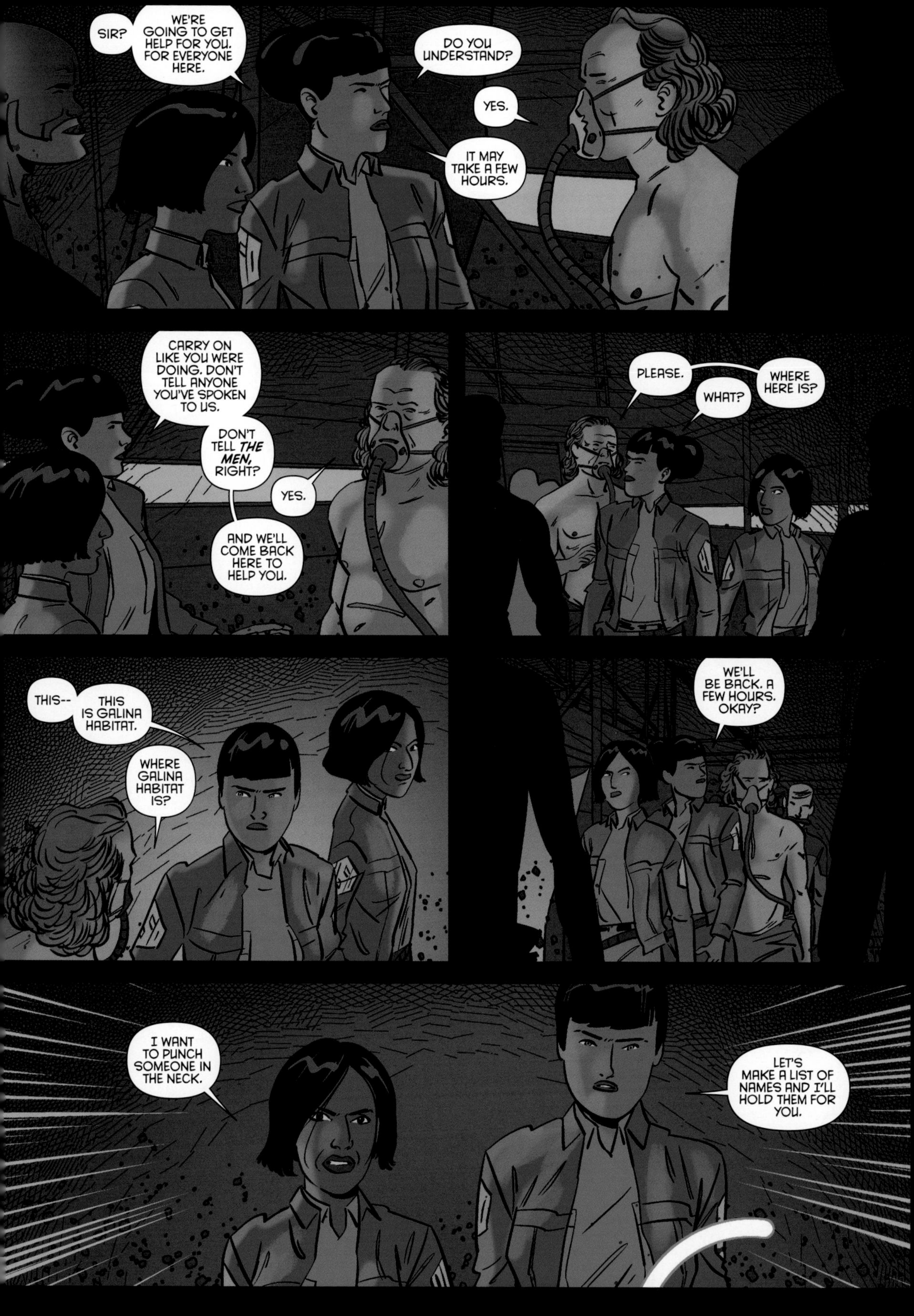
SIR?
WE'RE GOING TO GET HELP FOR YOU. FOR EVERYONE HERE.
DO YOU UNDERSTAND?
YES.
IT MAY TAKE A FEW HOURS.
CARRY ON LIKE YOU WERE DOING. DON'T TELL ANYONE YOU'VE SPOKEN TO US.
DON'T TELL *THE MEN,* RIGHT?
YES.
AND WE'LL COME BACK HERE TO HELP YOU.
PLEASE.
WHERE HERE IS?
WHAT?
THIS--
THIS IS GALINA HABITAT.
WHERE GALINA HABITAT IS?
WE'LL BE BACK. A FEW HOURS. OKAY?
I WANT TO PUNCH SOMEONE IN THE NECK.
LET'S MAKE A LIST OF NAMES AND I'LL HOLD THEM FOR YOU.

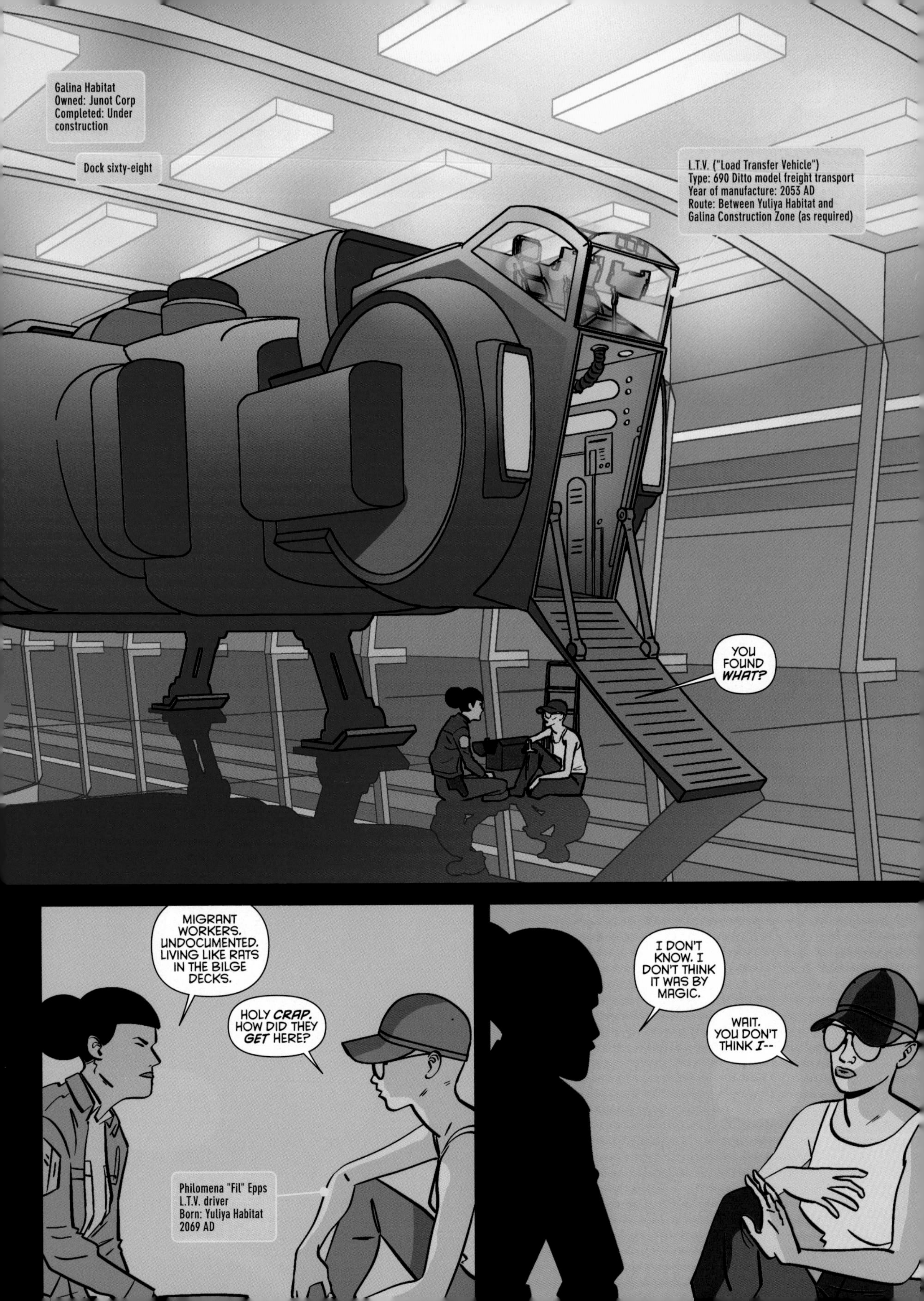
Galina Habitat
Owned: Junot Corp
Completed: Under construction
Dock sixty-eight
L.T.V. ("Load Transfer Vehicle")
Type: 690 Ditto model freight transport
Year of manufacture: 2053 AD
Route: Between Yuliya Habitat and Galina Construction Zone (as required)
YOU FOUND *WHAT?*
MIGRANT WORKERS. UNDOCUMENTED. LIVING LIKE RATS IN THE BILGE DECKS.
HOLY *CRAP.* HOW DID THEY *GET* HERE?
Philomena "Fil" Epps
L.T.V. driver
Born: Yuliya Habitat
2069 AD
I DON'T KNOW. I DON'T THINK IT WAS BY MAGIC.
WAIT. YOU DON'T THINK *I*--

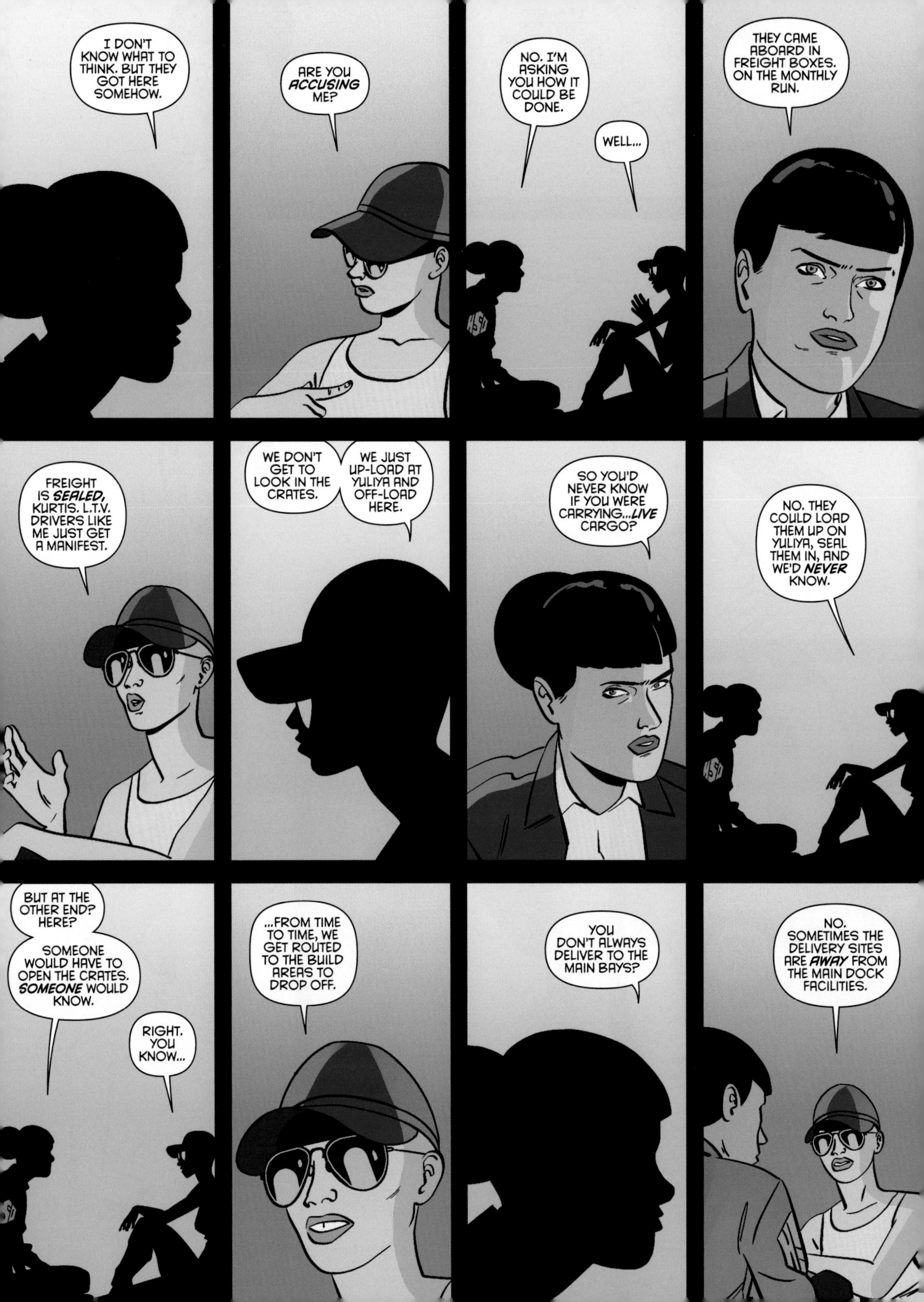

I DON'T KNOW WHAT TO THINK. BUT THEY GOT HERE SOMEHOW.
ARE YOU *ACCUSING* ME?
NO. I'M ASKING YOU HOW IT COULD BE DONE.
WELL...
THEY CAME ABOARD IN FREIGHT BOXES. ON THE MONTHLY RUN.
FREIGHT IS *SEALED,* KURTIS. L.T.V. DRIVERS LIKE ME JUST GET A MANIFEST.
WE DON'T GET TO LOOK IN THE CRATES.
WE JUST UP-LOAD AT YULIYA AND OFF-LOAD HERE.
SO YOU'D NEVER KNOW IF YOU WERE CARRYING...*LIVE* CARGO?
NO. THEY COULD LOAD THEM UP ON YULIYA, SEAL THEM IN, AND WE'D *NEVER* KNOW.
BUT AT THE OTHER END? HERE?
SOMEONE WOULD HAVE TO OPEN THE CRATES. *SOMEONE* WOULD KNOW.
RIGHT. YOU KNOW...
...FROM TIME TO TIME, WE GET ROUTED TO THE BUILD AREAS TO DROP OFF.
YOU DON'T ALWAYS DELIVER TO THE MAIN BAYS?
NO. SOMETIMES THE DELIVERY SITES ARE *AWAY* FROM THE MAIN DOCK FACILITIES.

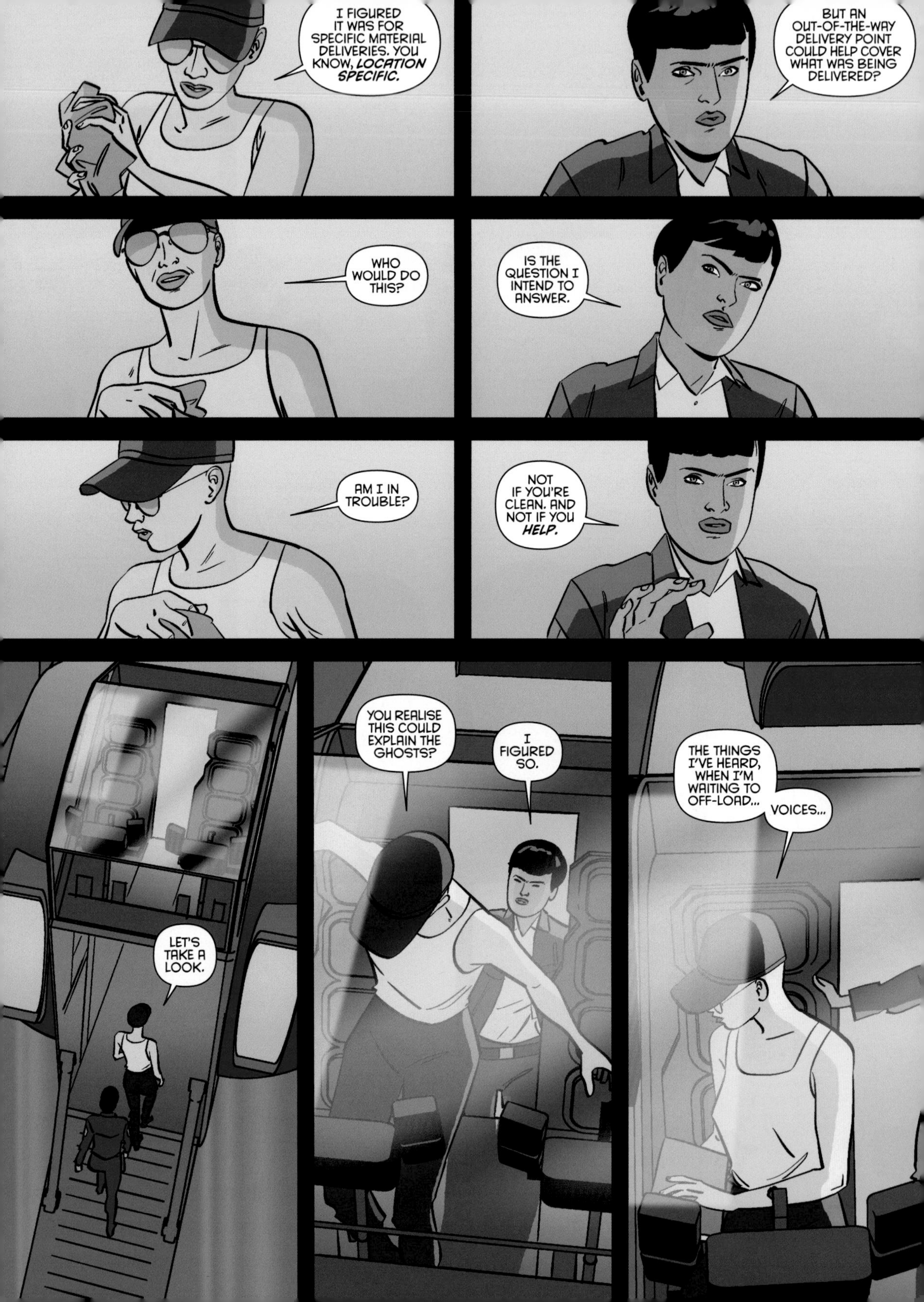
I FIGURED IT WAS FOR SPECIFIC MATERIAL DELIVERIES. YOU KNOW, *LOCATION SPECIFIC.*
BUT AN OUT-OF-THE-WAY DELIVERY POINT COULD HELP COVER WHAT WAS BEING DELIVERED?
WHO WOULD DO THIS?
IS THE QUESTION I INTEND TO ANSWER.
AM I IN TROUBLE?
NOT IF YOU'RE CLEAN. AND NOT IF YOU *HELP.*
LET'S TAKE A LOOK.
YOU REALISE THIS COULD EXPLAIN THE GHOSTS?
I FIGURED SO.
THE THINGS I'VE HEARD, WHEN I'M WAITING TO OFF-LOAD...
VOICES...

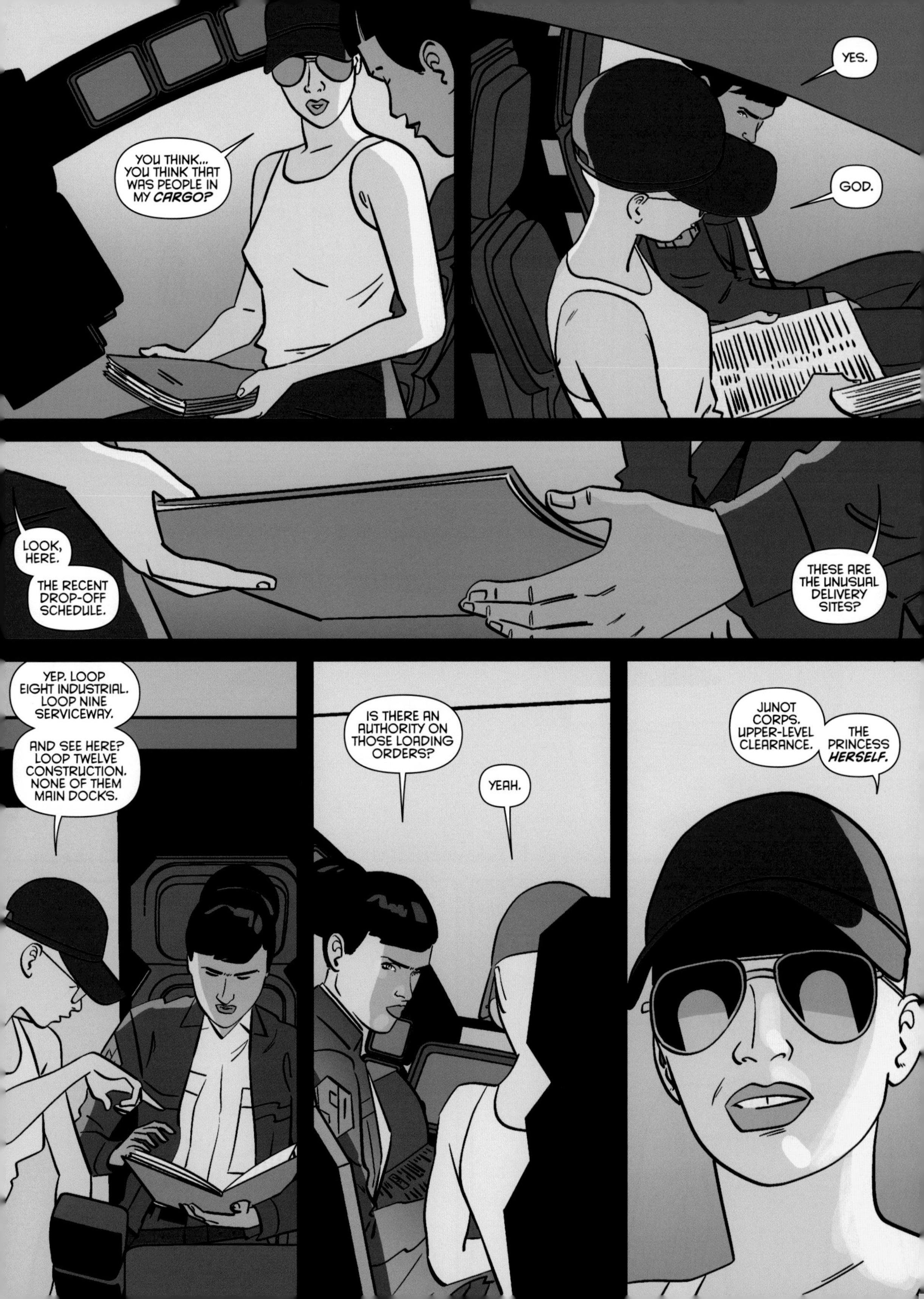
YOU THINK... YOU THINK THAT WAS PEOPLE IN MY *CARGO?*
YES.
GOD.
LOOK, HERE.
THE RECENT DROP-OFF SCHEDULE.
THESE ARE THE UNUSUAL DELIVERY SITES?
YEP. LOOP EIGHT INDUSTRIAL. LOOP NINE SERVICEWAY.
AND SEE HERE? LOOP TWELVE CONSTRUCTION. NONE OF THEM MAIN DOCKS.
IS THERE AN AUTHORITY ON THOSE LOADING ORDERS?
YEAH.
JUNOT CORPS. UPPER-LEVEL CLEARANCE.
THE PRINCESS *HERSELF.*

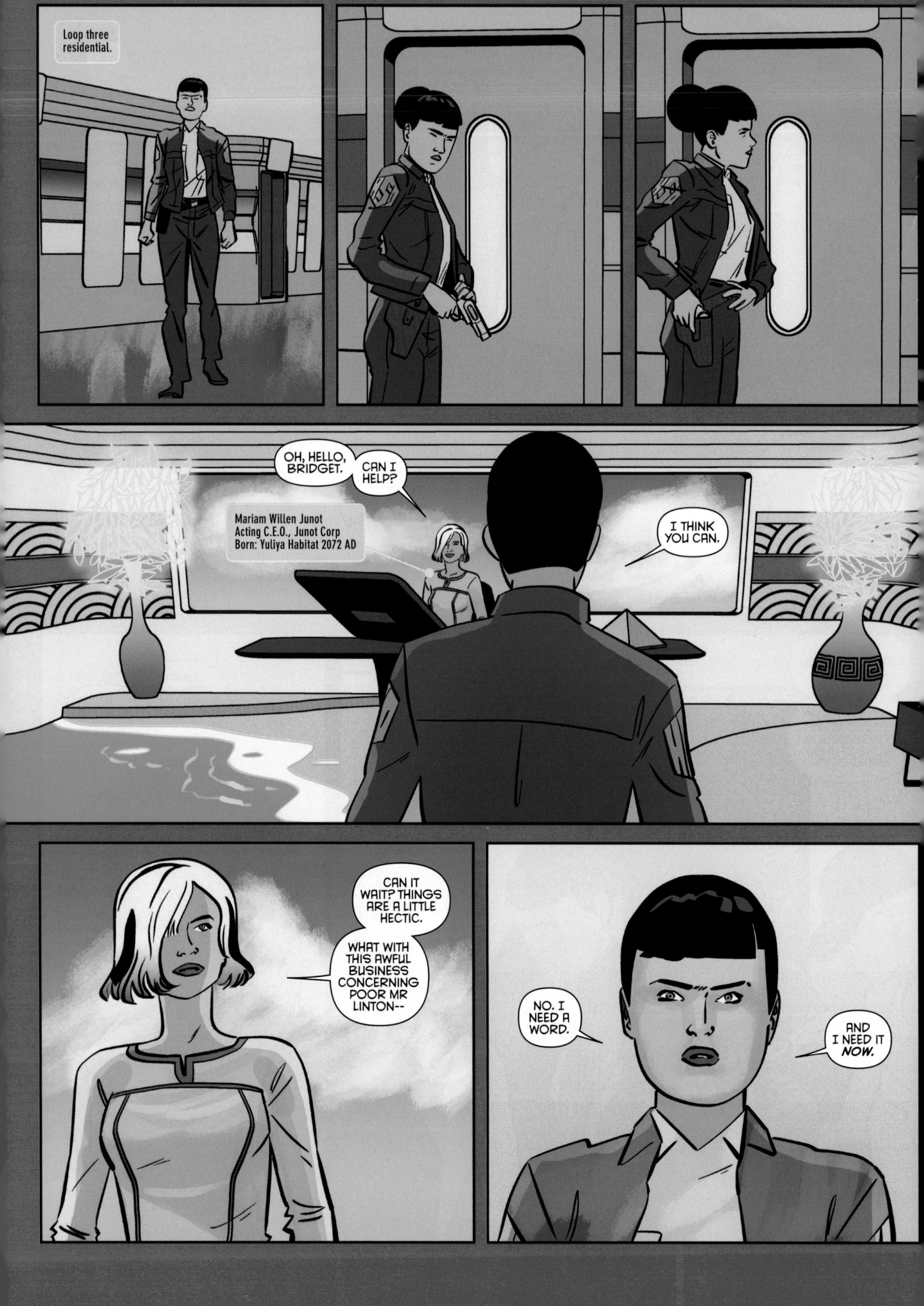
Loop three residential.
OH, HELLO, BRIDGET.
CAN I HELP?
Mariam Willen Junot
Acting C.E.O., Junot Corp
Born: Yuliya Habitat 2072 AD
I THINK YOU CAN.
CAN IT WAIT? THINGS ARE A LITTLE HECTIC.
WHAT WITH THIS AWFUL BUSINESS CONCERNING POOR MR LINTON--
NO. I NEED A WORD.
AND I NEED IT *NOW.*

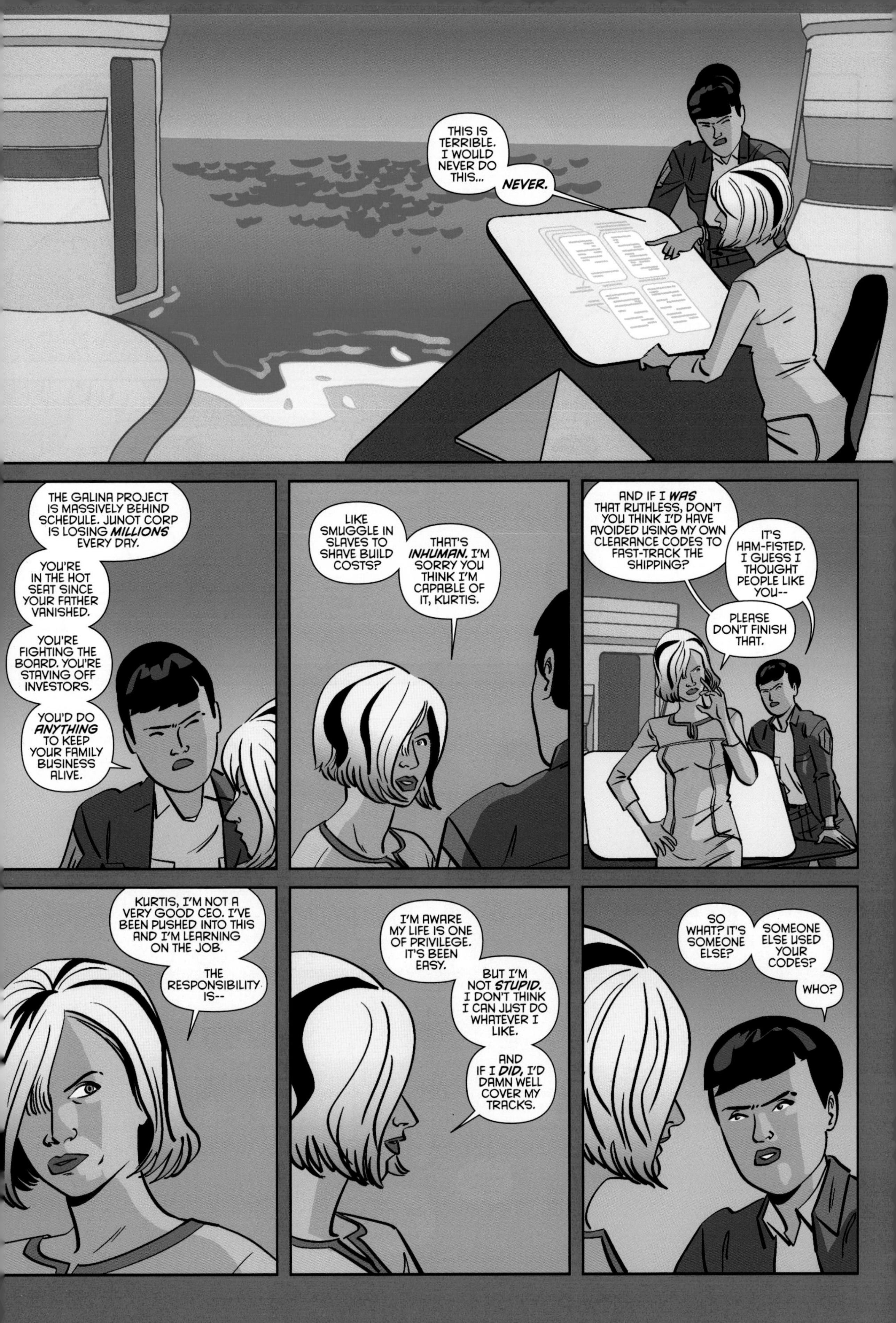

THIS IS TERRIBLE. I WOULD NEVER DO THIS... NEVER.
THE GALINA PROJECT IS MASSIVELY BEHIND SCHEDULE. JUNOT CORP IS LOSING MILLIONS EVERY DAY.
YOU'RE IN THE HOT SEAT SINCE YOUR FATHER VANISHED.
YOU'RE FIGHTING THE BOARD. YOU'RE STAVING OFF INVESTORS.
YOU'D DO ANYTHING TO KEEP YOUR FAMILY BUSINESS ALIVE.
LIKE SMUGGLE IN SLAVES TO SHAVE BUILD COSTS?
THAT'S INHUMAN. I'M SORRY YOU THINK I'M CAPABLE OF IT, KURTIS.
AND IF I WAS THAT RUTHLESS, DON'T YOU THINK I'D HAVE AVOIDED USING MY OWN CLEARANCE CODES TO FAST-TRACK THE SHIPPING?
IT'S HAM-FISTED. I GUESS I THOUGHT PEOPLE LIKE YOU--
PLEASE DON'T FINISH THAT.
KURTIS, I'M NOT A VERY GOOD CEO. I'VE BEEN PUSHED INTO THIS AND I'M LEARNING ON THE JOB.
THE RESPONSIBILITY IS--
I'M AWARE MY LIFE IS ONE OF PRIVILEGE. IT'S BEEN EASY.
BUT I'M NOT STUPID. I DON'T THINK I CAN JUST DO WHATEVER I LIKE.
AND IF I DID, I'D DAMN WELL COVER MY TRACKS.
SO WHAT? IT'S SOMEONE ELSE?
SOMEONE ELSE USED YOUR CODES?
WHO?

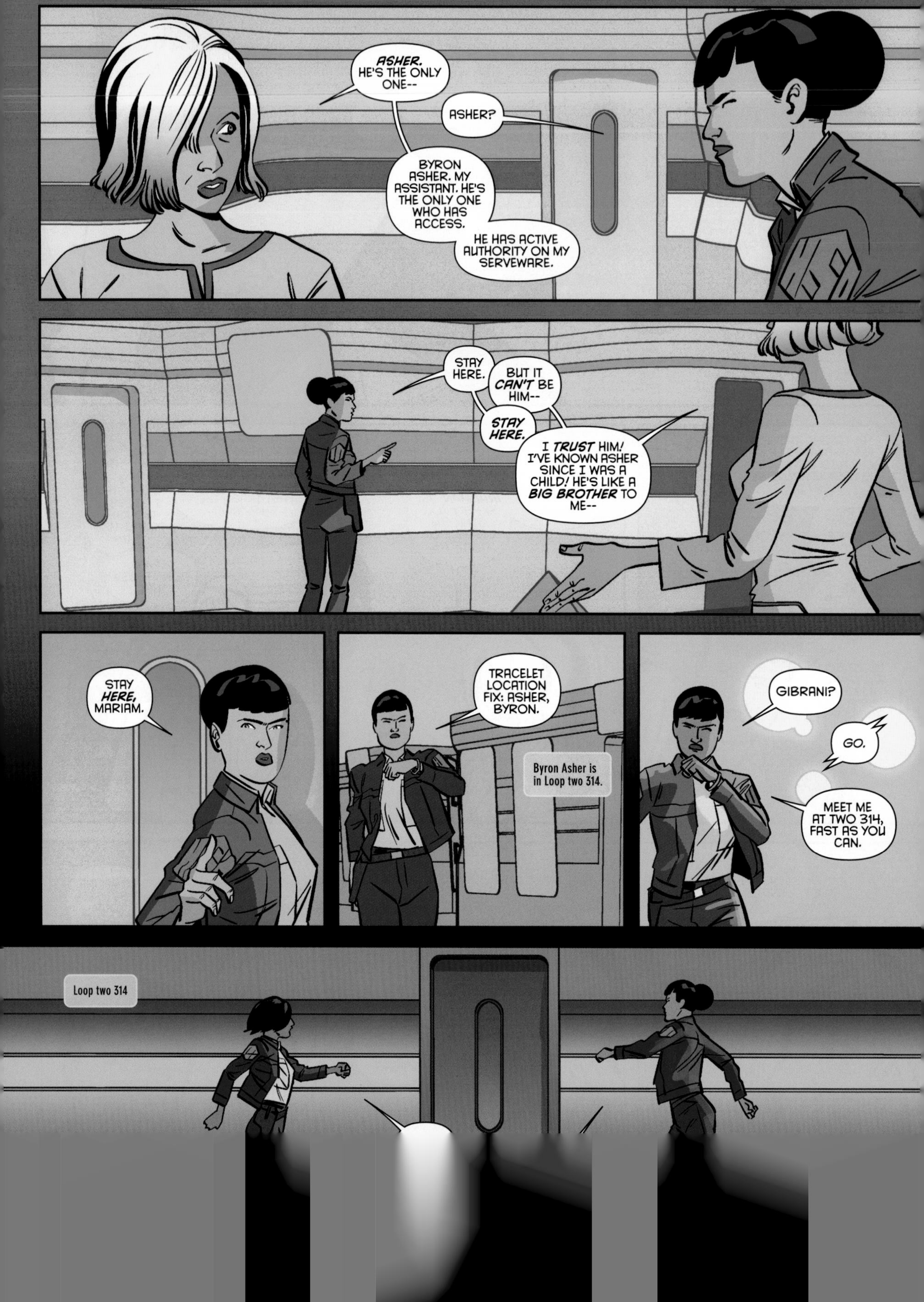
ASHER. HE'S THE ONLY ONE--
ASHER?
BYRON ASHER. MY ASSISTANT. HE'S THE ONLY ONE WHO HAS ACCESS.
HE HAS ACTIVE AUTHORITY ON MY SERVEWARE.
STAY HERE.
BUT IT CAN'T BE HIM--
STAY HERE.
I TRUST HIM! I'VE KNOWN ASHER SINCE I WAS A CHILD! HE'S LIKE A BIG BROTHER TO ME--
STAY HERE, MARIAM.
TRACELET LOCATION FIX: ASHER, BYRON.
Byron Asher is in Loop two 314.
GIBRANI?
GO.
MEET ME AT TWO 314, FAST AS YOU CAN.
Loop two 314

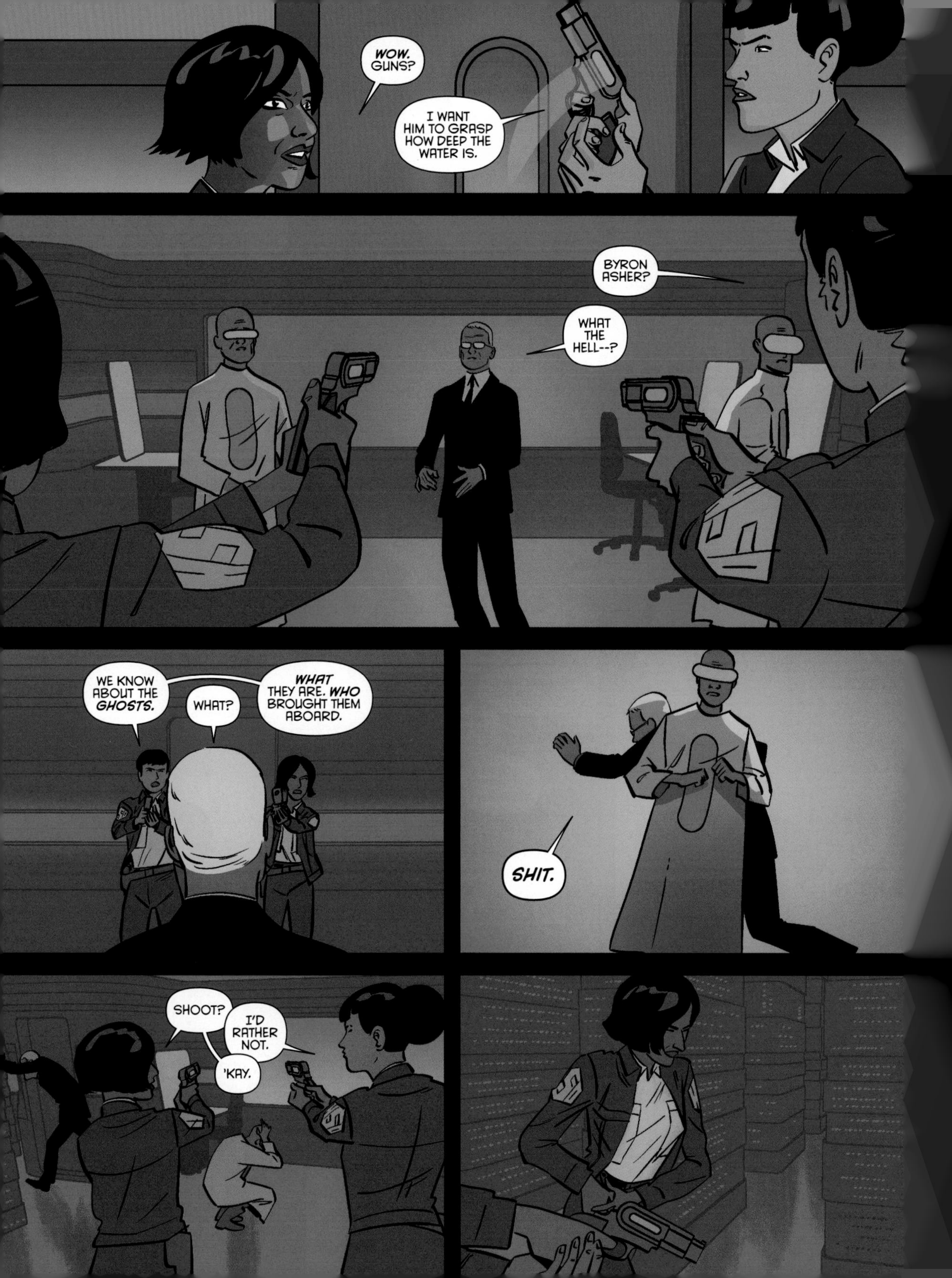

WOW. GUNS?
I WANT HIM TO GRASP HOW DEEP THE WATER IS.
BYRON ASHER?
WHAT THE HELL--?
WE KNOW ABOUT THE GHOSTS.
WHAT?
WHAT THEY ARE. WHO BROUGHT THEM ABOARD.
SHIT.
SHOOT?
I'D RATHER NOT.
'KAY.

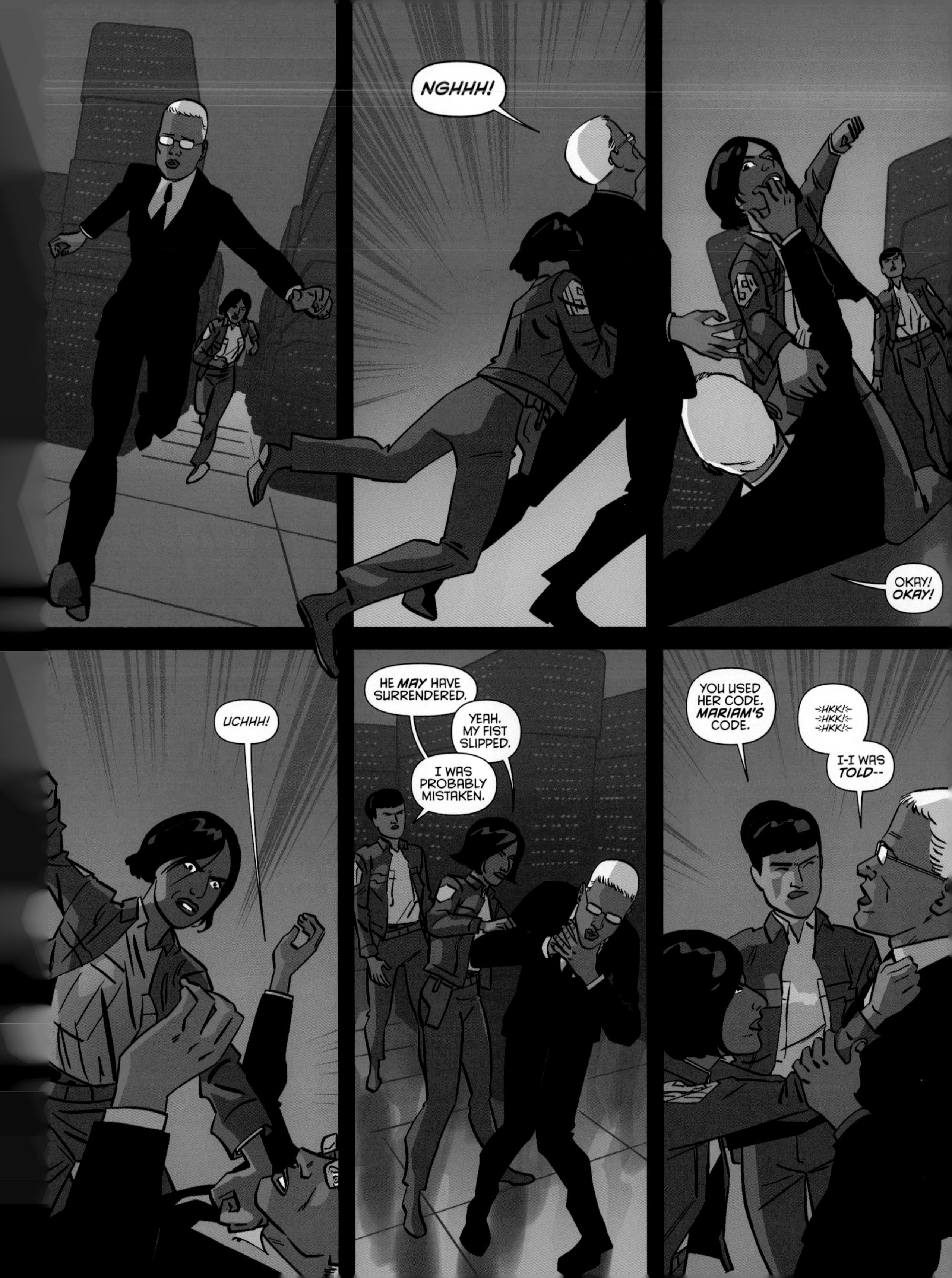
NGHHH!
OKAY! OKAY!
UCHHH!
HE MAY HAVE SURRENDERED.
YEAH. MY FIST SLIPPED.
I WAS PROBABLY MISTAKEN.
YOU USED HER CODE. MARIAM'S CODE.
HKK! HKK! HKK!
I-I WAS TOLD--

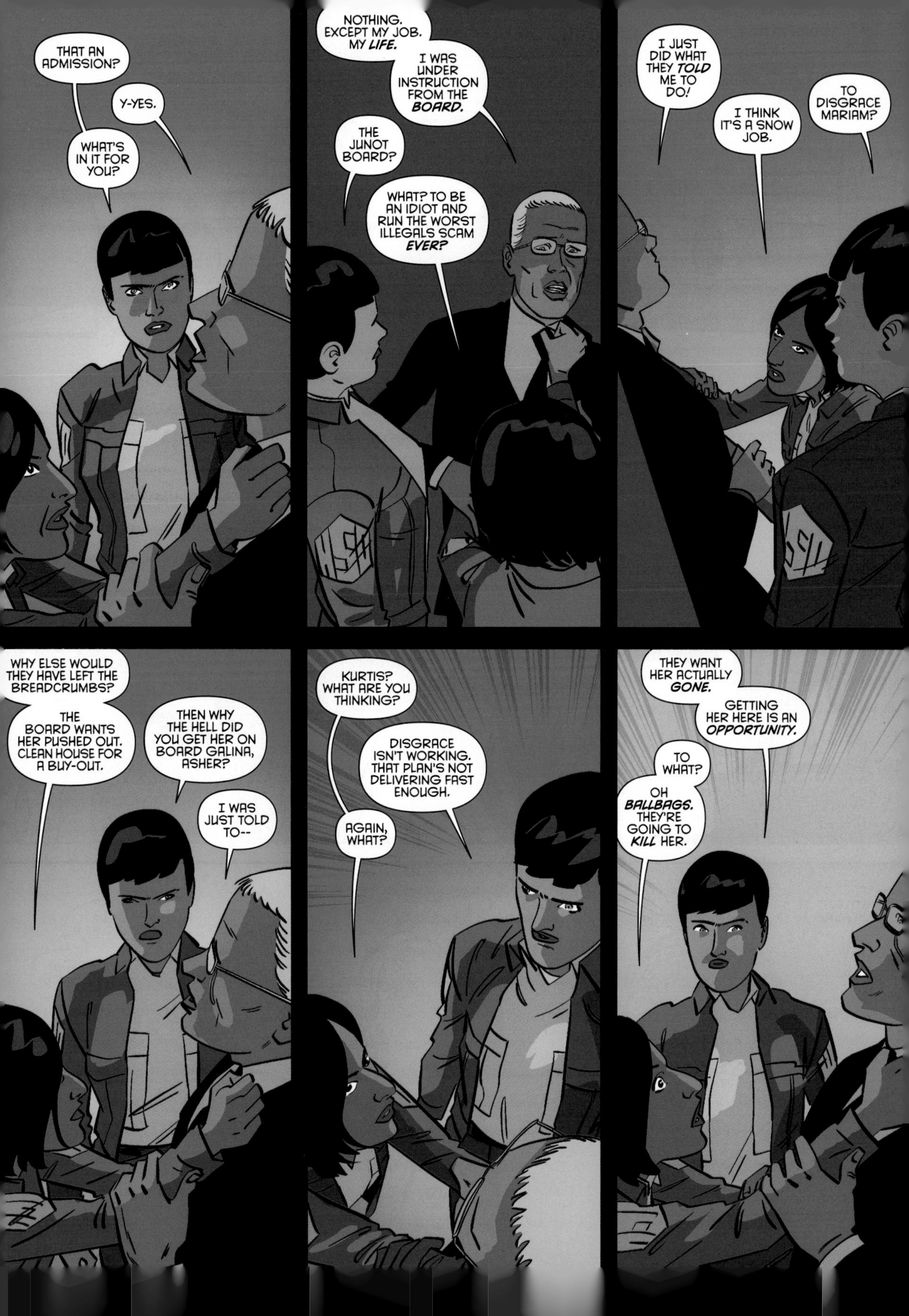
THAT AN ADMISSION?
Y-YES.
WHAT'S IN IT FOR YOU?
NOTHING. EXCEPT MY JOB. MY LIFE.
I WAS UNDER INSTRUCTION FROM THE BOARD.
THE JUNOT BOARD?
WHAT? TO BE AN IDIOT AND RUN THE WORST ILLEGALS SCAM EVER?
I JUST DID WHAT THEY TOLD ME TO DO!
I THINK IT'S A SNOW JOB.
TO DISGRACE MARIAM?
WHY ELSE WOULD THEY HAVE LEFT THE BREADCRUMBS?
THE BOARD WANTS HER PUSHED OUT. CLEAN HOUSE FOR A BUY-OUT.
THEN WHY THE HELL DID YOU GET HER ON BOARD GALINA, ASHER?
I WAS JUST TOLD TO--
KURTIS? WHAT ARE YOU THINKING?
DISGRACE ISN'T WORKING. THAT PLAN'S NOT DELIVERING FAST ENOUGH.
AGAIN, WHAT?
THEY WANT HER ACTUALLY GONE.
GETTING HER HERE IS AN OPPORTUNITY.
TO WHAT?
OH BALLBAGS. THEY'RE GOING TO KILL HER.

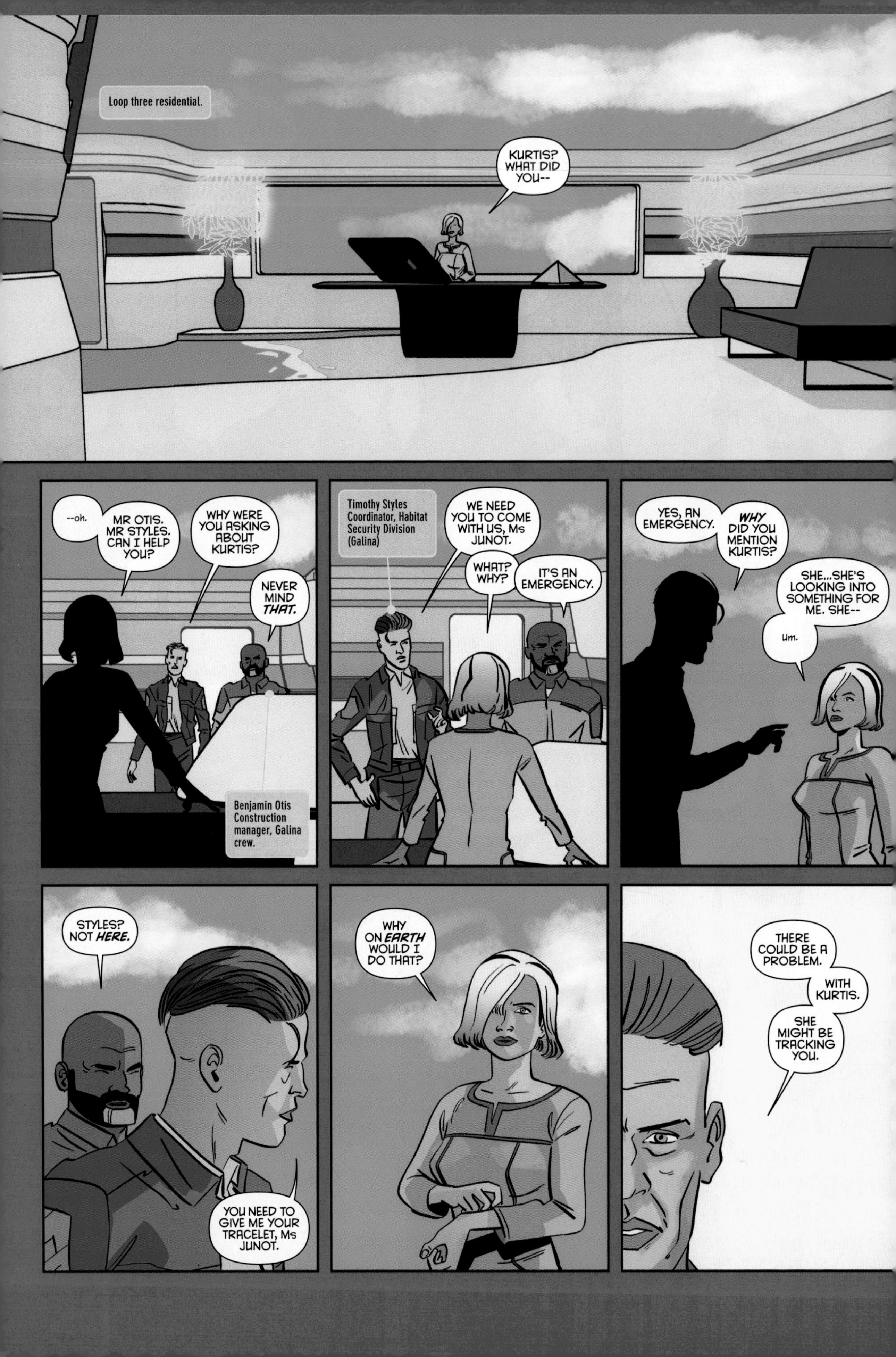
Loop three residential.
KURTIS? WHAT DID YOU--
--oh.
MR OTIS. MR STYLES. CAN I HELP YOU?
WHY WERE YOU ASKING ABOUT KURTIS?
NEVER MIND *THAT.*
Benjamin Otis Construction manager, Galina crew.
Timothy Styles Coordinator, Habitat Security Division (Galina)
WE NEED YOU TO COME WITH US, Ms JUNOT.
WHAT? WHY?
IT'S AN EMERGENCY.
YES, AN EMERGENCY.
WHY DID YOU MENTION KURTIS?
SHE...SHE'S LOOKING INTO SOMETHING FOR ME. SHE--
Um.
STYLES? NOT *HERE.*
YOU NEED TO GIVE ME YOUR TRACELET, Ms JUNOT.
WHY ON *EARTH* WOULD I DO THAT?
THERE COULD BE A PROBLEM.
WITH KURTIS.
SHE MIGHT BE TRACKING YOU.

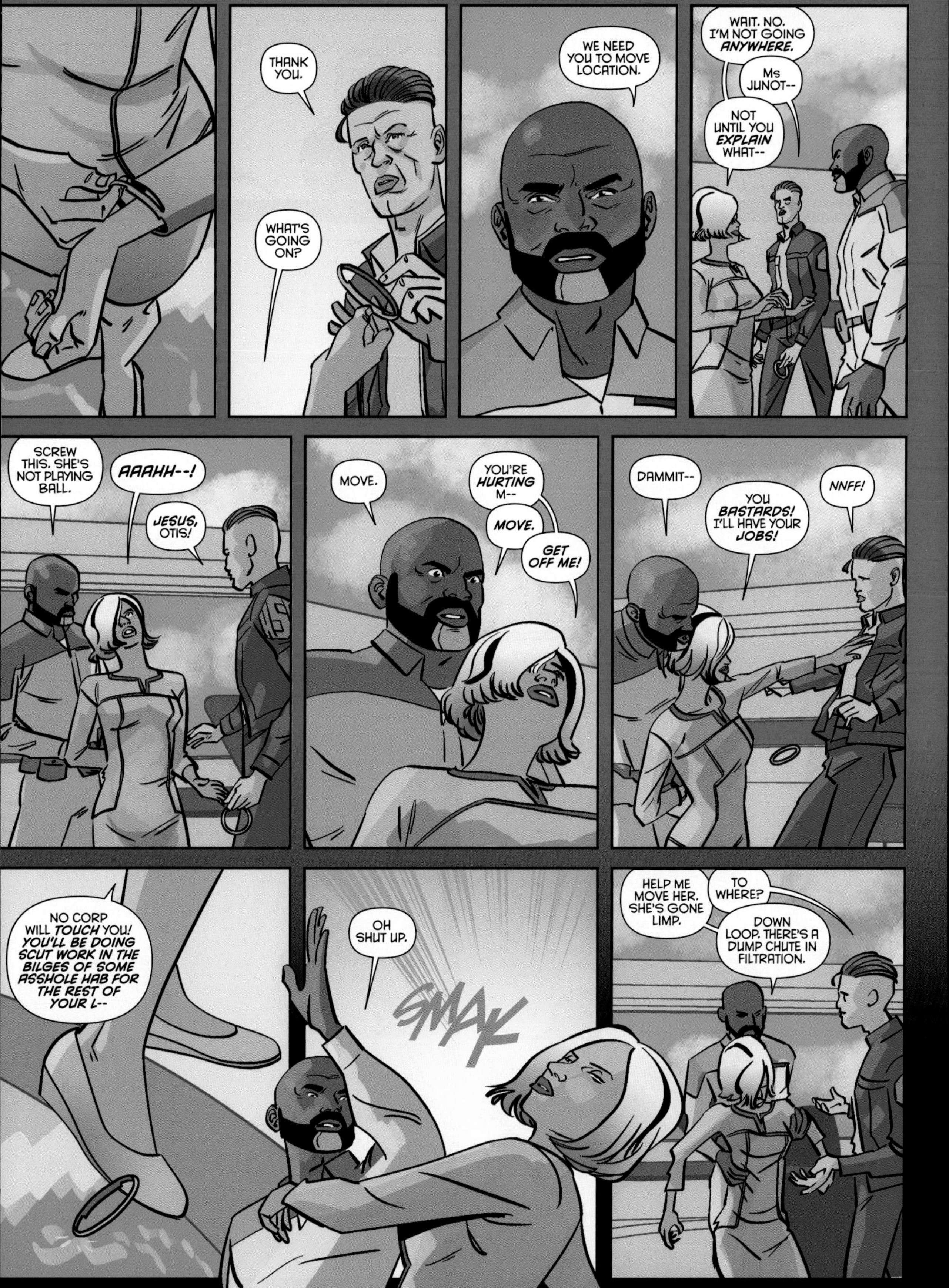
THANK YOU.
WHAT'S GOING ON?
WE NEED YOU TO MOVE LOCATION.
WAIT. NO. I'M NOT GOING *ANYWHERE.*
Ms JUNOT--
NOT UNTIL YOU *EXPLAIN* WHAT--
SCREW THIS. SHE'S NOT PLAYING BALL.
AAAHH--!
JESUS, OTIS!
MOVE.
YOU'RE *HURTING* M--
MOVE.
GET OFF ME!
DAMMIT--
YOU *BASTARDS!* I'LL HAVE YOUR *JOBS!*
NNFF!
NO CORP WILL *TOUCH* YOU! YOU'LL BE DOING SCUT WORK IN THE BILGES OF SOME ASSHOLE HAB FOR THE REST OF YOUR L--
OH SHUT UP.
SMAK
HELP ME MOVE HER. SHE'S GONE LIMP.
TO WHERE?
DOWN LOOP. THERE'S A DUMP CHUTE IN FILTRATION.

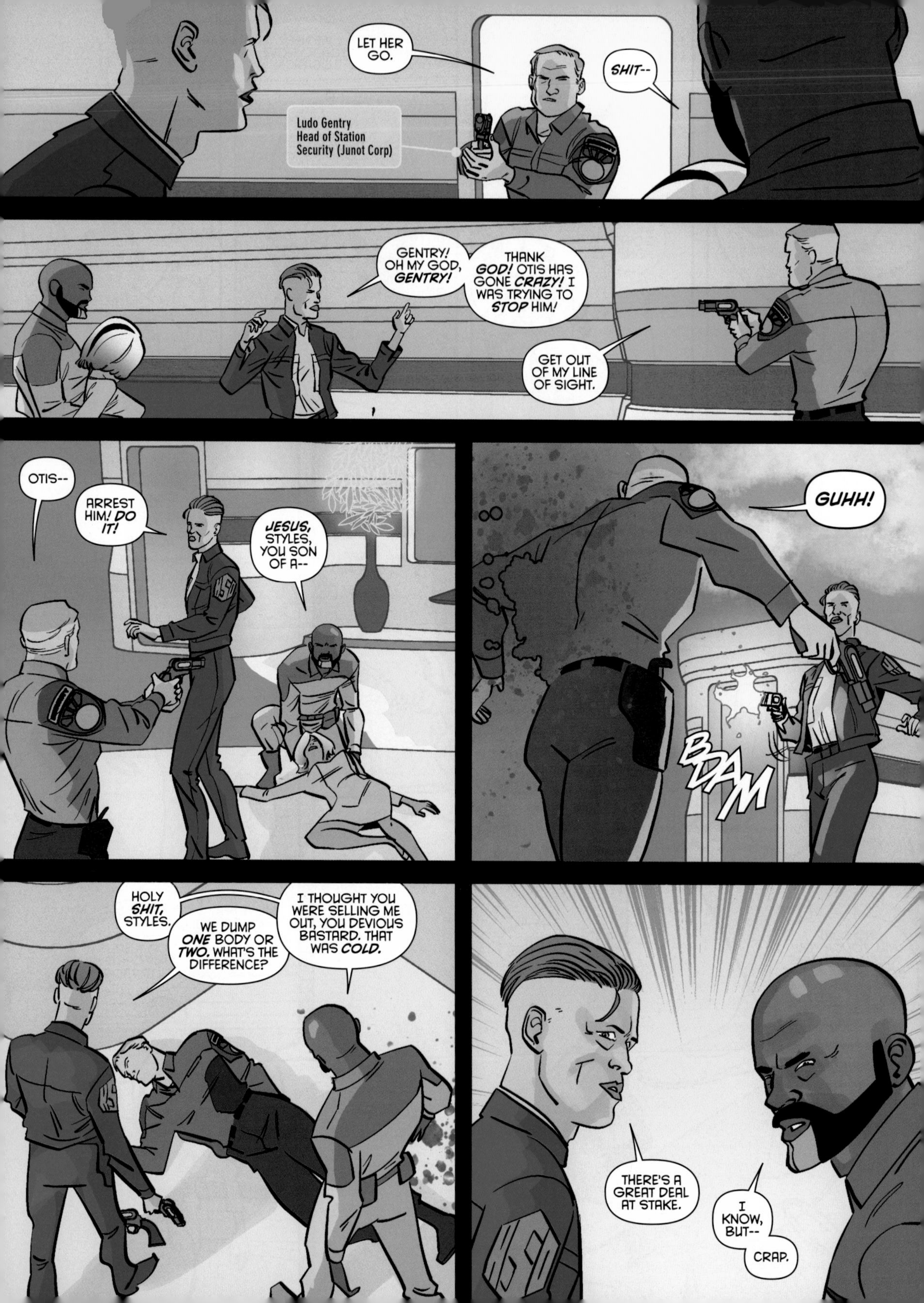
LET HER GO.
Ludo Gentry Head of Station Security (Junot Corp)
SHIT--
GENTRY! OH MY GOD, GENTRY!
THANK GOD! OTIS HAS GONE CRAZY! I WAS TRYING TO STOP HIM!
GET OUT OF MY LINE OF SIGHT.
OTIS--
ARREST HIM! DO IT!
JESUS, STYLES, YOU SON OF A--
GUHH!
BDAM
HOLY SHIT, STYLES.
I THOUGHT YOU WERE SELLING ME OUT, YOU DEVIOUS BASTARD. THAT WAS COLD.
WE DUMP ONE BODY OR TWO. WHAT'S THE DIFFERENCE?
THERE'S A GREAT DEAL AT STAKE.
I KNOW, BUT--
CRAP.

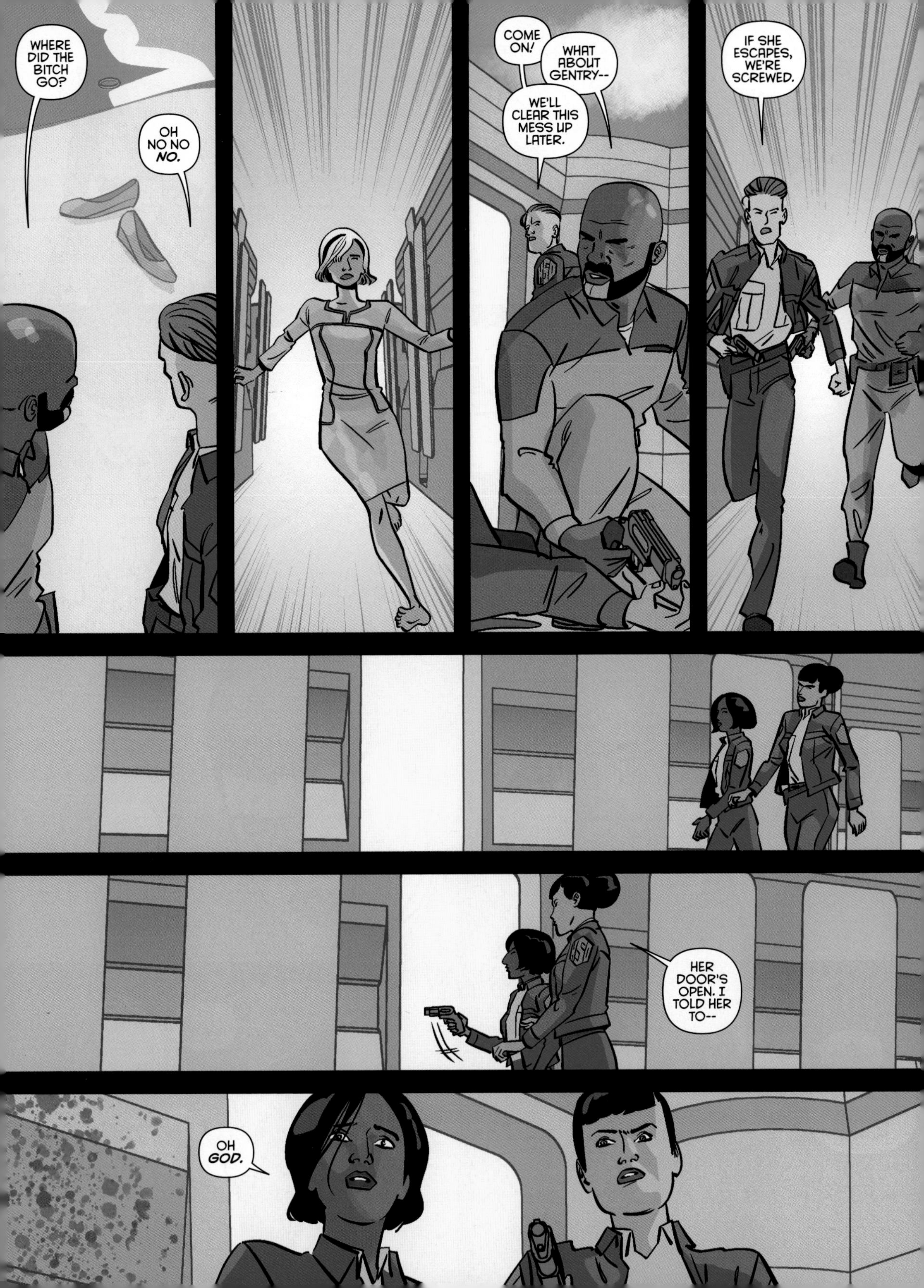

WHERE DID THE BITCH GO?
OH NO NO NO.
COME ON!
WHAT ABOUT GENTRY--
WE'LL CLEAR THIS MESS UP LATER.
IF SHE ESCAPES, WE'RE SCREWED.
HER DOOR'S OPEN. I TOLD HER TO--
OH GOD.

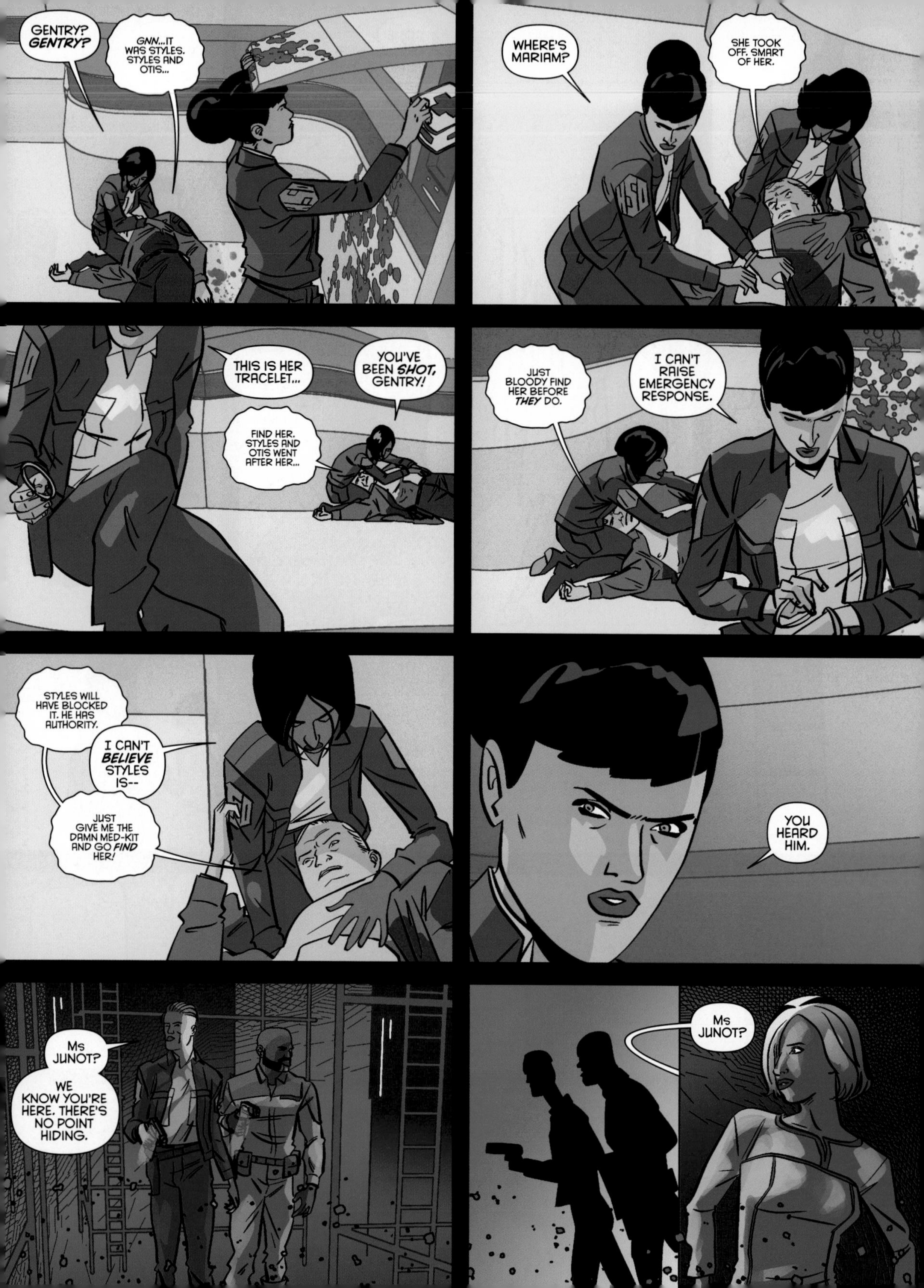
GENTRY? *GENTRY?*
GNN...IT WAS STYLES. STYLES AND OTIS...
WHERE'S MARIAM?
SHE TOOK OFF. SMART OF HER.
THIS IS HER TRACELET...
YOU'VE BEEN *SHOT*, GENTRY!
FIND HER. STYLES AND OTIS WENT AFTER HER...
I CAN'T RAISE EMERGENCY RESPONSE.
JUST BLOODY FIND HER BEFORE *THEY* DO.
STYLES WILL HAVE BLOCKED IT. HE HAS AUTHORITY.
I CAN'T *BELIEVE* STYLES IS--
JUST GIVE ME THE DAMN MED-KIT AND GO *FIND* HER!
YOU HEARD HIM.
Ms JUNOT?
WE KNOW YOU'RE HERE. THERE'S NO POINT HIDING.
Ms JUNOT?

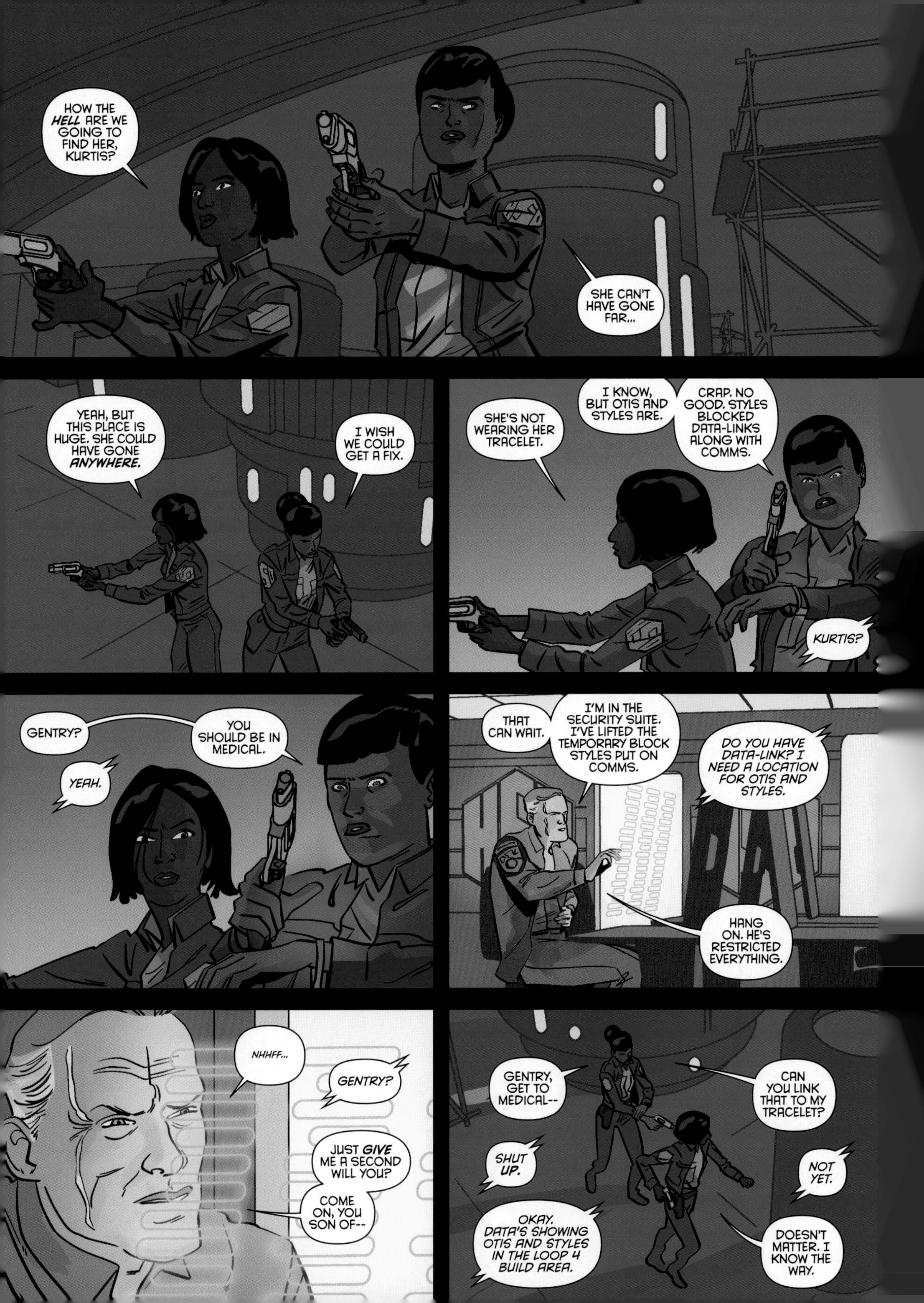
HOW THE *HELL* ARE WE GOING TO FIND HER, KURTIS?
SHE CAN'T HAVE GONE FAR...
YEAH, BUT THIS PLACE IS HUGE. SHE COULD HAVE GONE *ANYWHERE.*
I WISH WE COULD GET A FIX.
SHE'S NOT WEARING HER TRACELET.
I KNOW, BUT OTIS AND STYLES ARE.
CRAP. NO GOOD. STYLES BLOCKED DATA-LINKS ALONG WITH COMMS.
KURTIS?
GENTRY?
YOU SHOULD BE IN MEDICAL.
YEAH.
THAT CAN WAIT.
I'M IN THE SECURITY SUITE. I'VE LIFTED THE TEMPORARY BLOCK STYLES PUT ON COMMS.
DO YOU HAVE DATA-LINK? I NEED A LOCATION FOR OTIS AND STYLES.
HANG ON. HE'S RESTRICTED EVERYTHING.
NHHFF...
GENTRY?
JUST *GIVE* ME A SECOND WILL YOU?
COME ON, YOU SON OF--
GENTRY, GET TO MEDICAL--
CAN YOU LINK THAT TO MY TRACELET?
SHUT UP.
NOT YET.
OKAY. DATA'S SHOWING OTIS AND STYLES IN THE LOOP 4 BUILD AREA.
DOESN'T MATTER. I KNOW THE WAY.

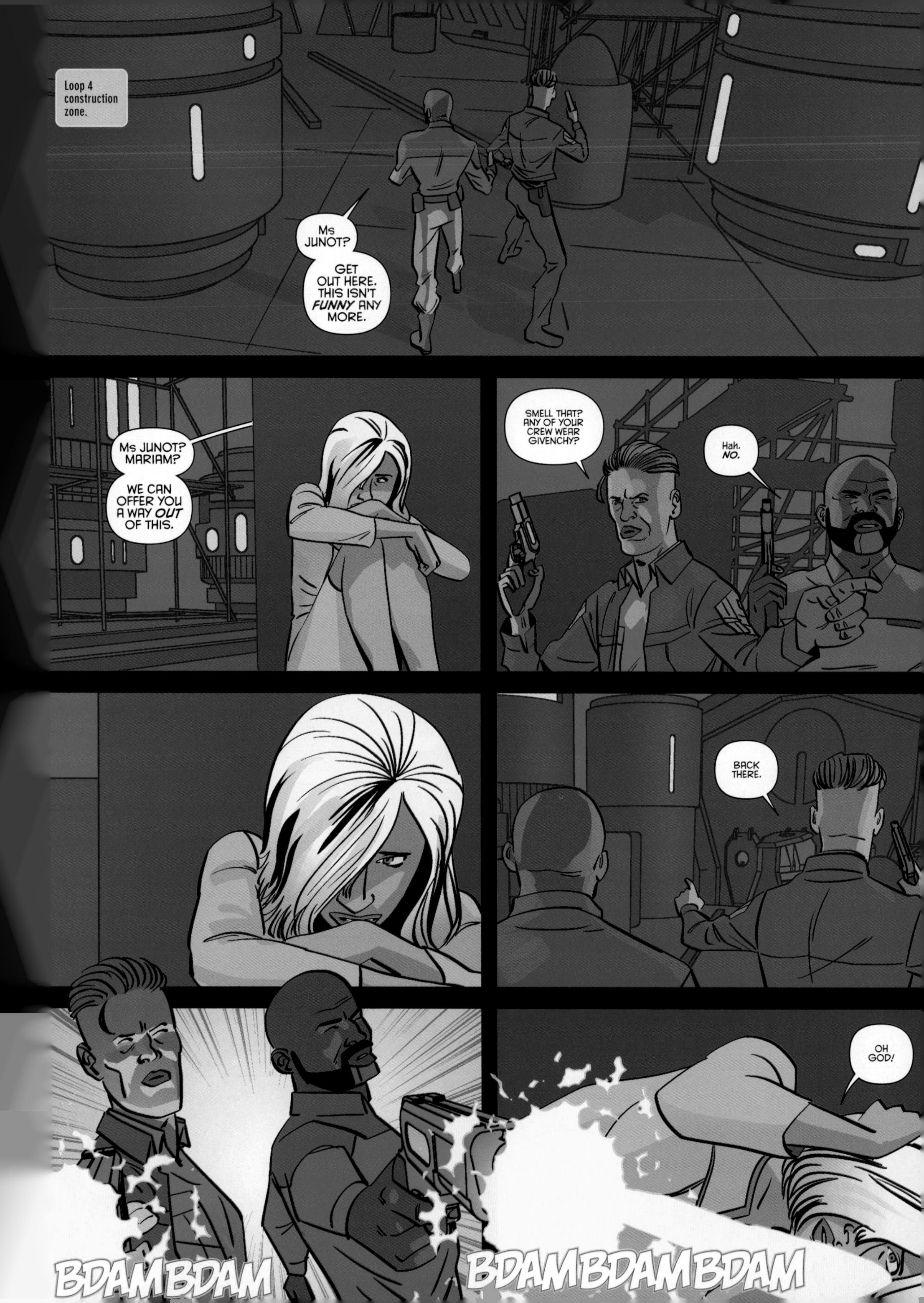

Loop 4 construction zone.
Ms JUNOT?
GET OUT HERE. THIS ISN'T *FUNNY* ANY MORE.
Ms JUNOT? MARIAM?
WE CAN OFFER YOU A WAY *OUT* OF THIS.
SMELL THAT? ANY OF YOUR CREW WEAR GIVENCHY?
Hah. *NO.*
BACK THERE.
BDAM BDAM
BDAM BDAM BDAM
OH GOD!

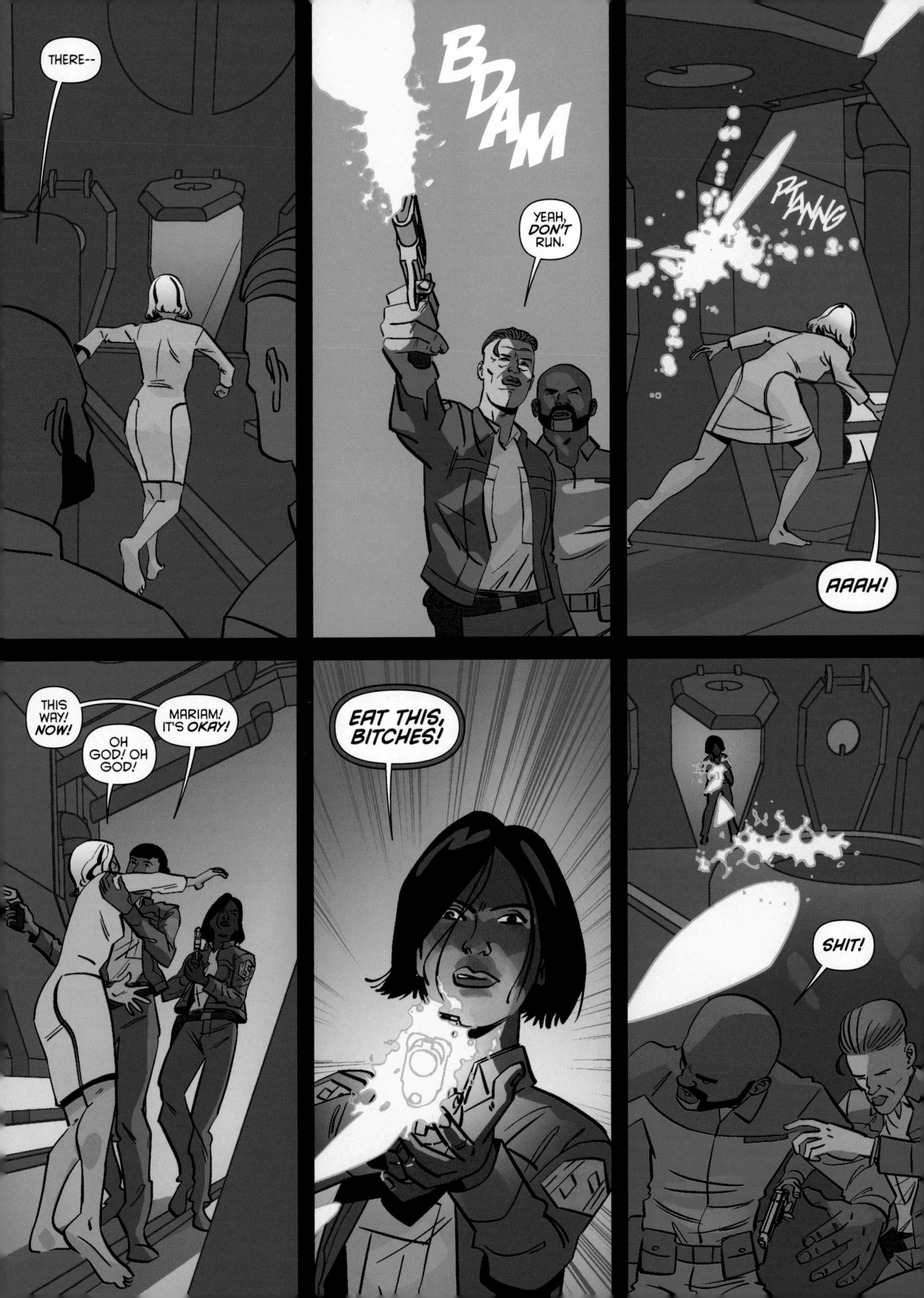
THERE--
BDAM
YEAH, DON'T RUN.
PKANNG
AAAH!
THIS WAY! NOW!
MARIAM! IT'S OKAY!
OH GOD! OH GOD!
EAT THIS, BITCHES!
SHIT!

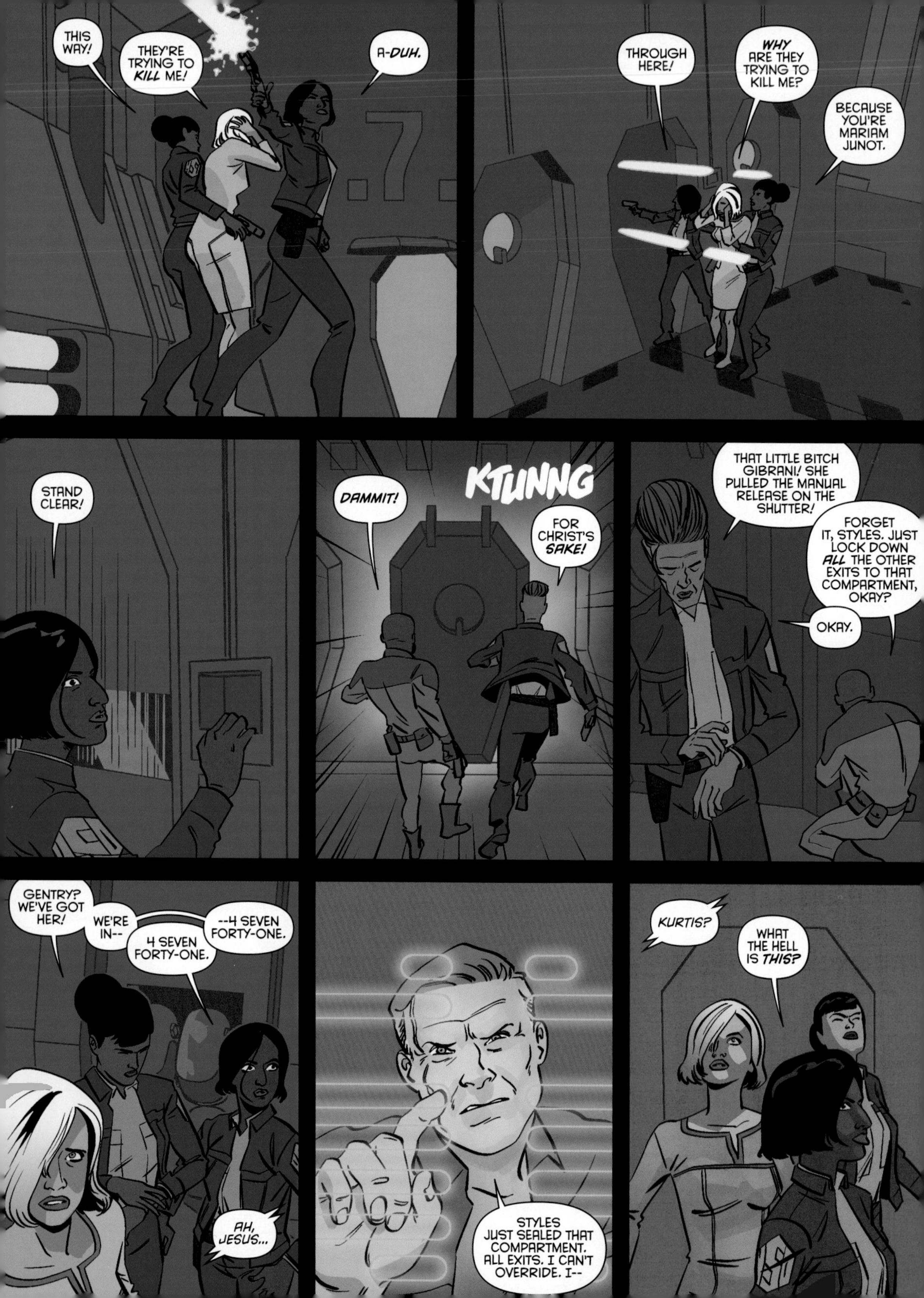
THIS WAY!
THEY'RE TRYING TO KILL ME!
A-DUH.
THROUGH HERE!
WHY ARE THEY TRYING TO KILL ME?
BECAUSE YOU'RE MARIAM JUNOT.
STAND CLEAR!
KTUNNG
DAMMIT!
FOR CHRIST'S SAKE!
THAT LITTLE BITCH GIBRANI! SHE PULLED THE MANUAL RELEASE ON THE SHUTTER!
FORGET IT, STYLES. JUST LOCK DOWN ALL THE OTHER EXITS TO THAT COMPARTMENT, OKAY?
OKAY.
GENTRY? WE'VE GOT HER!
WE'RE IN--
4 SEVEN FORTY-ONE.
--4 SEVEN FORTY-ONE.
AH, JESUS...
STYLES JUST SEALED THAT COMPARTMENT. ALL EXITS. I CAN'T OVERRIDE. I--
KURTIS?
WHAT THE HELL IS THIS?

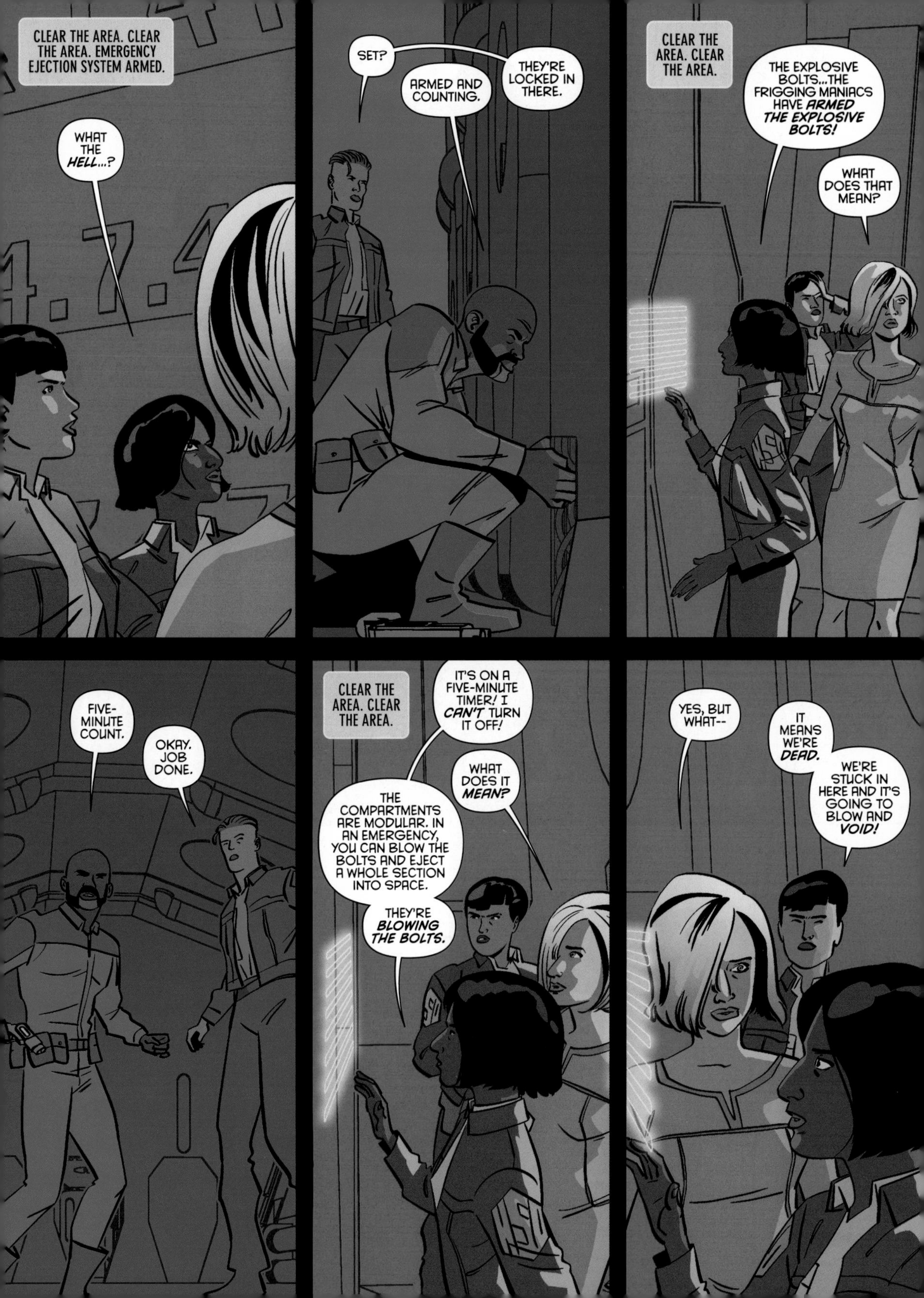

CLEAR THE AREA. CLEAR THE AREA. EMERGENCY EJECTION SYSTEM ARMED.
WHAT THE HELL...?
SET?
ARMED AND COUNTING.
THEY'RE LOCKED IN THERE.
CLEAR THE AREA. CLEAR THE AREA.
THE EXPLOSIVE BOLTS...THE FRIGGING MANIACS HAVE ARMED THE EXPLOSIVE BOLTS!
WHAT DOES THAT MEAN?
FIVE-MINUTE COUNT.
OKAY. JOB DONE.
CLEAR THE AREA. CLEAR THE AREA.
IT'S ON A FIVE-MINUTE TIMER! I CAN'T TURN IT OFF!
WHAT DOES IT MEAN?
THE COMPARTMENTS ARE MODULAR. IN AN EMERGENCY, YOU CAN BLOW THE BOLTS AND EJECT A WHOLE SECTION INTO SPACE.
THEY'RE BLOWING THE BOLTS.
YES, BUT WHAT--
IT MEANS WE'RE DEAD.
WE'RE STUCK IN HERE AND IT'S GOING TO BLOW AND VOID!

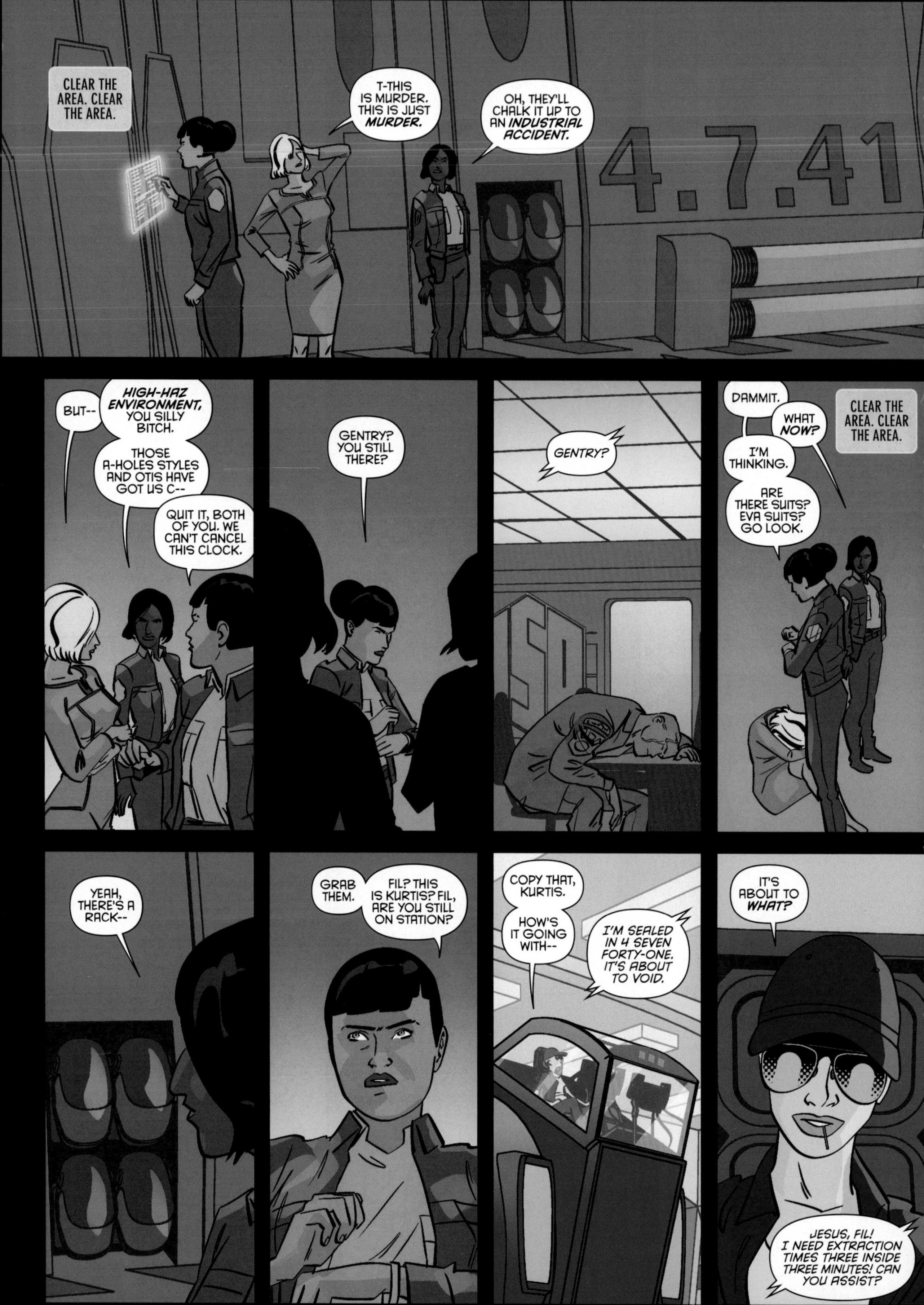
CLEAR THE AREA. CLEAR THE AREA.
T-THIS IS MURDER. THIS IS JUST MURDER.
OH, THEY'LL CHALK IT UP TO AN INDUSTRIAL ACCIDENT.
4.7.41
BUT--
HIGH-HAZ ENVIRONMENT, YOU SILLY BITCH.
THOSE A-HOLES STYLES AND OTIS HAVE GOT US C--
QUIT IT, BOTH OF YOU. WE CAN'T CANCEL THIS CLOCK.
GENTRY? YOU STILL THERE?
GENTRY?
DAMMIT.
WHAT NOW?
I'M THINKING.
ARE THERE SUITS? EVA SUITS? GO LOOK.
CLEAR THE AREA. CLEAR THE AREA.
YEAH, THERE'S A RACK--
GRAB THEM.
FIL? THIS IS KURTIS? FIL, ARE YOU STILL ON STATION?
COPY THAT, KURTIS.
HOW'S IT GOING WITH--
I'M SEALED IN 4 SEVEN FORTY-ONE. IT'S ABOUT TO VOID.
IT'S ABOUT TO WHAT?
JESUS, FIL! I NEED EXTRACTION TIMES THREE INSIDE THREE MINUTES! CAN YOU ASSIST?

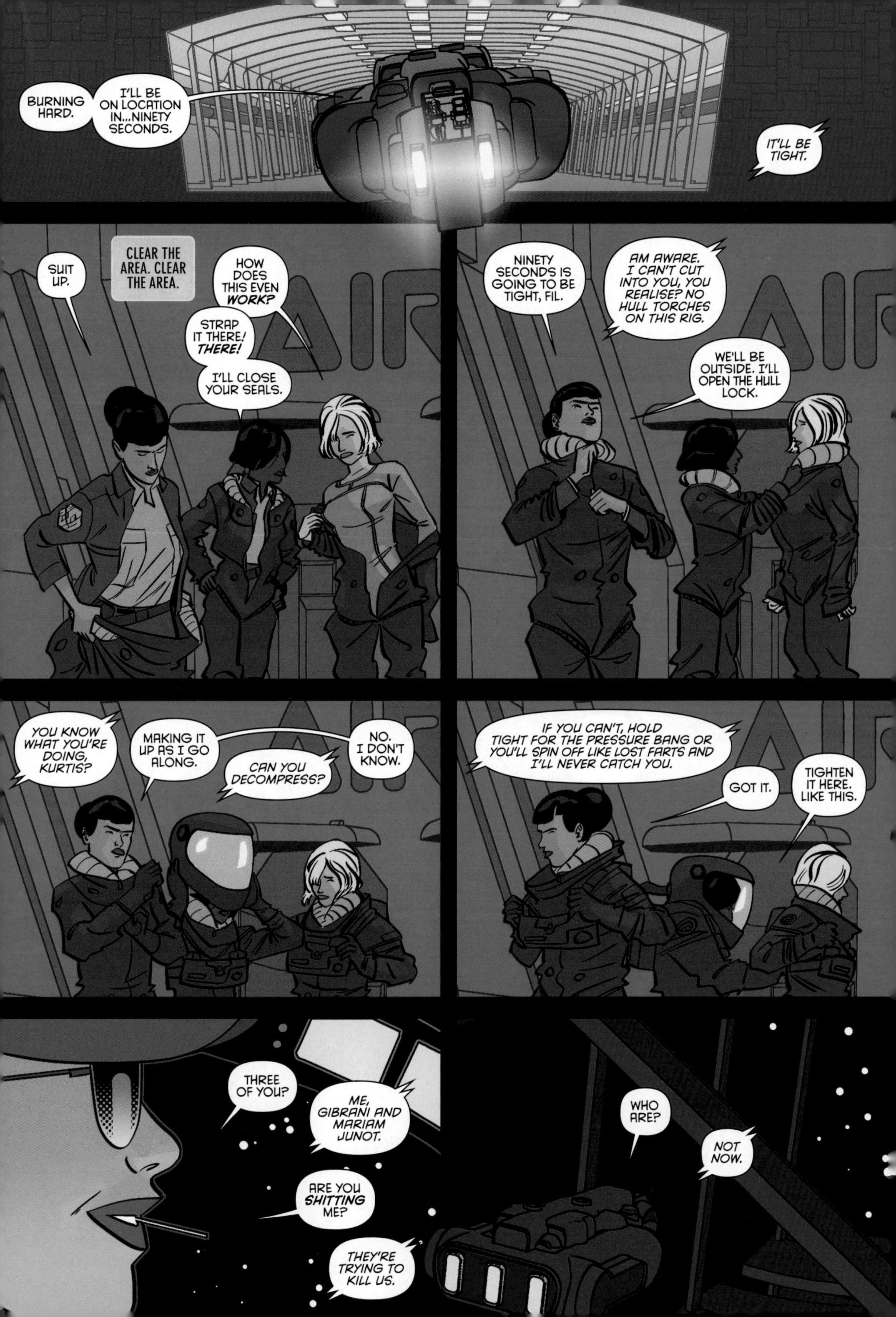

BURNING HARD.
I'LL BE ON LOCATION IN...NINETY SECONDS.
IT'LL BE TIGHT.
SUIT UP.
CLEAR THE AREA. CLEAR THE AREA.
HOW DOES THIS EVEN WORK?
STRAP IT THERE! THERE!
I'LL CLOSE YOUR SEALS.
NINETY SECONDS IS GOING TO BE TIGHT, FIL.
AM AWARE. I CAN'T CUT INTO YOU, YOU REALISE? NO HULL TORCHES ON THIS RIG.
WE'LL BE OUTSIDE. I'LL OPEN THE HULL LOCK.
YOU KNOW WHAT YOU'RE DOING, KURTIS?
MAKING IT UP AS I GO ALONG.
NO. I DON'T KNOW.
CAN YOU DECOMPRESS?
IF YOU CAN'T, HOLD TIGHT FOR THE PRESSURE BANG OR YOU'LL SPIN OFF LIKE LOST FARTS AND I'LL NEVER CATCH YOU.
GOT IT.
TIGHTEN IT HERE. LIKE THIS.
THREE OF YOU?
ME, GIBRANI AND MARIAM JUNOT.
ARE YOU SHITTING ME?
THEY'RE TRYING TO KILL US.
WHO ARE?
NOT NOW.

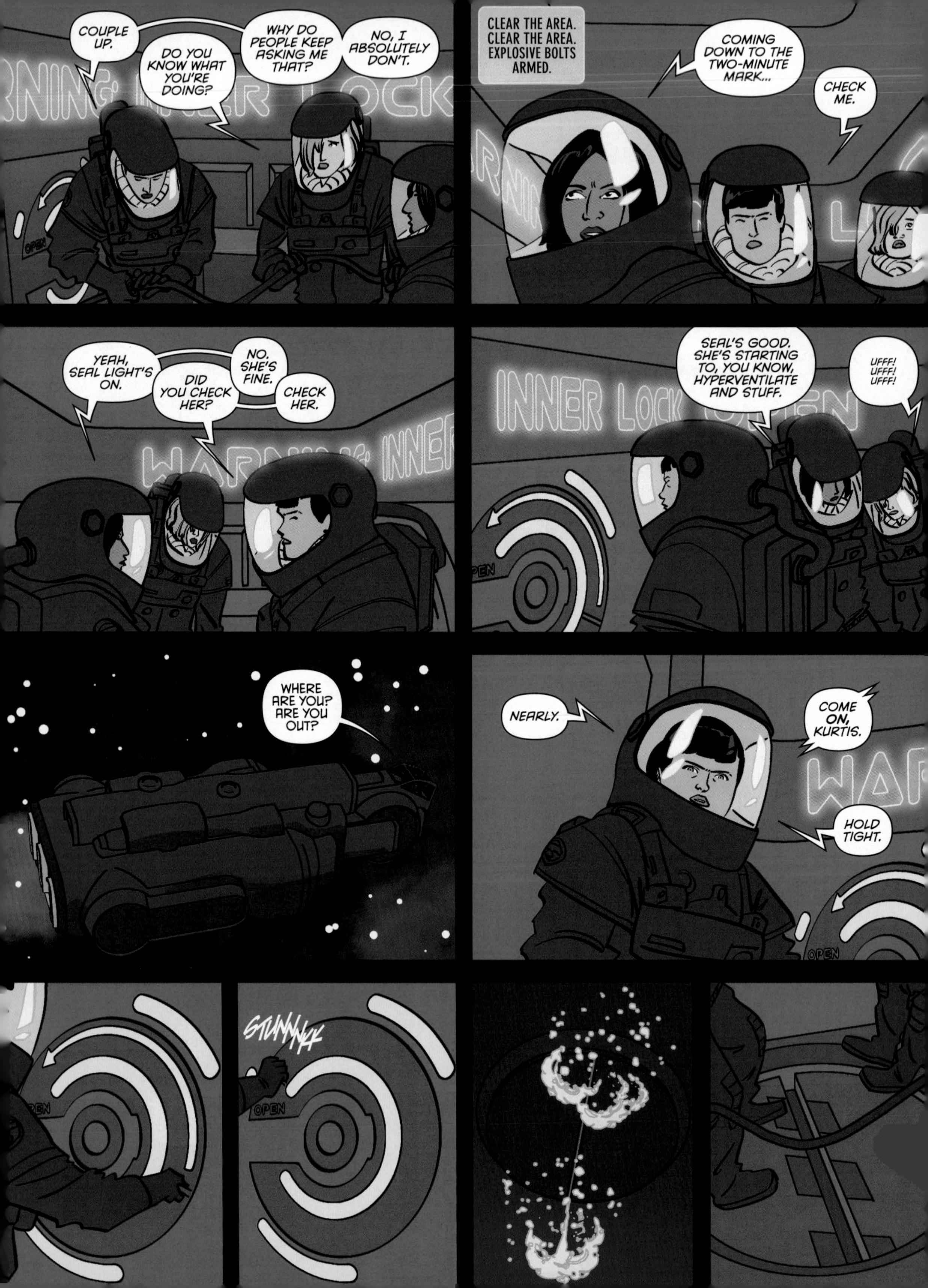
COUPLE UP.
DO YOU KNOW WHAT YOU'RE DOING?
WHY DO PEOPLE KEEP ASKING ME THAT?
NO, I ABSOLUTELY DON'T.
WARNING: INNER LOCK
CLEAR THE AREA. CLEAR THE AREA. EXPLOSIVE BOLTS ARMED.
COMING DOWN TO THE TWO-MINUTE MARK...
CHECK ME.
YEAH, SEAL LIGHT'S ON.
DID YOU CHECK HER?
NO. SHE'S FINE.
CHECK HER.
SEAL'S GOOD. SHE'S STARTING TO, YOU KNOW, HYPERVENTILATE AND STUFF.
UFFF! UFFF! UFFF!
INNER LOCK OPEN
WHERE ARE YOU? ARE YOU OUT?
NEARLY.
COME ON, KURTIS.
HOLD TIGHT.
OPEN
STUNNNK

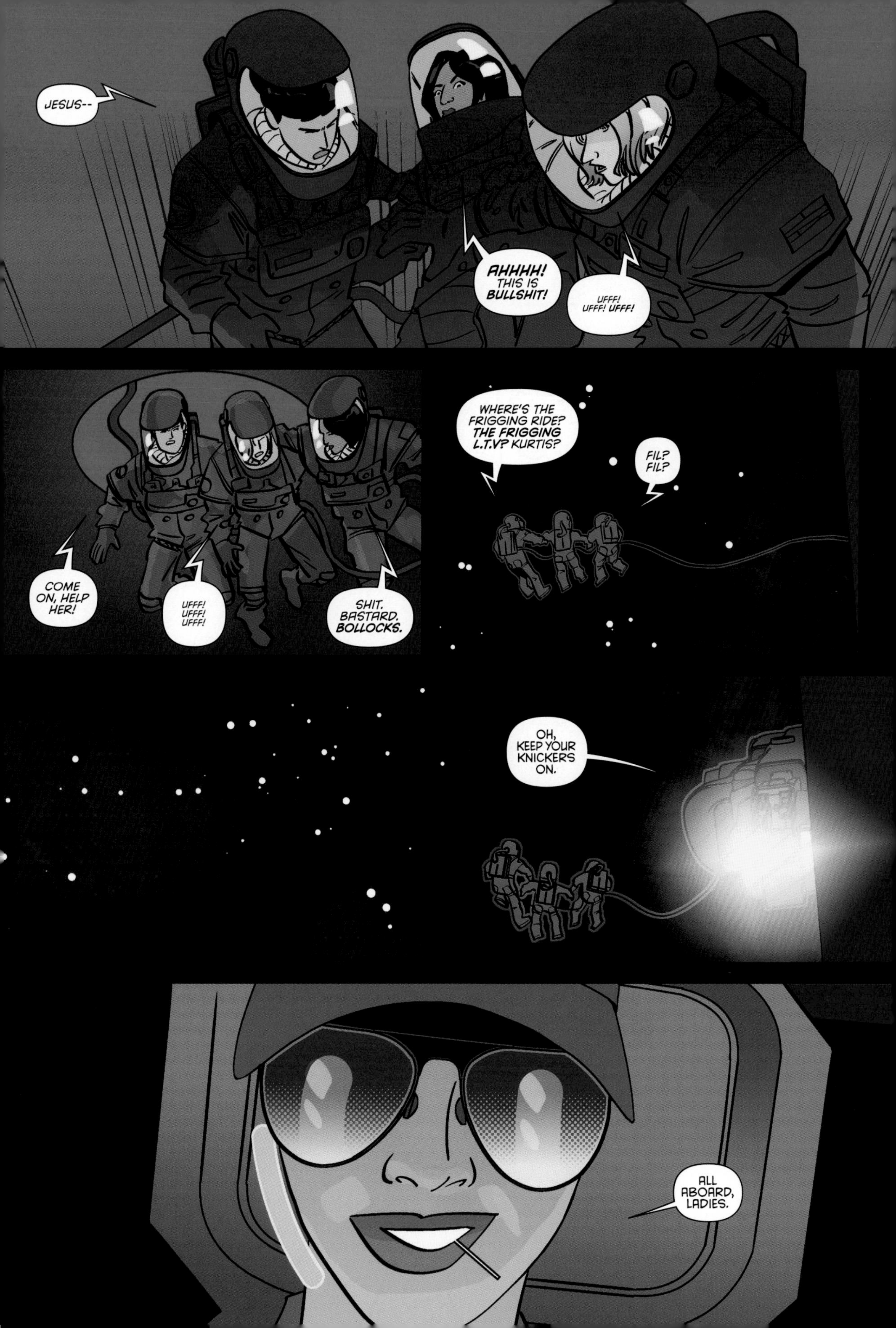
JESUS--
AHHHH! THIS IS BULLSHIT!
UFFF! UFFF! UFFF!
COME ON, HELP HER!
UFFF! UFFF! UFFF!
SHIT. BASTARD. BOLLOCKS.
WHERE'S THE FRIGGING RIDE? THE FRIGGING L.T.V? KURTIS?
FIL? FIL?
OH, KEEP YOUR KNICKERS ON.
ALL ABOARD, LADIES.

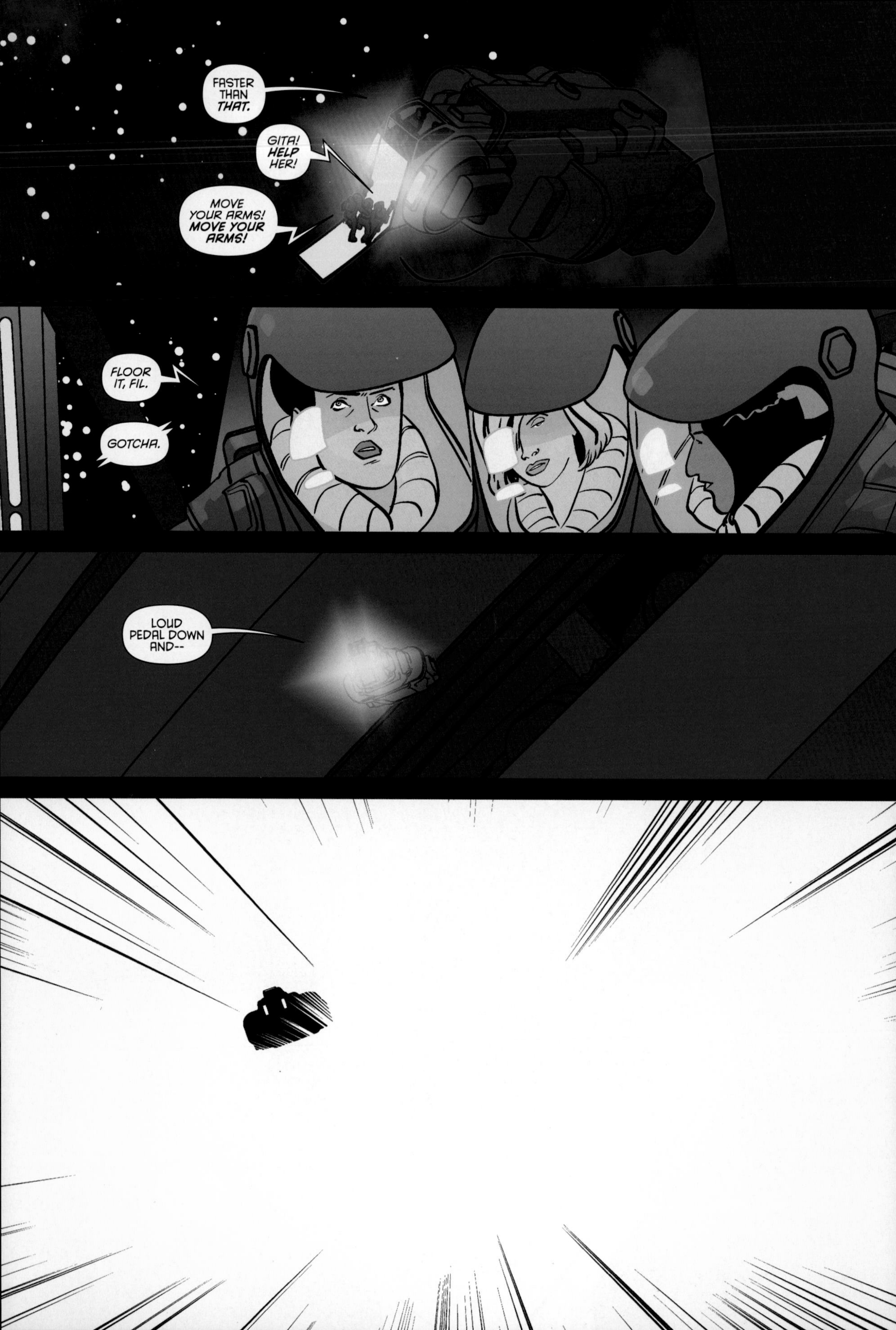
FASTER THAN *THAT.*
GITA! *HELP HER!*
MOVE YOUR ARMS! *MOVE YOUR ARMS!*
FLOOR IT, FIL.
GOTCHA.
LOUD PEDAL DOWN AND--

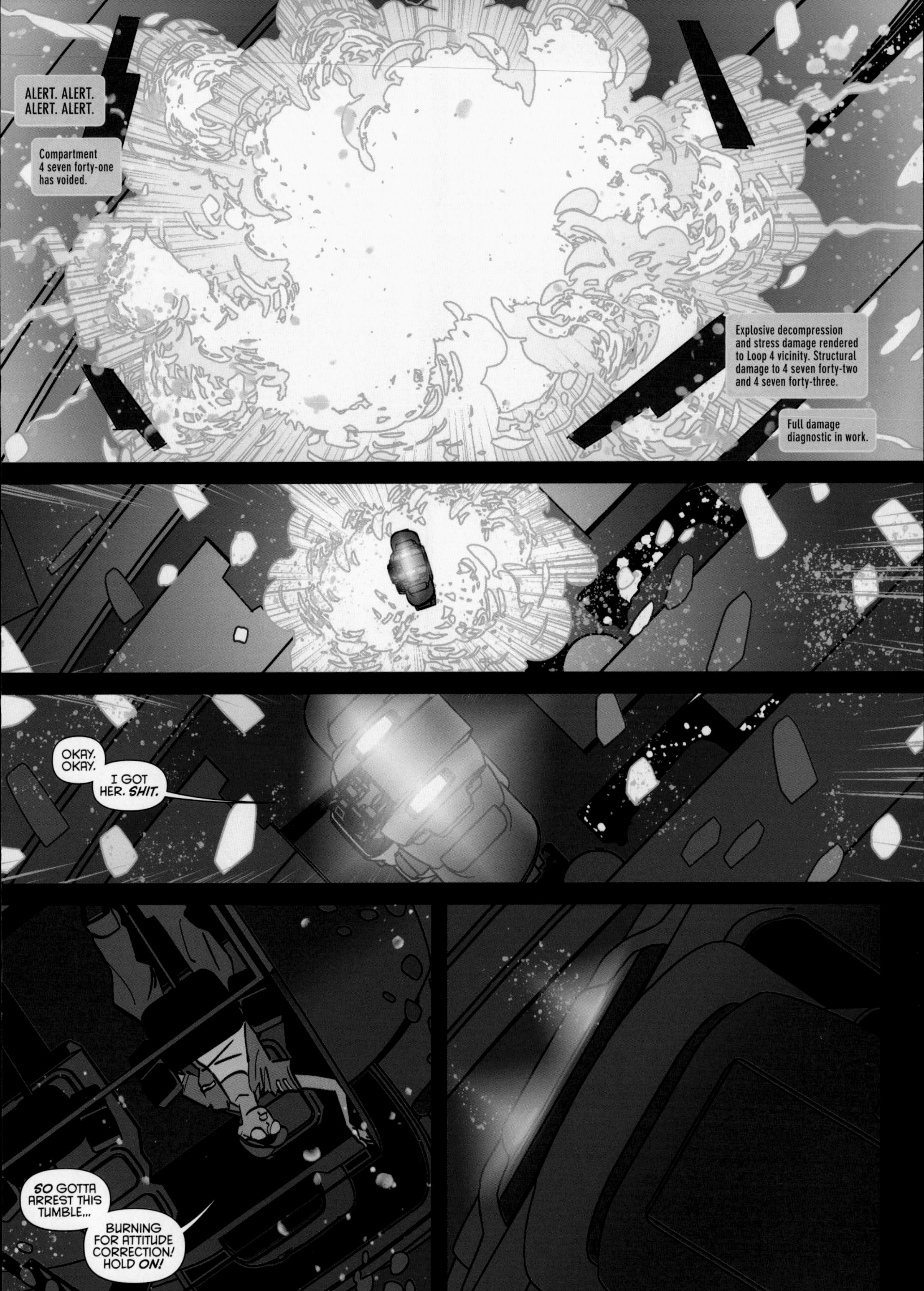
ALERT. ALERT. ALERT. ALERT.
Compartment 4 seven forty-one has voided.
Explosive decompression and stress damage rendered to Loop 4 vicinity. Structural damage to 4 seven forty-two and 4 seven forty-three.
Full damage diagnostic in work.
OKAY. OKAY.
I GOT HER. *SHIT.*
SO GOTTA ARREST THIS TUMBLE...
BURNING FOR ATTITUDE CORRECTION! HOLD *ON!*

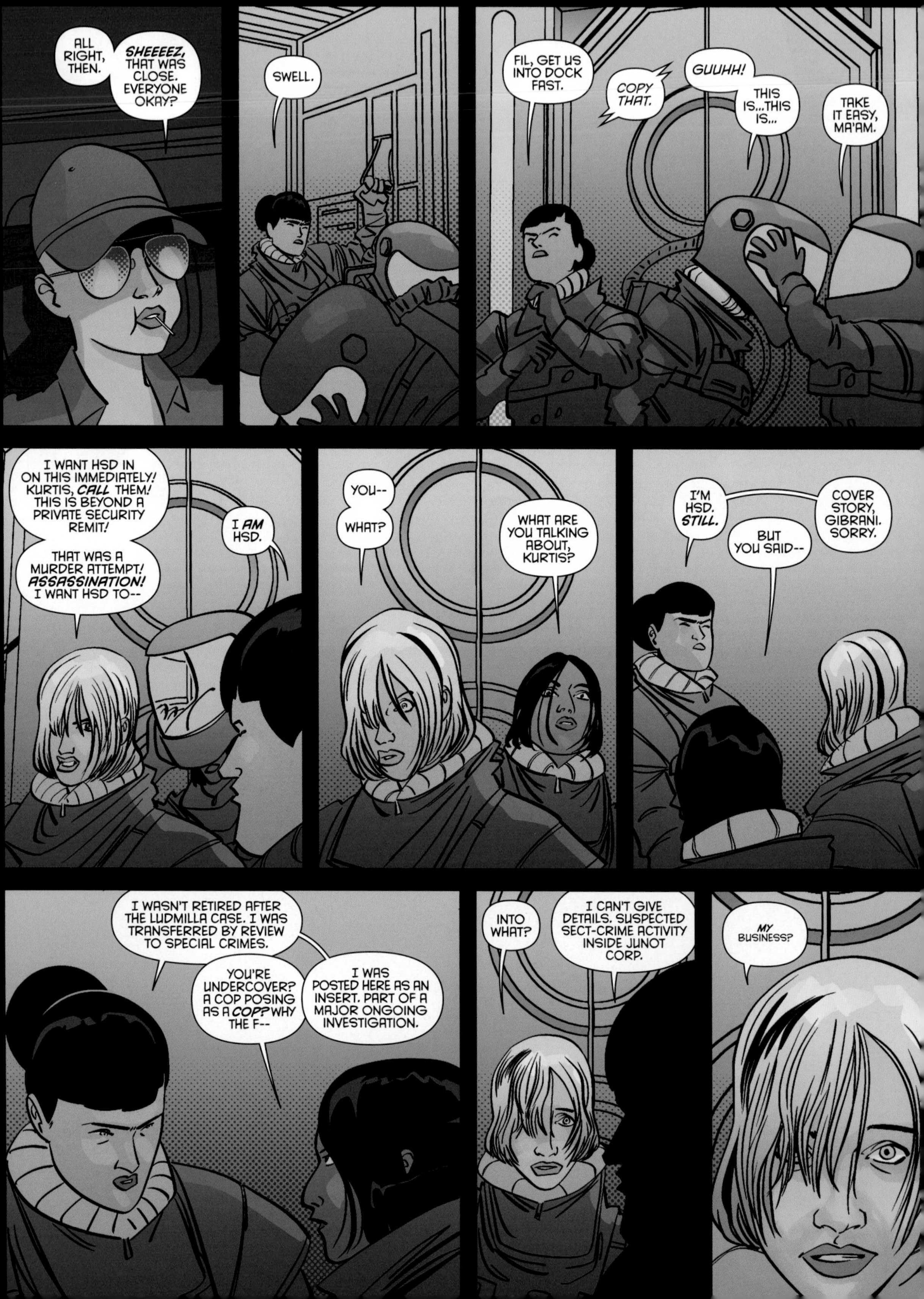
ALL RIGHT, THEN.
SHEEEEZ, THAT WAS CLOSE. EVERYONE OKAY?
SWELL.
FIL, GET US INTO DOCK FAST.
COPY THAT.
GUUHH!
THIS IS...THIS IS...
TAKE IT EASY, MA'AM.
I WANT HSD IN ON THIS IMMEDIATELY! KURTIS, CALL THEM! THIS IS BEYOND A PRIVATE SECURITY REMIT!
THAT WAS A MURDER ATTEMPT! ASSASSINATION! I WANT HSD TO--
I AM HSD.
YOU--
WHAT?
WHAT ARE YOU TALKING ABOUT, KURTIS?
I'M HSD. STILL.
COVER STORY, GIBRANI. SORRY.
BUT YOU SAID--
I WASN'T RETIRED AFTER THE LUDMILLA CASE. I WAS TRANSFERRED BY REVIEW TO SPECIAL CRIMES.
YOU'RE UNDERCOVER? A COP POSING AS A COP? WHY THE F--
I WAS POSTED HERE AS AN INSERT. PART OF A MAJOR ONGOING INVESTIGATION.
INTO WHAT?
I CAN'T GIVE DETAILS. SUSPECTED SECT-CRIME ACTIVITY INSIDE JUNOT CORP.
MY BUSINESS?

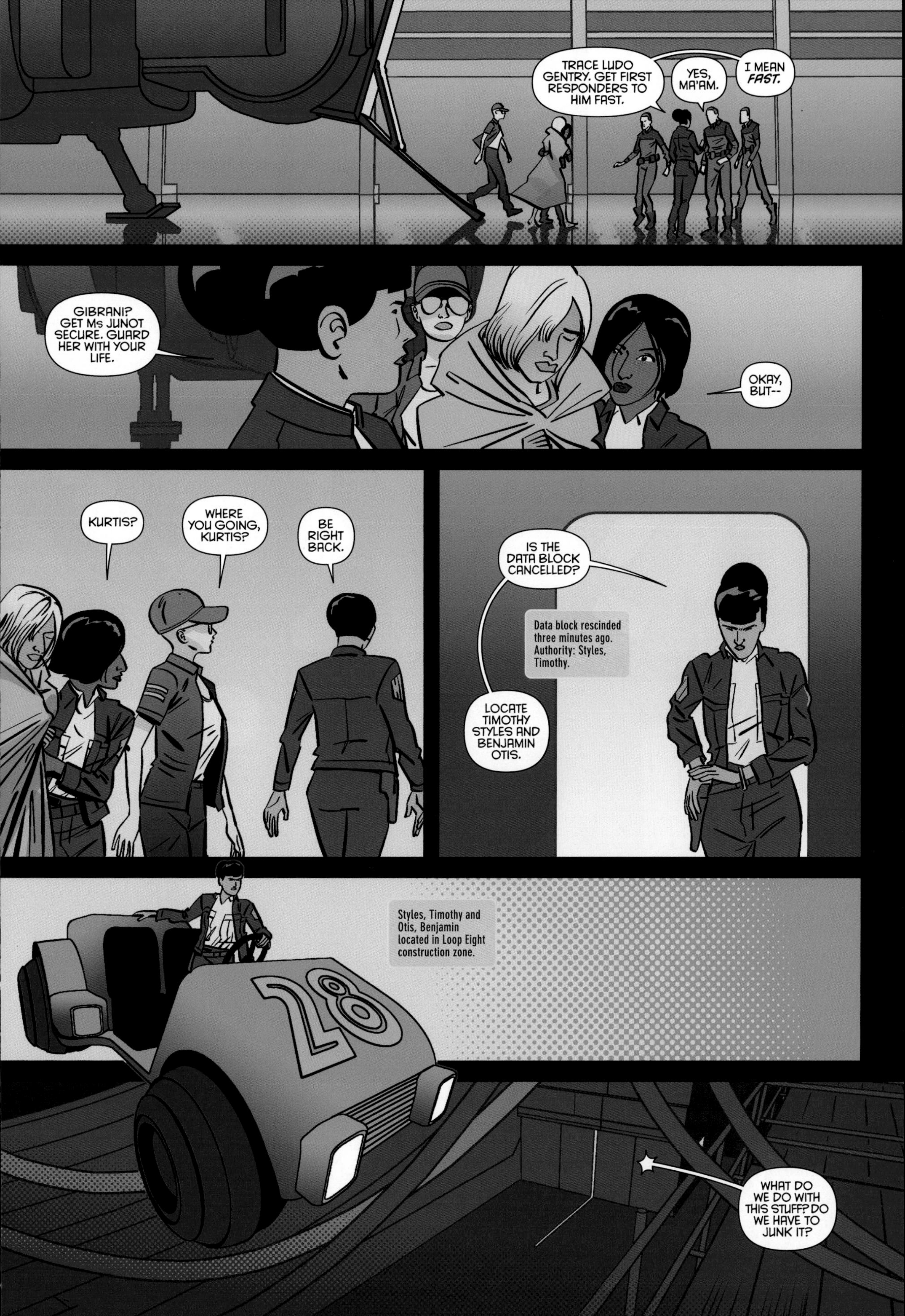
TRACE LUDO GENTRY. GET FIRST RESPONDERS TO HIM FAST.
YES, MA'AM.
I MEAN *FAST.*
GIBRANI? GET Ms JUNOT SECURE. GUARD HER WITH YOUR LIFE.
OKAY, BUT--
KURTIS?
WHERE YOU GOING, KURTIS?
BE RIGHT BACK.
IS THE DATA BLOCK CANCELLED?
Data block rescinded three minutes ago. Authority: Styles, Timothy.
LOCATE TIMOTHY STYLES AND BENJAMIN OTIS.
Styles, Timothy and Otis, Benjamin located in Loop Eight construction zone.
28
WHAT DO WE DO WITH THIS STUFF? DO WE HAVE TO JUNK IT?

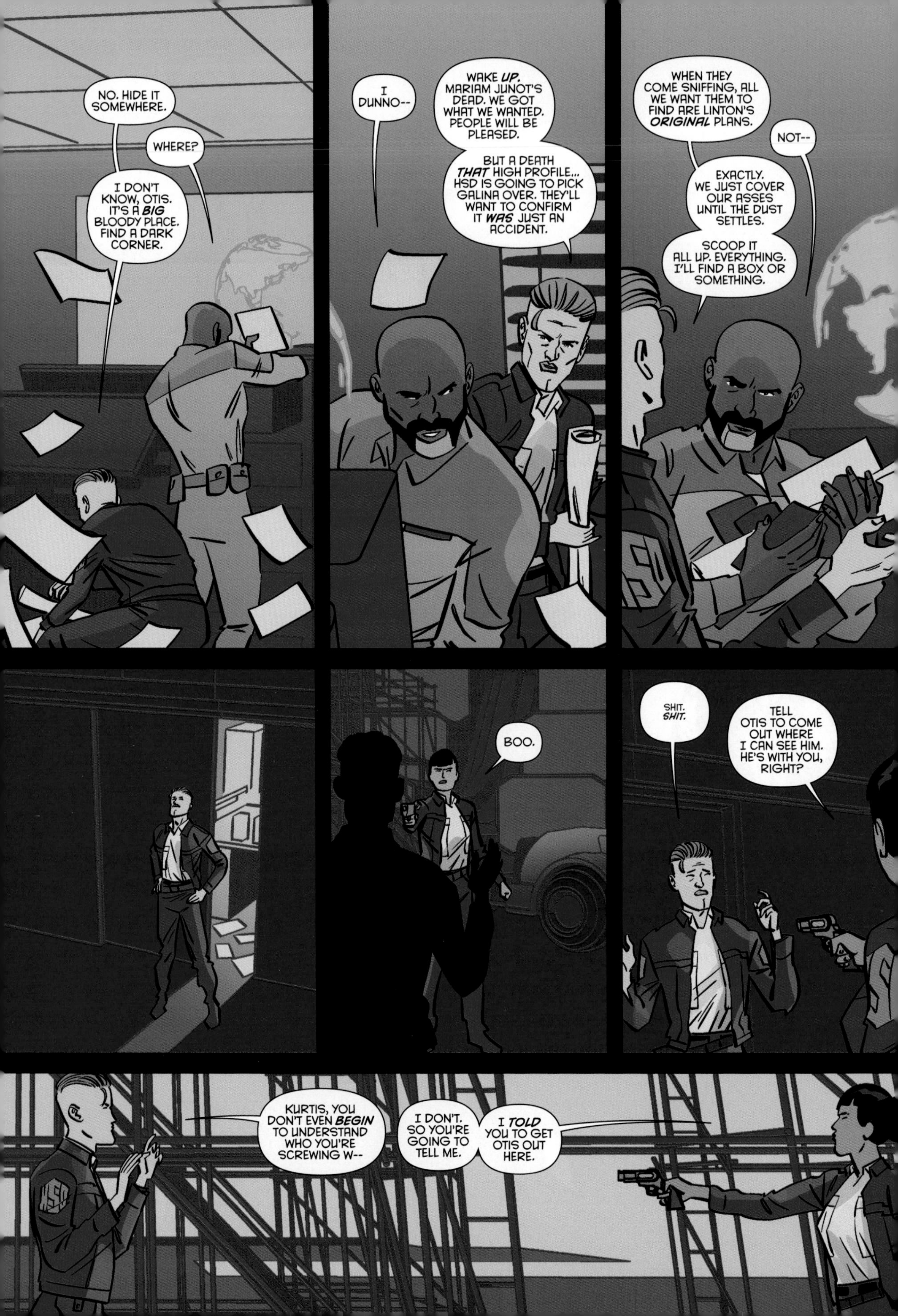
NO. HIDE IT SOMEWHERE.
WHERE?
I DON'T KNOW, OTIS. IT'S A *BIG* BLOODY PLACE. FIND A DARK CORNER.
I DUNNO--
WAKE *UP*. MARIAM JUNOT'S DEAD. WE GOT WHAT WE WANTED. PEOPLE WILL BE PLEASED.
BUT A DEATH *THAT* HIGH PROFILE... HSD IS GOING TO PICK GALINA OVER. THEY'LL WANT TO CONFIRM IT *WAS* JUST AN ACCIDENT.
WHEN THEY COME SNIFFING, ALL WE WANT THEM TO FIND ARE LINTON'S *ORIGINAL* PLANS.
NOT--
EXACTLY. WE JUST COVER OUR ASSES UNTIL THE DUST SETTLES.
SCOOP IT ALL UP. EVERYTHING. I'LL FIND A BOX OR SOMETHING.
BOO.
SHIT. *SHIT.*
TELL OTIS TO COME OUT WHERE I CAN SEE HIM. HE'S WITH YOU, RIGHT?
KURTIS, YOU DON'T EVEN *BEGIN* TO UNDERSTAND WHO YOU'RE SCREWING W--
I DON'T. SO YOU'RE GOING TO TELL ME.
I *TOLD* YOU TO GET OTIS OUT HERE.

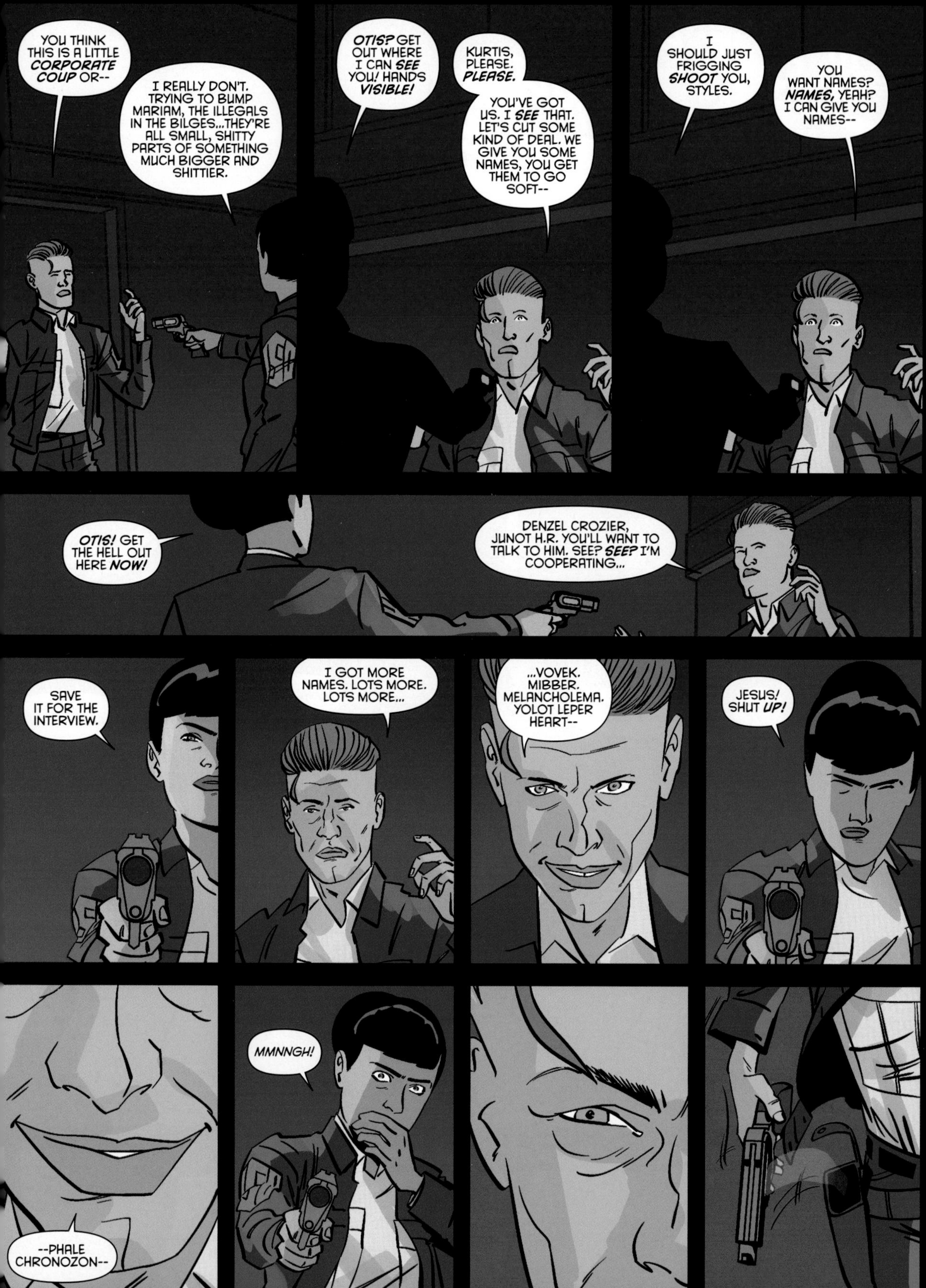
YOU THINK THIS IS A LITTLE *CORPORATE COUP* OR--
I REALLY DON'T. TRYING TO BUMP MARIAM, THE ILLEGALS IN THE BILGES...THEY'RE ALL SMALL, SHITTY PARTS OF SOMETHING MUCH BIGGER AND SHITTIER.
OTIS? GET OUT WHERE I CAN *SEE* YOU! HANDS *VISIBLE!*
KURTIS, PLEASE. *PLEASE.*
YOU'VE GOT US. I *SEE* THAT. LET'S CUT SOME KIND OF DEAL. WE GIVE YOU SOME NAMES, YOU GET THEM TO GO SOFT--
I SHOULD JUST FRIGGING *SHOOT* YOU, STYLES.
YOU WANT NAMES? *NAMES,* YEAH? I CAN GIVE YOU NAMES--
OTIS! GET THE HELL OUT HERE *NOW!*
DENZEL CROZIER, JUNOT H.R. YOU'LL WANT TO TALK TO HIM. SEE? *SEE?* I'M COOPERATING...
SAVE IT FOR THE INTERVIEW.
I GOT MORE NAMES. LOTS MORE. LOTS MORE...
...VOVEK. MIBBER. MELANCHOLEMA. YOLOT LEPER HEART--
JESUS! SHUT *UP!*
--PHALE CHRONOZON--
MMNNGH!

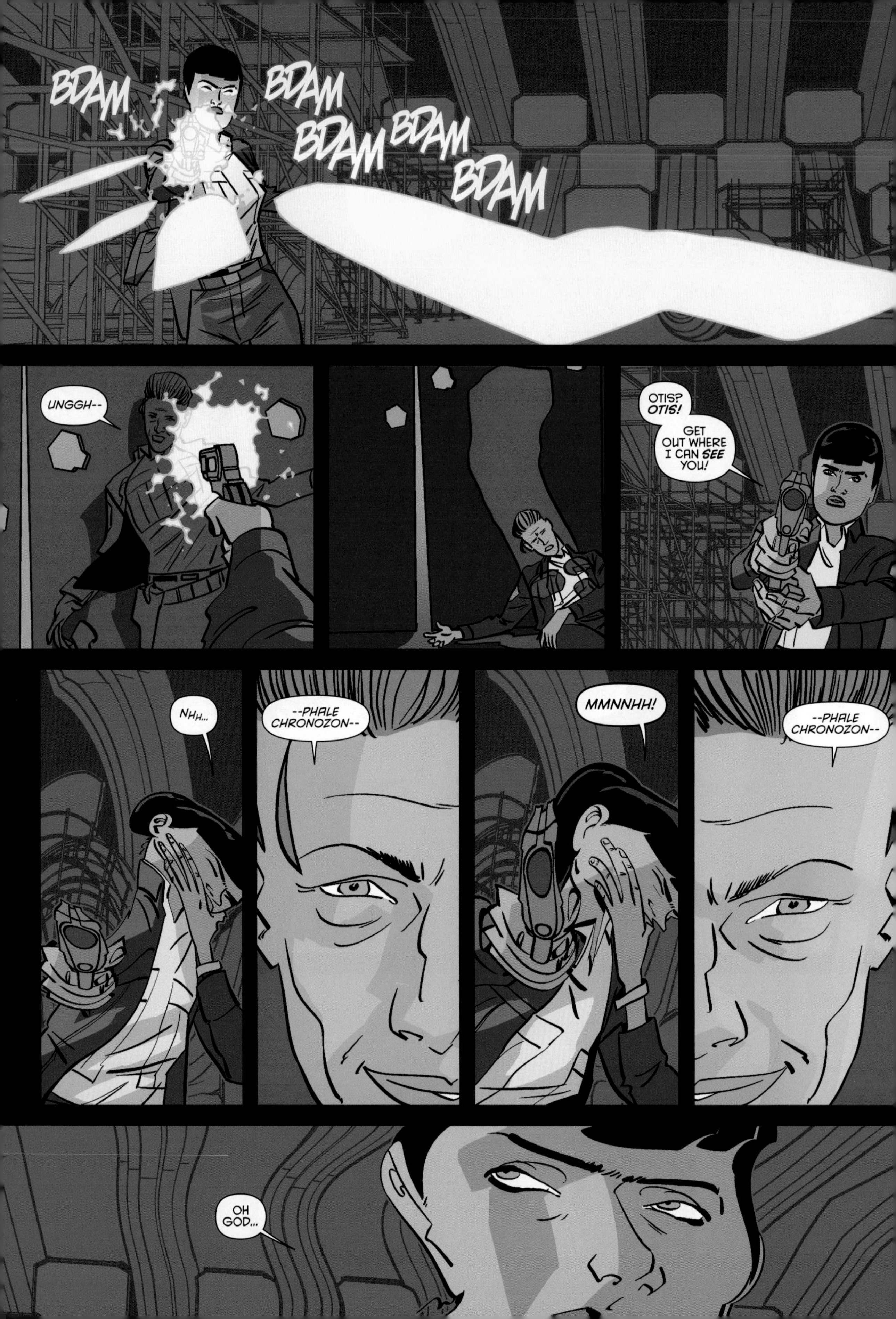
BDAM
BDAM
BDAM
BDAM
BDAM
UNGGH--
OTIS? OTIS!
GET OUT WHERE I CAN SEE YOU!
NHH...
--PHALE CHRONOZON--
MMNNHH!
--PHALE CHRONOZON--
OH GOD...

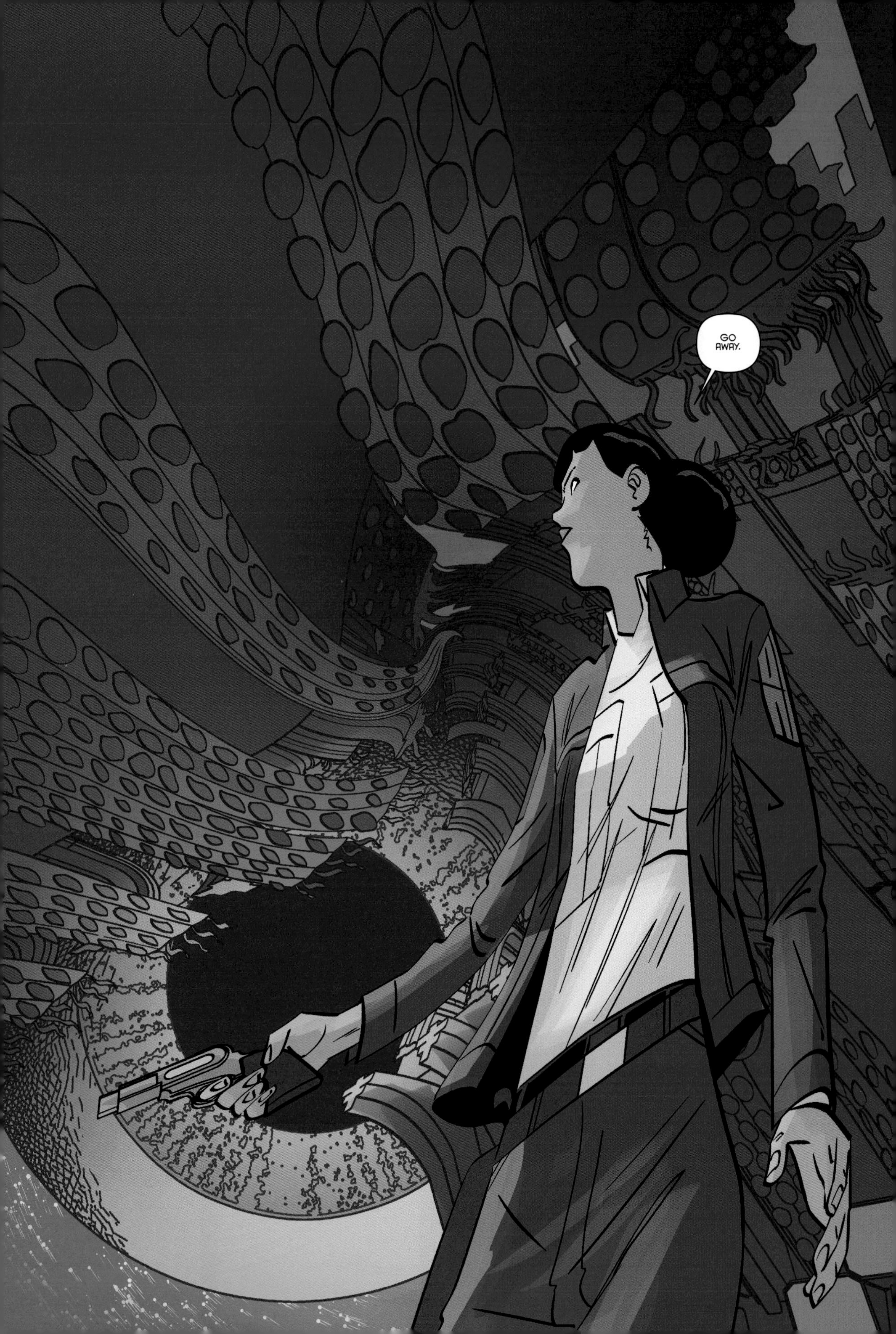
GO AWAY.

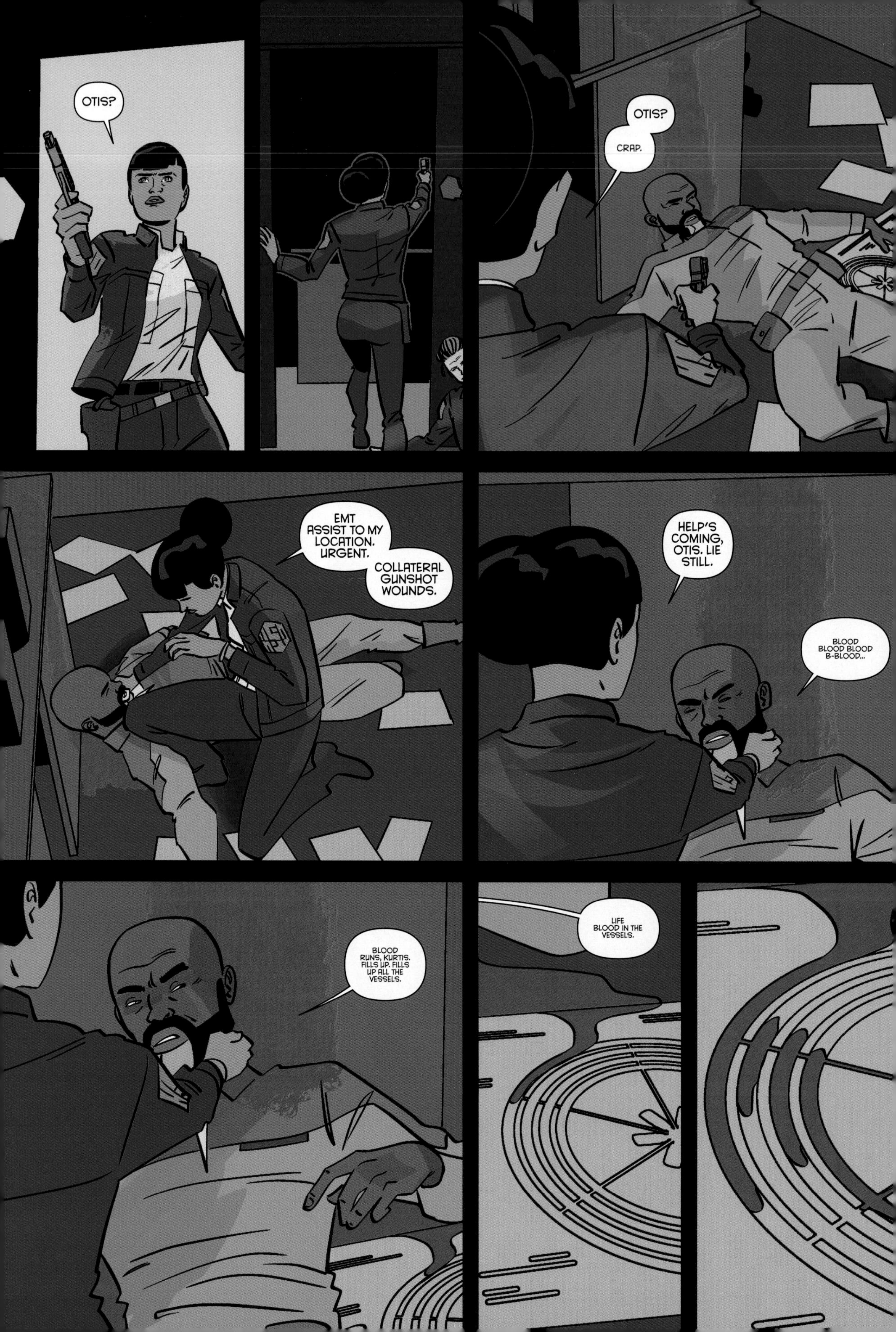
OTIS?
OTIS?
CRAP.
EMT ASSIST TO MY LOCATION. URGENT.
COLLATERAL GUNSHOT WOUNDS.
HELP'S COMING, OTIS. LIE STILL.
BLOOD BLOOD BLOOD B-BLOOD...
BLOOD RUNS, KURTIS. FILLS UP. FILLS UP ALL THE VESSELS.
LIFE BLOOD IN THE VESSELS.

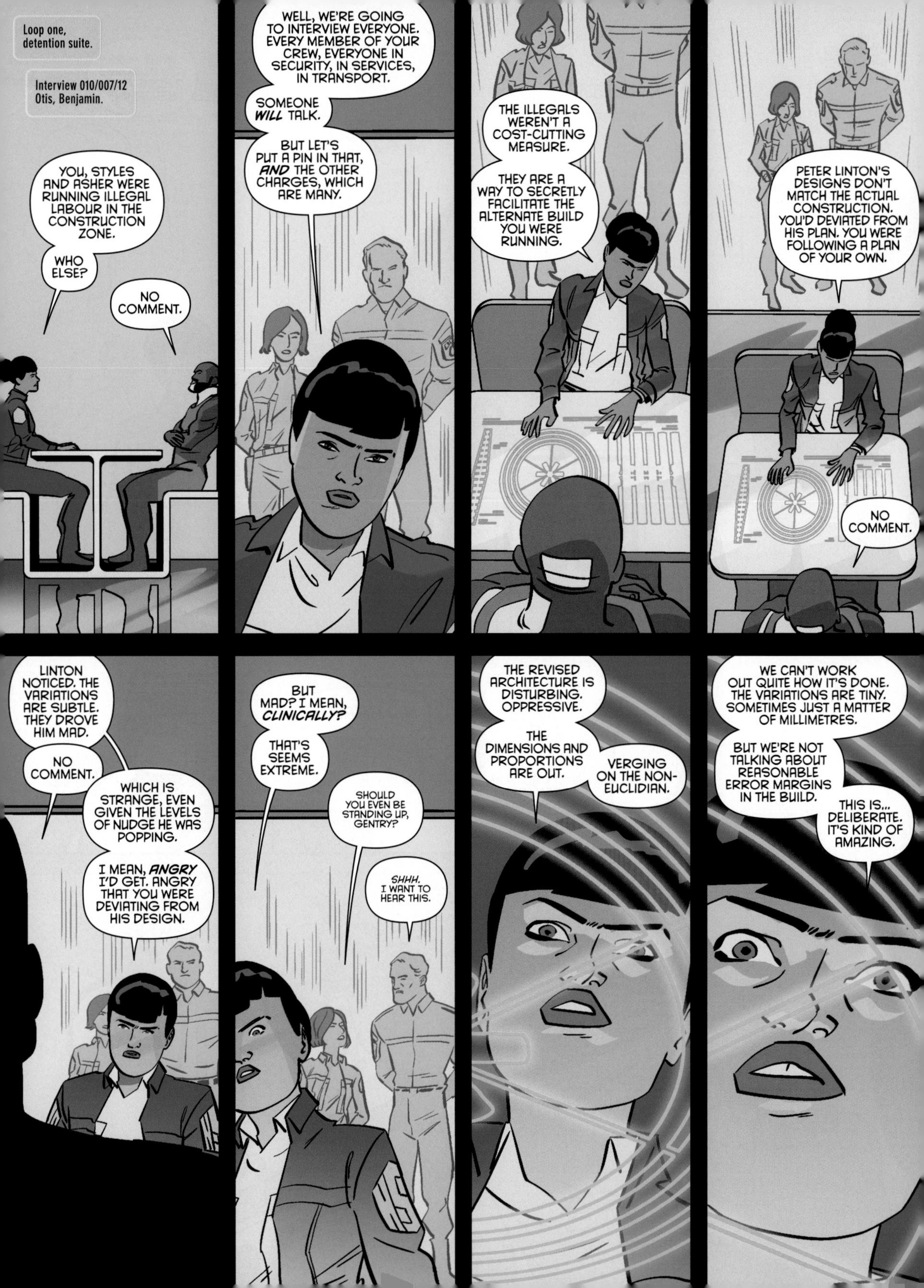
Loop one, detention suite.
Interview 010/007/12 Otis, Benjamin.
YOU, STYLES AND ASHER WERE RUNNING ILLEGAL LABOUR IN THE CONSTRUCTION ZONE.
WHO ELSE?
NO COMMENT.
WELL, WE'RE GOING TO INTERVIEW EVERYONE. EVERY MEMBER OF YOUR CREW, EVERYONE IN SECURITY, IN SERVICES, IN TRANSPORT.
SOMEONE *WILL* TALK.
BUT LET'S PUT A PIN IN THAT, *AND* THE OTHER CHARGES, WHICH ARE MANY.
THE ILLEGALS WEREN'T A COST-CUTTING MEASURE.
THEY ARE A WAY TO SECRETLY FACILITATE THE ALTERNATE BUILD YOU WERE RUNNING.
PETER LINTON'S DESIGNS DON'T MATCH THE ACTUAL CONSTRUCTION. YOU'D DEVIATED FROM HIS PLAN. YOU WERE FOLLOWING A PLAN OF YOUR OWN.
NO COMMENT.
LINTON NOTICED. THE VARIATIONS ARE SUBTLE. THEY DROVE HIM MAD.
NO COMMENT.
WHICH IS STRANGE, EVEN GIVEN THE LEVELS OF NUDGE HE WAS POPPING.
I MEAN, *ANGRY* I'D GET. ANGRY THAT YOU WERE DEVIATING FROM HIS DESIGN.
BUT MAD? I MEAN, *CLINICALLY?*
THAT'S SEEMS EXTREME.
SHOULD YOU EVEN BE STANDING UP, GENTRY?
SHHH. I WANT TO HEAR THIS.
THE REVISED ARCHITECTURE IS DISTURBING. OPPRESSIVE.
THE DIMENSIONS AND PROPORTIONS ARE OUT.
VERGING ON THE NON-EUCLIDIAN.
WE CAN'T WORK OUT QUITE HOW IT'S DONE. THE VARIATIONS ARE TINY. SOMETIMES JUST A MATTER OF MILLIMETRES.
BUT WE'RE NOT TALKING ABOUT REASONABLE ERROR MARGINS IN THE BUILD.
THIS IS... DELIBERATE. IT'S KIND OF AMAZING.

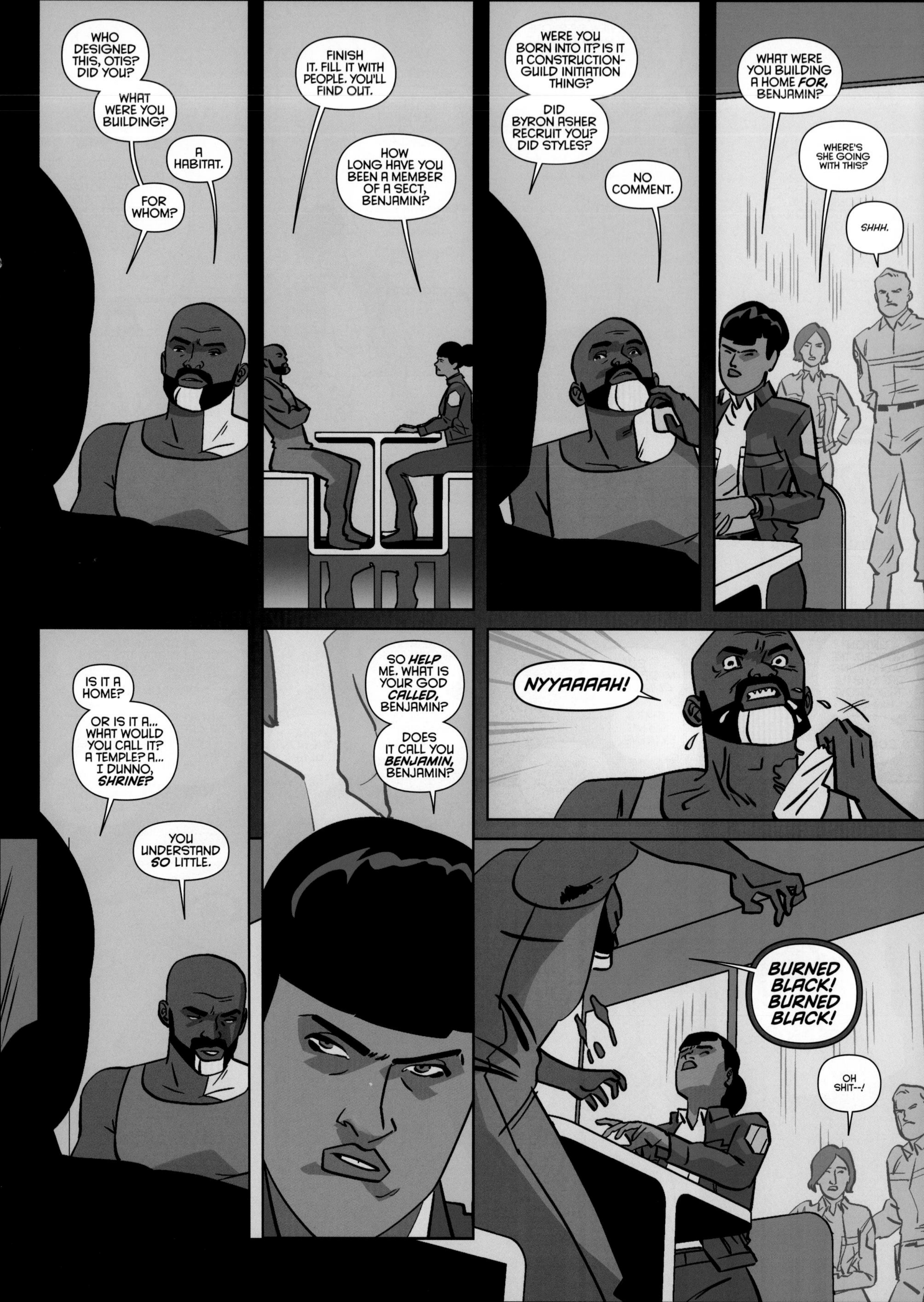
WHO DESIGNED THIS, OTIS? DID YOU?
WHAT WERE YOU BUILDING?
A HABITAT.
FOR WHOM?
FINISH IT. FILL IT WITH PEOPLE. YOU'LL FIND OUT.
HOW LONG HAVE YOU BEEN A MEMBER OF A SECT, BENJAMIN?
WERE YOU BORN INTO IT? IS IT A CONSTRUCTION-GUILD INITIATION THING?
DID BYRON ASHER RECRUIT YOU? DID STYLES?
NO COMMENT.
WHAT WERE YOU BUILDING A HOME *FOR,* BENJAMIN?
WHERE'S SHE GOING WITH THIS?
SHHH.
IS IT A HOME?
OR IS IT A... WHAT WOULD YOU CALL IT? A TEMPLE? A... I DUNNO, *SHRINE?*
YOU UNDERSTAND *SO* LITTLE.
SO *HELP* ME. WHAT IS YOUR GOD *CALLED,* BENJAMIN?
DOES IT CALL YOU *BENJAMIN,* BENJAMIN?
NYYAAAAH!
BURNED BLACK! BURNED BLACK!
OH SHIT--!

IT'LL BURN OUT YOUR DUMB BRAIN! BURN IT BLACK!

NGHH!

KURTIS!

UHNN!

BACK OFF! BACK OFF! BACK OFF!

THE UNREACH! THE UNREACH! HANGING IN THE SUN, WAITING TO BE BORN!

COMING TO TAKE US HOME--

GLLRRKK--

GET OFF THE TABLE AND BACK UP TO THE WALL, OTIS!

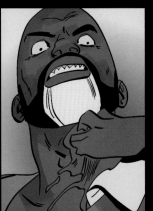

OH SHITTING HELL!

JESUS--

GLLAAAHHKK!

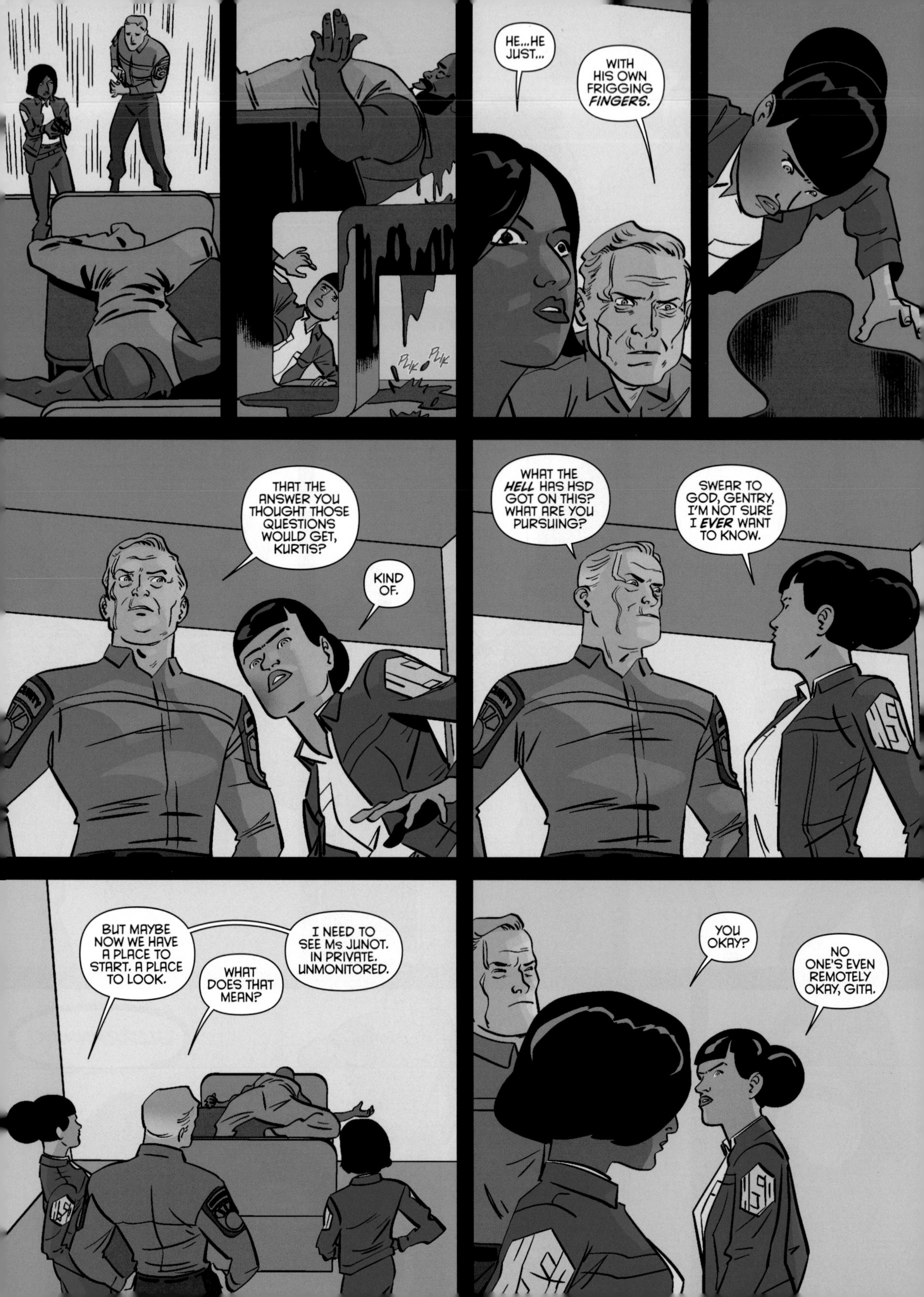
PLIK PLIK
HE...HE JUST...
WITH HIS OWN FRIGGING *FINGERS.*
THAT THE ANSWER YOU THOUGHT THOSE QUESTIONS WOULD GET, KURTIS?
KIND OF.
WHAT THE *HELL* HAS HSD GOT ON THIS? WHAT ARE YOU PURSUING?
SWEAR TO GOD, GENTRY, I'M NOT SURE I *EVER* WANT TO KNOW.
BUT MAYBE NOW WE HAVE A PLACE TO START. A PLACE TO LOOK.
WHAT DOES THAT MEAN?
I NEED TO SEE Ms JUNOT. IN PRIVATE. UNMONITORED.
YOU OKAY?
NO ONE'S EVEN REMOTELY OKAY, GITA.

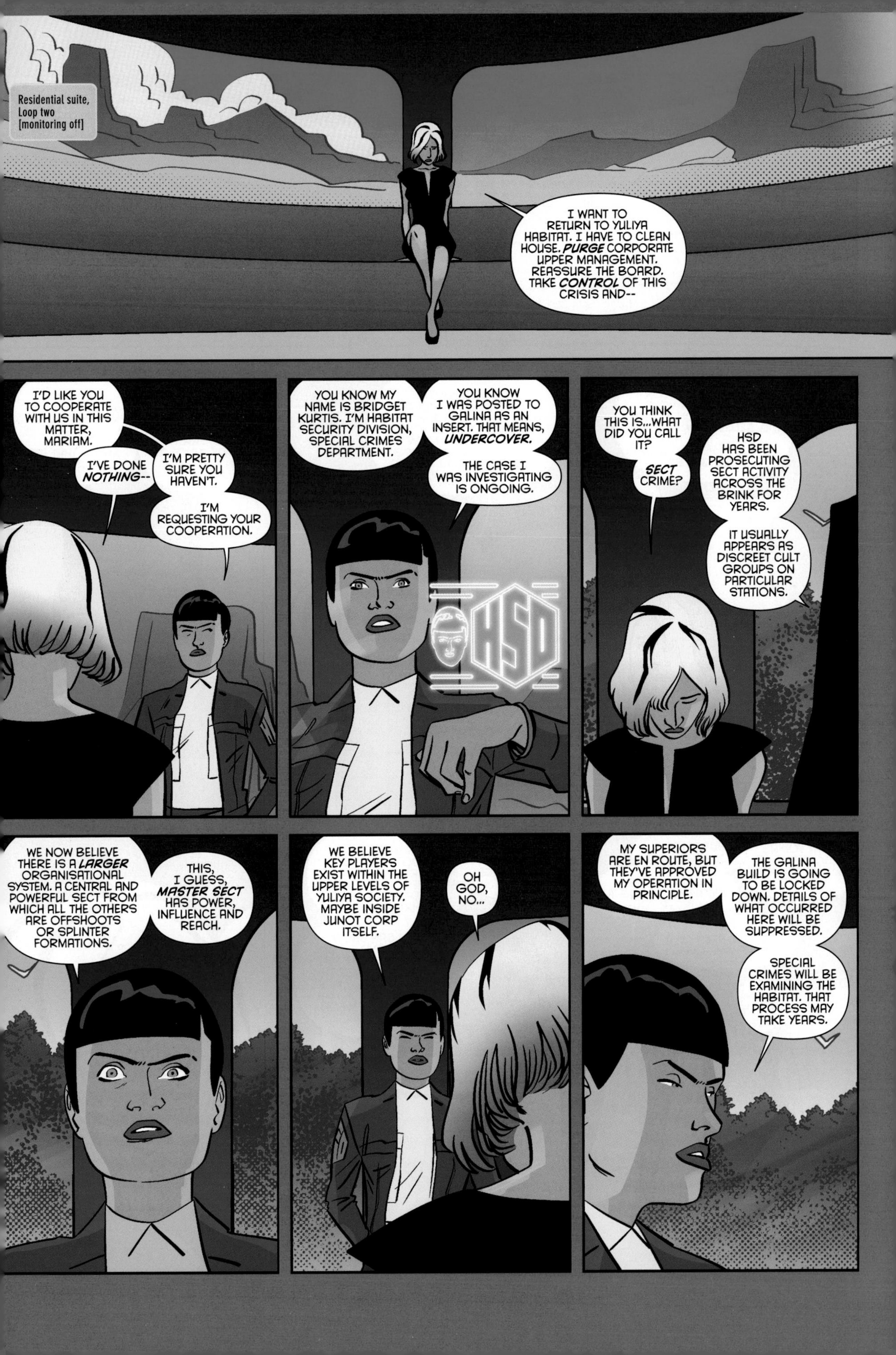

Residential suite, Loop two [monitoring off]
I WANT TO RETURN TO YULIYA HABITAT. I HAVE TO CLEAN HOUSE. PURGE CORPORATE UPPER MANAGEMENT. REASSURE THE BOARD. TAKE CONTROL OF THIS CRISIS AND--
I'D LIKE YOU TO COOPERATE WITH US IN THIS MATTER, MARIAM.
I'VE DONE NOTHING--
I'M PRETTY SURE YOU HAVEN'T.
I'M REQUESTING YOUR COOPERATION.
YOU KNOW MY NAME IS BRIDGET KURTIS. I'M HABITAT SECURITY DIVISION, SPECIAL CRIMES DEPARTMENT.
YOU KNOW I WAS POSTED TO GALINA AS AN INSERT. THAT MEANS, UNDERCOVER.
THE CASE I WAS INVESTIGATING IS ONGOING.
HSD
YOU THINK THIS IS...WHAT DID YOU CALL IT?
SECT CRIME?
HSD HAS BEEN PROSECUTING SECT ACTIVITY ACROSS THE BRINK FOR YEARS.
IT USUALLY APPEARS AS DISCREET CULT GROUPS ON PARTICULAR STATIONS.
WE NOW BELIEVE THERE IS A LARGER ORGANISATIONAL SYSTEM. A CENTRAL AND POWERFUL SECT FROM WHICH ALL THE OTHERS ARE OFFSHOOTS OR SPLINTER FORMATIONS.
THIS, I GUESS, MASTER SECT HAS POWER, INFLUENCE AND REACH.
WE BELIEVE KEY PLAYERS EXIST WITHIN THE UPPER LEVELS OF YULIYA SOCIETY. MAYBE INSIDE JUNOT CORP ITSELF.
OH GOD, NO...
MY SUPERIORS ARE EN ROUTE, BUT THEY'VE APPROVED MY OPERATION IN PRINCIPLE.
THE GALINA BUILD IS GOING TO BE LOCKED DOWN. DETAILS OF WHAT OCCURRED HERE WILL BE SUPPRESSED.
SPECIAL CRIMES WILL BE EXAMINING THE HABITAT. THAT PROCESS MAY TAKE YEARS.

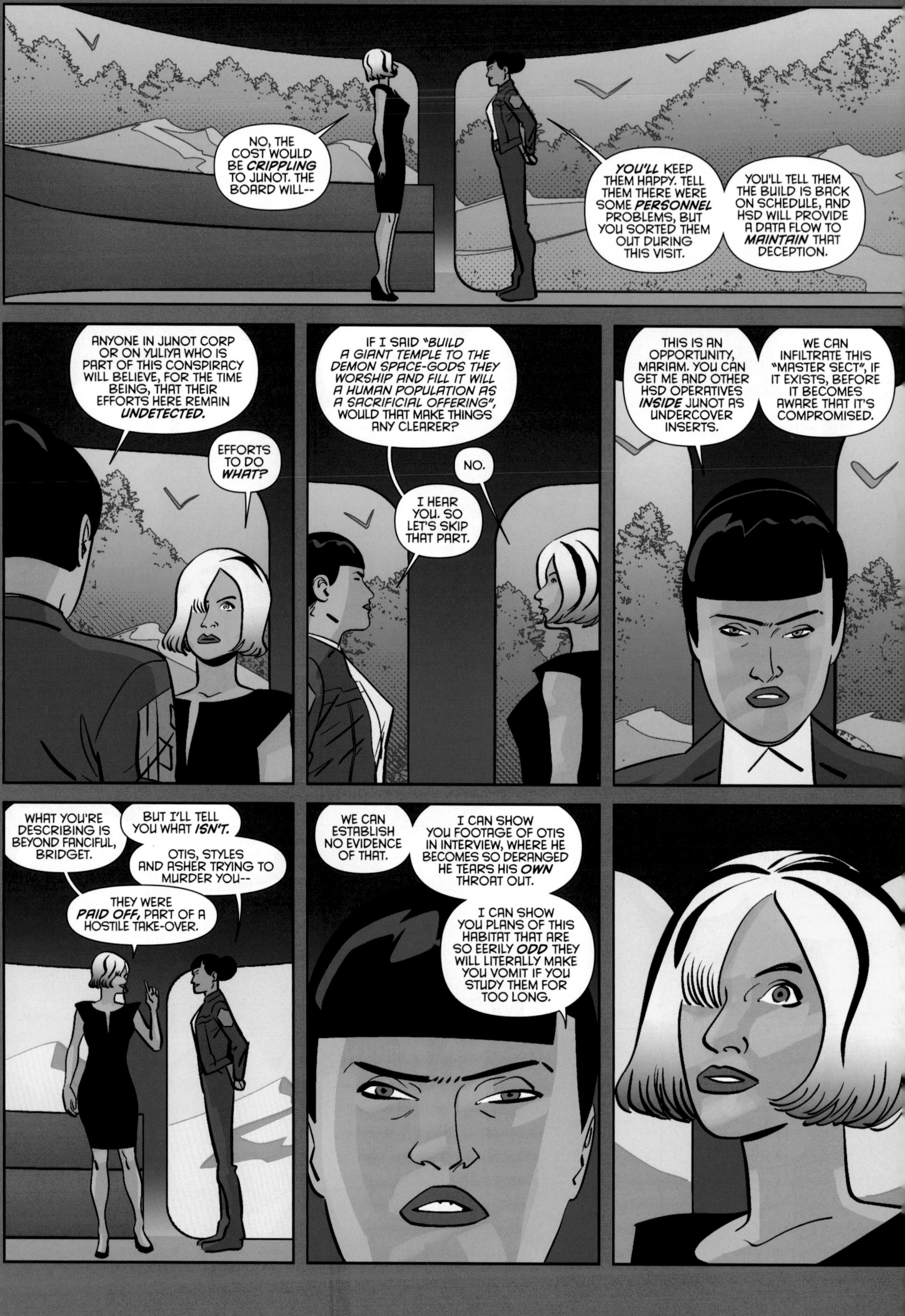
NO, THE COST WOULD BE CRIPPLING TO JUNOT. THE BOARD WILL--
YOU'LL KEEP THEM HAPPY. TELL THEM THERE WERE SOME PERSONNEL PROBLEMS, BUT YOU SORTED THEM OUT DURING THIS VISIT.
YOU'LL TELL THEM THE BUILD IS BACK ON SCHEDULE, AND HSD WILL PROVIDE A DATA FLOW TO MAINTAIN THAT DECEPTION.
ANYONE IN JUNOT CORP OR ON YULIYA WHO IS PART OF THIS CONSPIRACY WILL BELIEVE, FOR THE TIME BEING, THAT THEIR EFFORTS HERE REMAIN UNDETECTED.
EFFORTS TO DO WHAT?
IF I SAID "BUILD A GIANT TEMPLE TO THE DEMON SPACE-GODS THEY WORSHIP AND FILL IT WILL A HUMAN POPULATION AS A SACRIFICIAL OFFERING", WOULD THAT MAKE THINGS ANY CLEARER?
NO.
I HEAR YOU. SO LET'S SKIP THAT PART.
THIS IS AN OPPORTUNITY, MARIAM. YOU CAN GET ME AND OTHER HSD OPERATIVES INSIDE JUNOT AS UNDERCOVER INSERTS.
WE CAN INFILTRATE THIS "MASTER SECT", IF IT EXISTS, BEFORE IT BECOMES AWARE THAT IT'S COMPROMISED.
WHAT YOU'RE DESCRIBING IS BEYOND FANCIFUL, BRIDGET.
BUT I'LL TELL YOU WHAT ISN'T.
OTIS, STYLES AND ASHER TRYING TO MURDER YOU--
THEY WERE PAID OFF, PART OF A HOSTILE TAKE-OVER.
WE CAN ESTABLISH NO EVIDENCE OF THAT.
I CAN SHOW YOU FOOTAGE OF OTIS IN INTERVIEW, WHERE HE BECOMES SO DERANGED HE TEARS HIS OWN THROAT OUT.
I CAN SHOW YOU PLANS OF THIS HABITAT THAT ARE SO EERILY ODD THEY WILL LITERALLY MAKE YOU VOMIT IF YOU STUDY THEM FOR TOO LONG.

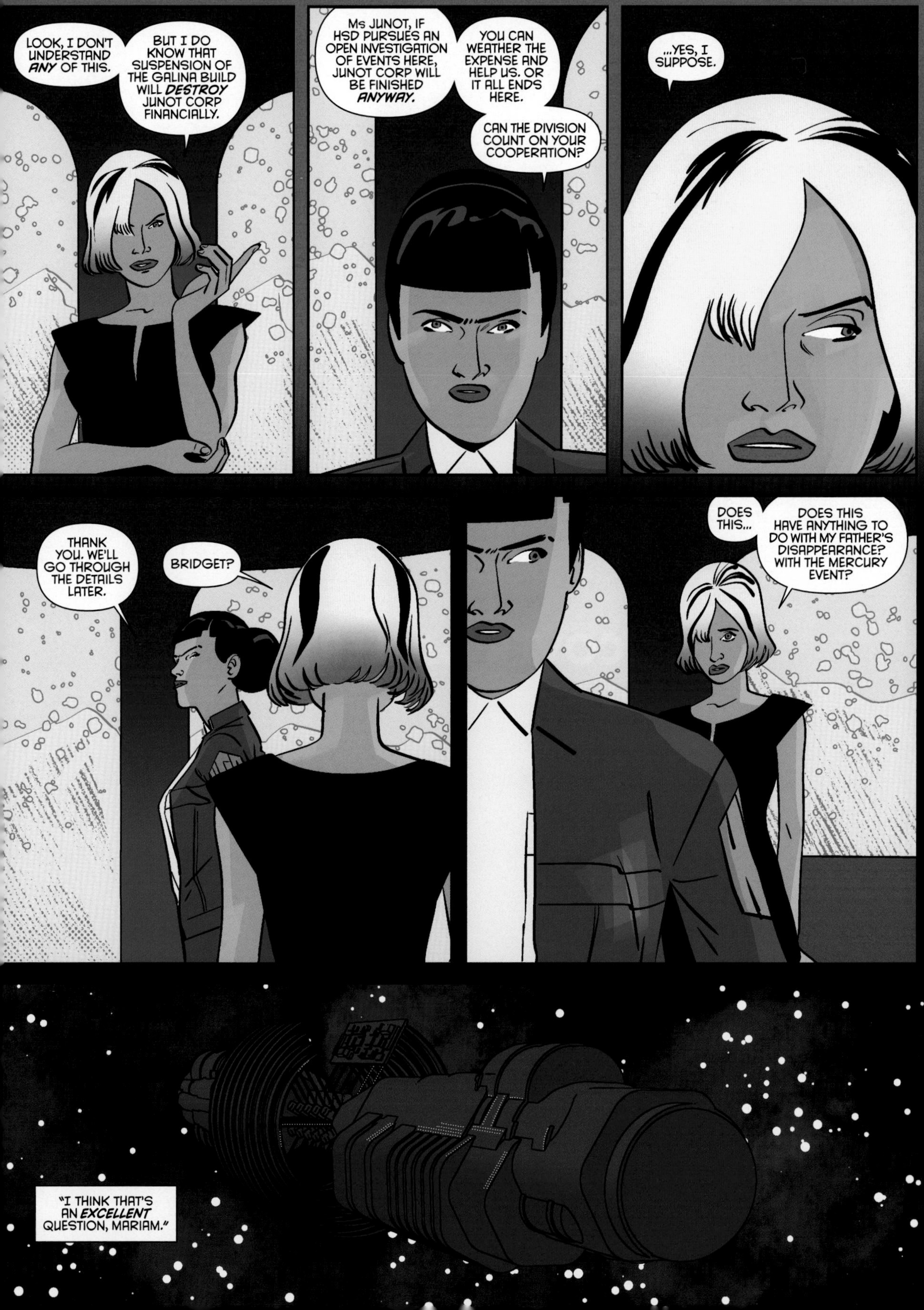
LOOK, I DON'T UNDERSTAND *ANY* OF THIS.
BUT I DO KNOW THAT SUSPENSION OF THE GALINA BUILD WILL *DESTROY* JUNOT CORP FINANCIALLY.
Ms JUNOT, IF HSD PURSUES AN OPEN INVESTIGATION OF EVENTS HERE, JUNOT CORP WILL BE FINISHED *ANYWAY.*
YOU CAN WEATHER THE EXPENSE AND HELP US. OR IT ALL ENDS HERE.
CAN THE DIVISION COUNT ON YOUR COOPERATION?
...YES, I SUPPOSE.
THANK YOU. WE'LL GO THROUGH THE DETAILS LATER.
BRIDGET?
DOES THIS...
DOES THIS HAVE ANYTHING TO DO WITH MY FATHER'S DISAPPEARANCE? WITH THE MERCURY EVENT?
"I THINK THAT'S AN *EXCELLENT* QUESTION, MARIAM."

COVER GALLERY

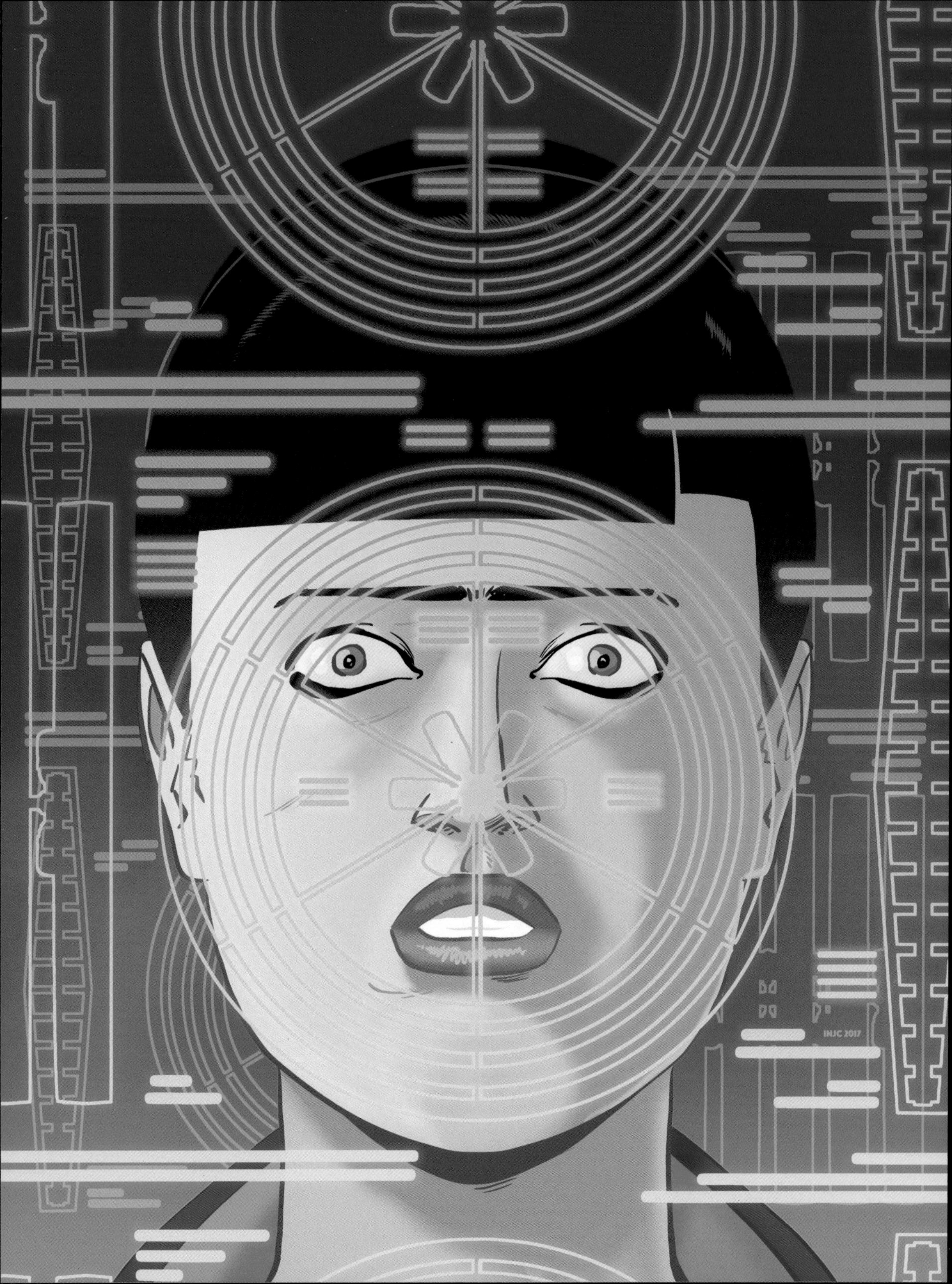
INJC 2017

2000 AD Prog 2030: Cover by **I.N.J. Culbard**

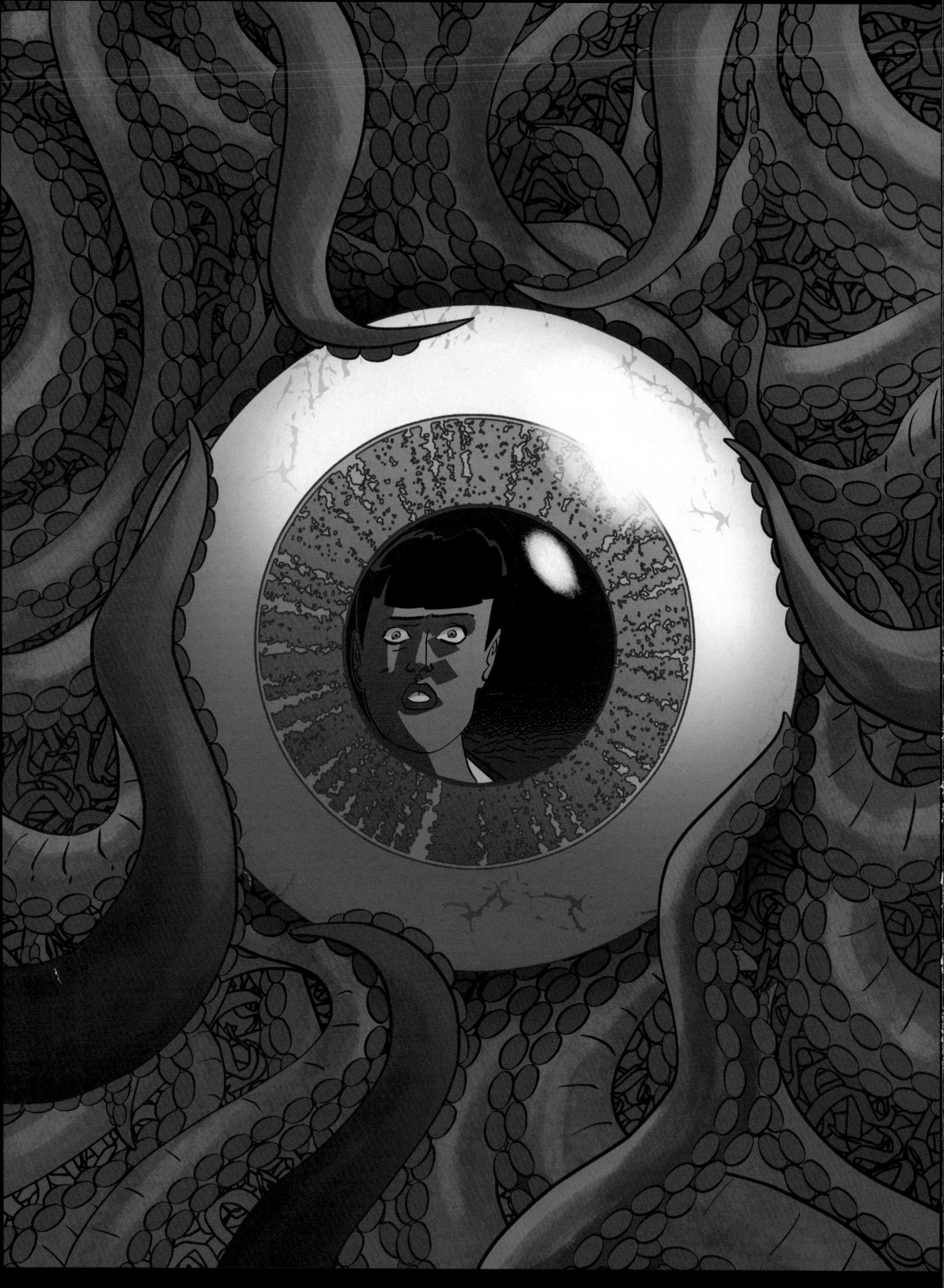

2000 AD Prog 2039: Cover by **I.N.J. Culbard**

DAN ABNETT

Dan Abnett is a seven-times New York Times bestselling author and an award-winning comic book writer. He has written over fifty novels, including the acclaimed Gaunt's Ghosts series, the Eisenhorn and Ravenor trilogies, volumes of the million-selling Horus Heresy series, *The Silent Stars Go By* (*Doctor Who*), *Rocket Raccoon and Groot: Steal the Galaxy*, *The Avengers: Everybody Wants To Rule The World*, *The Wield*, *Triumff: Her Majesty's Hero*, and *Embedded*. In comics, he is known for his work on *The Legion of Super-Heroes, Aquaman, The Titans, Nova, Wild's End*, and *The New Deadwardians*. His 2008 run on *The Guardians of the Galaxy* for Marvel formed the inspiration for the blockbuster movie. A regular contributor to the UK's long-running 2000 AD, he is the creator of series including *Grey Area, Lawless, Brink, Kingdom* and the classic *Sinister Dexter*. He has also written extensively for the games industry, including *Shadow of Mordor* and *Alien:Isolation*.

Dan lives and works in the UK. Follow him on Twitter @VincentAbnett